Google® Powered

Google® Powered

Productivity with Online Tools

Jerri L. Ledford

BICENTENNIAL 1807 WILEY 2007 BICENTENNIAL

Wiley Publishing, Inc.

Google® Powered: Productivity with Online Tools

Published by
Wiley Publishing, Inc.
10475 Crosspoint Boulevard
Indianapolis, IN 46256
www.wiley.com

Published simultaneously in Canada

ISBN: 978-0-470-10965-6

Manufactured in the United States of America

10 9 8 7 6 5 4 3 2 1

Library of Congress Cataloging-in-Publication Data

Ledford, Jerri L.
Google powered : productivity with on-line tools / by Jerri L. Ledford.
p. cm.
Includes index.
ISBN-13: 978-0-470-10965-6 (paper/website)
ISBN-10: 0-470-10965-3 (paper/website)
1. Google. 2. Web search engines. 3. Internet searching. I. Title.
ZA4234.G64L43 2007
025.04—dc22
2006036461

For Rick,
because I know you'll read it

About the Author

Jerri Ledford has been a freelance business technology writer for more than ten years. During that time, over 700 of her articles, profiles, news stories, and reports have appeared online and in print. Her publishing credits include *Intelligent Enterprise, Network World, Information Security Magazine, DCM Magazine, CRM Magazine,* and *IT Manager's Journal.*

Jerri also develops and teaches technology training courses for both consumer and business users. Some of the course topics she's been involved with include: security, customer service, career skills, and technology for companies such as IBT Financial, Writer's Village University, Beacon Hill Financial Services, Hewlett Packard, and CNET. She is the author of *The Rational Guide to Preventing Identity Theft* (Mann Publishing, 2005), *Cut the Cord! The Consumer's Guide to VoIP* (Course PTR, 2005), *The Personal Cybersecurity Bible* (Course PTR, 2005), *The Gadget Geek's Guide to Your Sony PlayStation Portable* (Course PTR, 2006), *Google Analytics* (with Mary Tyler, Wiley, 2006), and *25 Home Automation Projects for the Evil Genius* (McGraw-Hill, 2006).

In her off-time Jerri travels between Alabama, Mississippi, and Tennessee, where she enjoys hiking, spending time on the beach, and other travel — that is, when she's not playing with her electronic gadgets. She is fondly referred to as "tech support" by friends and family members.

Credits

Acquisitions Editor
Katie Mohr

Development Editor
William Bridges

Technical Editor
Yvette Deluca

Copy Editor
Nancy Rapoport

Editorial Manager
Mary Beth Wakefield

Production Manager
Tim Tate

Vice President and Executive Group Publisher
Richard Swadley

Vice President and Executive Publisher
Joseph B. Wikert

Compositor
Maureen Forys,
Happenstance Type-O-Rama

Proofreader
Kathryn Duggan

Indexer
Melanie Belkin

Anniversary Logo Design
Richard Pacifico

Contents

Acknowledgments

I always struggle with the acknowledgments in a book because so many people make it possible for the book to be created. I don't even know the names of many of those people, so if you're not mentioned here, I apologize. And I want you to know how very much I appreciate every effort that you put into making this an excellent reference for readers.

Names I do know include Bill Bridges and Yvette Deluca. Bill is the world's best development editor. He knows his stuff, he makes my stuff shine, and we have a lot of fun along the way. Thanks, Bill, again.

Yvette is an amazing tech editor who wasn't one bit afraid to show me just where I screwed up. Folks, she's saved you a lot of headaches, and I owe her a debt of gratitude. Yvette, I hope we get to work together again. I really appreciate all you've done for me.

There's a whole team of people at Wiley who deserve big kudos: Katie Mohr, Mary Beth Wakefield, David Mayhew, and probably a dozen other people. Your efforts are always amazing, your attitudes always wonderful, and your help always appreciated. Thanks so very much.

At Google there's also a whole team: Alex Ortiz and Brett Cosby (again), David Glazer, Carl Sjogreen, Brandon McCormick, Lauren Smith, and Jennifer Mazzon — you've all been super-responsive. Thanks for your help. Thanks for sharing your knowledge. And thanks for being excited about the project.

On the personal side, I could write pages and pages of thanks. Authors need interaction, and the people around them make all the difference during the writing of a book. Jennifer and Rick, you guys are amazing. I love our weekly dinners, our friendships, and your belief in me. I can't ever tell you thank you enough.

Curtis, Sean, and Jennifer — my original cheering team. You're always there with a good word and a hug. What more can a girl ask for? Thank you.

I could go on a lot longer — Connie, Beckie, Mom and Dad, Neil Salkind, Lynn Haller, and a few dozen other folks! I won't, though, because I know you're ready to get on with the important stuff. But allow me one more...

Thank *you* for buying and reading the book. I hope it's everything you were expecting when you made the decision to add it to your collection.

Introduction

Microsoft's schedule for the coming year includes a release of its new version of the Microsoft Office suite to accompany the new Windows Vista, which is Microsoft's new operating system. The program comes with lots of bells and whistles — and a pretty hefty price tag!

There has to be a better way to have all of the office programs that you need without breaking the bank, right?

There is. And Google provides it. In a flurry of activity over the past couple of years, Google has purchased a variety of Web-based programs that make it possible for you to have all the tools you need without shelling out even one thin dime. Really.

Among the different products Google has acquired are a word-processing program, a spreadsheet application, an e-mail application, a calendaring application, a note-taking program, a VoIP (Voice over Internet Protocol) program, and a program that will help you manage and share your digital pictures.

All these applications are covered in this book, some in more detail than others. The idea is to get you quickly up to speed so you can begin using the programs and replace those other costly office programs before you have to shell out a few hundred dollars to upgrade.

What you won't find in this book are modifications for the programs or much more than a glance at Google's search capabilities. There are plenty of other books that cover that information. I'd like to help you get started with something new.

Overview of the Book and Technology

These days it seems that Google has a hand in everything. And the fact that the company is taking a stab at office programs only makes sense. After all, what better way to improve your productivity than to take your office applications online and cut the time it takes to share and collaborate on documents and projects? It makes sense, and it also makes sense that Google, the King of the Internet, would be the company to go there.

In this book, you'll find everything you need to know to get started using the various programs that Google offers for office productivity. It's a basic book, written mostly for beginners, but even advanced users might learn a thing or two.

Each of the eight office-related Google programs is covered. And each program is given its own section so that you can flip back to the section you need without having to read through the whole book again.

It's guaranteed that Google will change these programs. Most of them are still in beta testing at the time of this writing. To help you keep up with changes to the applications, I've set up a companion Web site. You can find it at `http://googleproductivitytools.com`. There you'll find announcements about changes and additions, and additional tips and tricks about the program. For the programs still in beta testing, there may also be invitations available on the site.

How This Book Is Organized

As of this writing, Google hasn't combined these programs into a single suite of applications. There have been some combinations (such as the Writely/Spreadsheets combination that led to Google Docs & Spreadsheets), but for the most part, these are all separate applications.

For that reason, you'll find that this book is broken into nine parts. Here's a quick look at what you'll find in each part:

- **Part I: Getting to Know Google** — This is a short section that introduces you to some of the more specific aspects of what you can and can't do with Google and how to get around the Google Web site.
- **Part II: Google Docs** — This is the first half of the Google Docs & Spreadsheets program, which specifically covers creating documents. You'll find information on how to get started using the program, how to navigate it, and how to use the features of the program. There are also suggestions for the extras that you can accomplish with Google Docs.
- **Part III: Google Spreadsheets** — The second part of Google Docs & Spreadsheets is the spreadsheet application and that's what you'll find covered in this section. Again, you'll find information on how to get started using Google Spreadsheets, how to get around in the program, and how to collaborate with others on spreadsheets.
- **Part IV: Google Page Creator** — This section covers Google's Web page creation and publishing program. You learn how to get around in the

program and how to use it to quickly create professional Web pages that you can publish for free on Google Pages.

- **Part V: Google Calendar** — Google Calendar is a neat application that integrates with your Gmail application. In this part of the book, you learn everything you need to know about using Google Calendar to keep you moving along on time and as planned.
- **Part VI: Google Notebook** — Are you a note-taker? And do you wish there were some way you could take notes while you're surfing the Internet? If so, this program is for you and in this section you learn all about getting around Google Notebook, using it to take notes, and collaborating with others or publishing your notebooks to the Web.
- **Part VII: Google Talk** — Google is all about communications. It began with search, but now there's a lot more to it, such as the Google Talk program that lets you talk to your friends using voice, chat, or e-mail. And in this section of the book, you learn all about using these different techniques through this one program. You'll be communicating with everyone in no time.
- **Part VIII: Gmail** — E-mail is the life blood of most organizations (and personal lives). This section of the book shows you how to use Gmail, an e-mail program that makes others pale by comparison. By the time you finish this section, you'll be navigating and using Gmail like a real pro.
- **Part IX: Picasa** — Have you been sucked into the digital camera craze yet? If you have, you should definitely read this section on Picasa, Google's answer to photo organization and sharing. In this section, you learn everything you need to know to upload pictures to Picasa, organize and share those pictures, and even to post pictures to your blog with a few mouse clicks.

If you're considering moving to Web-based productivity applications, then you should definitely read through this book at least once. Other productivity applications are available online, but none of them has quite the appeal that Google's office tools have.

Read through everything at least once. If you've used any of the applications covered here before, you may find some of the information a little repetitive, but there are nuggets for you advanced folks, too. And everyone needs a little refresher now and again, as a reminder of features that may have been forgotten.

After you've read through the book, it will still be a useful reference, so keep it on the shelf near the computer. Then when you get stuck using one of the programs covered here, you can quickly flip to the appropriate section.

A few other things you may find useful in the book's organization are the hints, tips, notes, warnings, and sidebars that are included. These are important bits of information that you don't want to miss. They may tell you an alternative way to do something, or how to accomplish tasks faster, or they may give you notes about the programs, or even warnings about what you shouldn't do.

The sidebars include information about additional Google programs that you may find useful and places to look for more information on topics that are related to, but not central to, using the Google office programs.

Who Should Read This Book

So now you're wondering if this book is for you, right? Let me help you out a little. The book is written first and foremost for beginning Google tools users. If you're an advanced user, you'll probably still find some useful information, but you'll also find some of the information a little repetitive.

In addition to being for beginning users, the information included in this book is also geared to help both the business user and the home user. You'll find examples that apply to both groups, although I'll admit it leans heavily toward the small business side. Both types of users should benefit from the information that's included, however, because in most cases the examples can be applied to both business and home activities.

Finally, if you're not sure you're comfortable using Web-based applications, then you should read the book. By the time you're finished, you'll understand the benefits and the pitfalls of using such office applications. And what's more, you'll know how to use them and can test them all out for yourself.

Tools You Will Need

Every time I see a section heading that says "Tools You'll Need," I picture a garage full of tools that I have no clue how to use. But here's some good news. This is not what you're up against when you're using Google's office tools.

The tools that you'll need to use the applications covered in this book are pretty basic — a computer, an Internet connection, and a Web browser. If you're buying the book, it's a good bet you already have all these tools at your disposal. So, what are you waiting for?

Moving On

That's it. I'll shut up now and let you read on. There's a lot of information to cover, and I don't want to waste your time.

Eight programs. A little time. No money. That's what it will take for you to do nearly everything you could with a more expensive office suite. Treasures await.

PART

I

Getting to Know Google

Google. Unless you live in a cave, you've probably heard the name. In fact, it's one of the most frequently (and most globally) used search engines. Google wasn't the first search engine to hit the Internet, but it's one of the best. And did you know there's more to it than just search capabilities?

There is. A lot more. And in the chapters that follow, you'll learn just how much Google makes available to you. In this section of the book, you'll also find out how to get connected with Google so that you can start taking advantage of all the programs the company has to offer.

CHAPTER 1

Buried Treasures

Muck around on the Google Web pages long enough, and you're bound to find a program you didn't know Google made available. You probably know that Google search technology is among the best (and most used) in the world. But did you know that Google has a program that will let you search for a local business, map it, and even zoom in or out on the map so you can find it? You can even access this information from your smartphone or wireless-enabled PocketPC.

That's the promise of Google: buried treasures. The folks over at Google (there are more than 6,500 Google employees now) are constantly working on something new and exciting to help you find information, do business faster, or connect to the world more easily. And that means there's always something more just around the corner.

Google Is More Than Search

In 1995, two guys who didn't even like each other all that much — Larry Page and Sergey Brin — managed to come together on one topic: They agreed that searches could be performed faster and return better results, if only the software would enable it. An application called BackRub was born out of that agreement, and today it's the biggest player in search. Wait, that's not exactly how it happened. Yes, a search engine called BackRub was designed by Brin and Page, but eventually it was renamed Google, a play on the mathematical term "googol," which is a number that consists of a 1 followed by 100 zeros. (Try figuring equations with numbers in *that* range!) The idea was that the name Google would represent the organization's mission to classify the immense amounts of data available on the Web.

So in the beginning, Google *was* just search. And it was very good at it. The company started in a college dorm room, used a garage as a first office, and eventually "Google-ized" the Silicon Graphics, Inc., campus in Mountain View, California. It became a giant because of the search algorithms that were developed in those early days and then were continuously improved upon by the brightest minds in technology. But did you know there's more to Google than just search?

There really is. In the years since its inception in 1995, Google has expanded and improved. The company has bought out other companies and added to its offerings. Each of the programs now included in Google's huge portfolio has a search capability as a basis for its operation. Maybe it's simply searching documents, or perhaps it's searching for a title or a term, but you can bet that anything coming out of the Google portfolio will have search built into it in some fashion.

But don't be fooled into thinking that's all you get. Many of the applications coming out of Google right now are useful for far more than just search. I'm writing this book from the Google Docs & Spreadsheets application that Google is beta-testing. It's about 60 percent complete, and fully functional as far as I can tell. Yes, some of the functionality that you'll find in Microsoft Word just doesn't exist in the Docs half of the program, but for the price (FREE!), it's an excellent application. I cover Google Docs & Spreadsheets more in Parts II and III, so that's all I'll say for now.

What's more, Google is now a household term that people use as both a noun and a verb. As of mid-2006, it's officially a word in the dictionary, as well. You can "Google" any term that comes to mind and something can even be described as "Googlesque." So today, Google *is* search, but it's also much more.

So, what else does Google offer that you might find useful? The following is a list of Google programs that you can pick and choose from. Some are very search-specific (such as Froogle), while others include some elements of search but will help you with other activities, such as keeping your calendar.

- **AdWords:** An advertising/marketing program
- **Alerts:** A reminder service
- **Analytics:** A Web site metrics collection and analysis program
- **Blog Search:** A blog search service
- **Blogger:** A blogging tool

- **Book Search:** A book search service
- **Calendar:** A Web-based calendar application
- **Catalogs:** A catalog search service
- **Checkout:** An e-commerce checkout application
- **Desktop:** A collection of tools to make your desktop more user-friendly
- **Directory:** A service that allows you to browse the Internet by topic
- **Earth:** A combination of satellite imagery and mapping applications referred to as a "3D interface to the planet"
- **Finance:** A financial news and information service
- **Froogle:** An e-commerce price-based comparison service
- **Gmail:** An e-mail application
- **Google Docs & Spreadsheets:** A Web-based word-processing and spreadsheets application
- **Groups:** A mailing-list service
- **Images:** A picture-specific search service
- **Local:** A local search service
- **Maps:** A Web-based mapping application
- **Maps for Mobile:** A mapping application for mobile devices
- **Mobile:** A collection of Google-related mobile applications
- **News:** A Web-based news service
- **Notebook:** A note-taking and information collection application
- **Page Creator:** A Web-design application
- **Picasa:** A photo-editing and sharing application
- **Scholar:** A search service specifically for scholarly papers
- **SketchUp:** A 3D modeling application
- **SMS:** A text message–based search service for mobile devices
- **Specialized Searches:** A search service for specific topics
- **Talk:** An instant messaging and Internet telephony application
- **Toolbar:** A toolbar that puts Google search capabilities in your Web browser
- **Translate:** A Web-based language translation service
- **Video:** A video sharing application
- **Web Search:** A Web-search service that indexes billions of Web pages

I've probably missed some additional programs in the preceding list, which doesn't even include the programming-based applications that enable you to design your own plug-ins for Google. The point is, Google has programs that will help you do lots of stuff better, or faster, or more conveniently. And the best part of these programs, again, is that they're FREE.

What You Can Do with Google

Okay, so that's a lot of programs. But what can you do with them? None of them are fully functional, right? Wrong. Many are fully functional. For example, Google's Page Creator can help you to quickly build and publish a Web page, and you'll find everything that you need to do it included in the program.

One great part of all of these programs is that they're Web-based. What that means (and this is especially true for the programs covered in this book) is that you have access to your information from any computer, anywhere in the world. You don't have to carry a computer with you if you're going to Florida or the Bahamas for a vacation. If you need any of the information that you've created or added to Google programs, all you have to do is find a cyber cafe and log in. Your documents and publications will all be right there. No need to carry disks, USB drives, or any other equipment that's going to weigh you down.

With Google you can also be more productive. Some of the programs covered in this book allow simultaneous editing. You and three or four colleagues can work on the same document, at the same time, and immediately see the changes. It doesn't matter if you're in the United States and your colleagues are in Japan, Russia, and Spain. You can work together as if you were sitting side by side. You don't have to wait five hours or even five minutes for feedback on your changes to a document. Your colleagues can see your changes immediately, and can respond to them just as quickly.

One more thing Google does is guard your bottom line. Because Google programs are free, that means you're not shelling out hundreds of dollars for the privilege of working. Instead, you and every other person in your company can access these programs right from the Internet; the only cost to you is the Internet connection, which presumably you're already paying for. Bottom line is no worry.

That's not to say these programs aren't useful to home users, too. The benefits of Google applications are just as relevant if you're using the programs for personal rather than business reasons. You can bring your friends into the mix as you collaborate on the greatest party of the year, or share your work-in-progress with your critique group. You can even use Picasa to manipulate and share your favorite photos. The possibilities with Google are endless.

What's Not Covered Here

I can hear you already: "That's a long list of programs to cover all in one book." You're right. It's too long and it wouldn't do the programs justice, so I've chosen just the programs that will help you be more productive while saving you from having to purchase high-cost, proprietary software: Google Docs & Spreadsheets, Page Creator, Calendar, Notebook, Talk, Picasa, and Gmail.

The programs should give you a fully functional office suite when used together:

- **Google Docs & Spreadsheets:** The Google answer to Microsoft Word and Excel. These two programs aren't as functional as their Microsoft rivals, but what's there should be all you need for basic data processing, blogging, and spreadsheet functionality.
- **Page Creator:** Google's Page Creator is an online tool for designing and publishing Web sites. It takes just minutes to set up an attractive Web site using this program, and although it's not as functional as some Web page design programs, the What You See Is What You Get (WYSIWYG) interface is easy to use.
- **Calendar:** Need to keep track of your day-to-day appointments? Google Calendar is a decent calendar application that lets you quickly see what you have scheduled for the day. It's missing a few of the nicer functions of Microsoft Outlook, but it's functional (and useful) nonetheless.
- **Notebook:** One problem that many people come up against as they're searching the Web or using an Internet-based application is that they need somewhere to put notes about what they're learning or need to know. Google offers Google Notebook to help you with that. Save all or parts of Web pages and add notes to them, or just create your own notes in the program. Then, when you need to access your information, it shouldn't be too hard to find.
- **Talk:** Everyone needs to stay connected. Google Talk offers a variety of ways to do that, from chats and instant messaging to VoIP services that are easy to use.
- **Gmail:** Of course, no office suite is complete without some e-mail application. Gmail may be the newest e-mail app on the Web, but unofficially it's the granddaddy of them all. Gmail has a never-toss-just-search philosophy about e-mail, so you never again have to worry about another accidentally deleted e-mail. And if security is your concern, you'll be most pleased with the Gmail spam filter. It's amazing.

- **Picasa:** Digital photos are quickly taking the place of their paper-based counterparts, and everyone wants an application that will let them manipulate photos. Picasa is that application. You can even use Picasa to share your digital photos with other people.

All of that still doesn't tell you what's not covered here. And there's quite a lot that's not. Some things you probably won't see (or won't see more than a note about) are AdWords and Google Analytics. AdWords is an advertising application from Google, and Google Analytics is about tracking your Web site traffic. Both might be useful in your daily business flow, but there's just not enough room to cover them here. Besides, great books have already been written about both applications.

LEARN MORE ABOUT ADWORDS AND GOOGLE ANALYTICS

If you're really interested in reading more about Google's AdWords program or the Google Analytics application, that information is easy enough to find. Here are some books that I recommend as a jumping-off point. And don't forget to review the help files for both applications. You'll find these books full of information that you don't want to miss.

- ***Winning Results with Google AdWords*, by Andrew Goodman. McGraw-Hill Osborne Media, ISBN: 0072257024.**
- ***Google Analytics*, by Mary Tyler and Jerri Ledford. Wiley, ISBN: 0470053852.**
- ***Building Your Business with Google For Dummies*, by Brad Hill. Wiley, ISBN: 0764571435.**

Other programs you probably won't even see mentioned include Catalogs, Scholarly, Directory, and most of the Search applications that Google has in its repertoire. These programs are beyond the scope of this book, but if you're interested in learning more about them, there's plenty of information to be found on the Google Products page online at `www.google.com/intl/en/options/`.

You might find the other programs mentioned here and there. There may even be a note or sidebar included about how those programs can help to improve your experiences with Google. But this book really is about the different productivity tools available from Google, so that's mostly what you'll find in the chapters that follow.

CHAPTER

2

Getting Started with Google

One of the most appealing aspects of Google's applications is that in most cases they're accessible to anyone who wants to give them a try. If they're not, it's usually because the application is so new that the powers that be over at Google are phasing in the number of users.

Beginning with Gmail, Google has allowed a limited number of users to sign up for applications while they are still in beta testing. Once the limited number is reached, new users are allowed to access an application only by invitation until the beta testing on the application is complete. At that time, Google opens the application to general use.

Whether you're one of the first users to access a new application, a user who's fortunate enough to land an invitation (because you know "in-people"), or someone coming to a program after the application has been opened to the general public, the first step is to create a Google account.

You Need a Google Account

I would equate Google to a kingdom full of rich wonders. The problem with kingdoms is that very often they're protected by locked doors. Google is, too. The good news is that anyone can get keys to the kingdom. The only requirement is that you register for a Google account, a process that requires a few minutes of your time and a couple of simple pieces of information:

1. Go to `www.google.com`.
2. Click the Sign In link in the top-right corner. You'll be taken to a page that displays the log-in box for those with a Google account.
3. To register a new Google account, click the Create an account now link located below the sign-in box.
4. You are taken to the Create an account screen. Fill in your e-mail address, choose a password, and select your location. You must also decide if you want personalized search capabilities enabled. Such capabilities are based on your personal usage habits. (For more information on passwords, see the sidebar "Password Tips.")
5. Now, enter the verification word, and read and agree to the terms of service and then click "I accept. Create my account now."
6. You should be taken to a page like the one shown in Figure 2-1. Now you have to wait until your verification e-mail is delivered.

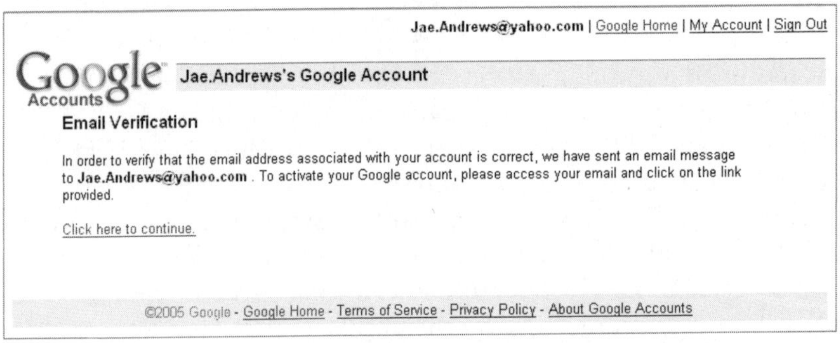

Figure 2-1: You are required to verify your account before it is activated.

7. Once the verification e-mail arrives, click the link included in the message. Alternatively, you can copy the link included in the message and paste it into the address bar of your Web browser. Your account is then verified, and you're now the proud owner of a Google account.

NOTE **Be sure you read the terms of service carefully before you click the button to accept the terms of service and create a new account.**

PASSWORD TIPS

It seems simple, but your password is your protection from unauthorized people accessing your Google account. When creating a password for your new Google account, use the following tips to ensure you're as protected as possible:

- **Create a password using a mix of numbers, letters, and punctuation marks.**
- **Use both lowercase and capital letters.**
- **Create a unique acronym by using a familiar phrase that can be represented by numbers and letters. For example, "Tomorrow is only a day away," could be used to create the password: TiO1dA.**
- **Never user personal information such as birth dates, anniversary dates, or Social Security numbers to create passwords.**
- **Avoid repetitive characters (i.e., 112233aabbcc), sequential numbers or letters (i.e., 1234 or abcd), and keyboard patterns (i.e., qwerty).**
- **Create passwords that are no less than six characters long. Eight or ten characters is a better choice.**

Your passwords are your last line of defense between you and some nefarious soul who would love to gain access to your personal information. Make sure you take the time to create the most secure password you can. And remember, never share your passwords or write them down for others to find.

Your Google account may not look like much, but there's more to it than meets the eye. Remember that this is your key to the kingdom. The wonders lie inside the castle walls.

Getting Around Google's Pages

By design, when you go to the Google page (`www.google.com`), the interface is kept simple. That's because many people who navigate to that page are going there simply to perform a Web search. But now that you have a Google account, you might like to spice up that page a bit.

Personalizing Google

Google gives you a couple of options for adding interest to the front page of your Google account. The first option is to set your global preference for your Google applications. You can do this by clicking the Preferences link to the right of the Google search box (see Figure 2-2).

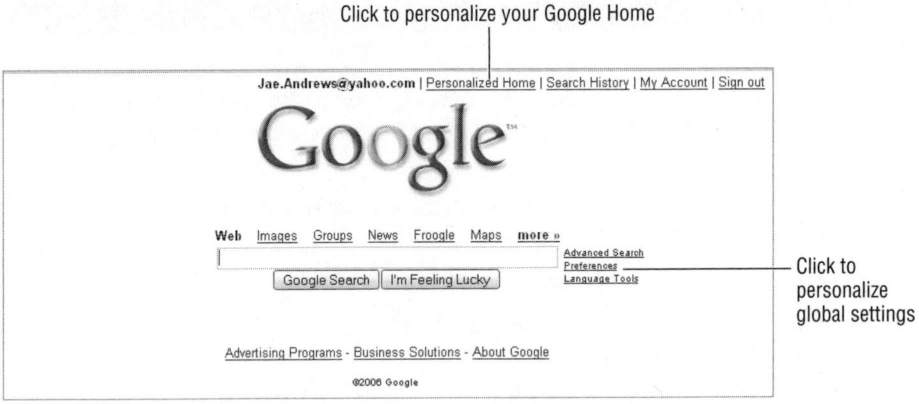

Figure 2-2: Personalize the Google home page to accentuate your personal style.

When you click the Preferences link, you are taken to a page where you can set your interface language, search language (you can leave search results from specific languages out of the results returned), SafeSearch Filtering preferences, number of results shown, and the behavior of the results window. When you've made your selections, click Save Preferences and your preferences are saved and you're returned to the main search page. (This works, however, only if you have cookies enabled, as explained by the note at the bottom of the Google page.)

The next, and most exciting, personalization option that Google offers is the ability to create a Personalized Home on Google. A Personalized Home is a Google front page that directly reflects your personality, and the activities that you use Google to complete. It's not nearly as Spartan as the default Google home page, but it's far more useful.

To create your Personalized Home, click the Personalized Home link on the top right of the page. You are taken to a page from which you can select different types of content to include on the page. What's included in this first selection menu is only the beginning.

Many more modules are available that are designed to perform all sorts of functions, from showing you the time to connecting you with your calendar, Gmail, and even the RSS feeds you may subscribe to. Choose from the available modules to personalize your page with information that's relevant to your style and personality. When you're finished, your personalized Google page might look similar to the one shown in Figure 2-3.

In true Google form, you can also change any of the content on your Personalized Home anytime you get bored with what's there. To remove an item from the page, simply click the small X next to each item, and to add new items, click the Add content link in the upper-left corner.

Figure 2-3: Your Personalized Home will reflect how you use Google.

Finding Google Applications

Now that you've got your page all set up to your liking, it's time to find all of the goodies that Google has tucked away here and there. On that main Google page, you have access to a few neat programs, such as Images, Groups, News, Froogle, and Maps. But there's far more to be found at Google if you click the more link.

When you click the link to see more of Google's products, you are taken to a page that shows you a listing of many of the applications that Google makes available. But it's still not a complete list. Even more programs are hidden deeper in the maze of Google pages.

For example, if you click the Google Labs link, you are taken to a listing of some of the programs that Google Labs has created or is currently working on. This is a good place to find some of the neat new stuff that Google has in store for the near future. Many applications start out in Google Labs and eventually graduate to general use.

Even with all of those options, there are still Google products that you might not find listed. But here's a little trick: You can access a description of all of the Google products from the company's Press Center. So, for the fullest description of what Google has available to serve the needs and wants of its customers, go to `www.google.com/press/descriptions.html`.

So many little gems are hidden here and there in Google-land that you'll spend hours just marveling at everything that's available. When you're done, come on back and I'll tell you a little more.

Google Extras

No doubt you've found a program or two that you didn't know existed or at the very least didn't know Google was responsible for. There are plenty of them out there, some more useful than others, and most won't be covered in this book.

But before I move on, there are a couple you might be interested in hearing about. These are the types of programs that have no direct bearing on your day-to-day activities, but could come in handy when you find yourself in need of inspiration.

The first of these tools is Google Zeitgeist. This is a handy ranking of the top-ranking search queries of the week, month, and year, both domestically and internationally. So, why should you care? You may not. But if you want to know what's on the mind of people who use Google, the Zeitgeist is the best place to find out. And you can go directly to Google Zeitgeist at the following Web address: `www.google.com/press/zeitgeist.html`.

Google Trends is another program you might find interesting. It enables you to see how often people have searched for topics of interest to you over time. A good use for Google Trends is if you're considering a marketing campaign. You can use Google Trends to let you know how or how often keywords associated with your marketing campaign might be searched for. If you're interested in Google Trends, you can find it at `www.google.com/trends`.

Two final jewels that might interest you are Google Blog and Google Groups. Actually, there are nearly 30 official Google blogs and probably even more groups. The blogs can all be accessed from the main Google Blog at `http://googleblog.blogspot.com/`.

Google is constantly changing. These blogs are the best way to keep up with what's happening at Google now and what's coming in the future. You'll also find tips and examples of how to use the various programs covered by each of the blogs.

Google-related groups, which are mailing lists that you can join, are also a useful tool if you want to know more about product features or how others use various features of a particular product. You can find Google Groups at `http://groups.google.com/?hl=en`. To find groups related to a specific Google product, search for that product or browse the group categories by clicking the Browse group categories link near the bottom of the page.

Google has so much to offer that you could spend days just browsing through the various programs and information related to those programs. Eventually, however, you'll probably need to get something done. Whether it's write a letter to a colleague or friend, create a Web site, keep up with appointments, or have a phone conversation, Google has the tools you need. Keep reading. Before the journey is over, I'll cover the tools that will increase your productivity the most.

PART

II

Google Docs

Information is everything. That's the mantra today's society lives by. And in living by it, we're constantly under pressure not only to create information but also to digitize what we create so that anyone, anywhere in the world, can access it.

Google's word-processing program, Google Docs, is one-half of a program that provides a solution to that problem. (The other half of the program — Google Spreadsheets — is covered in Part III of this book.) Together, Google Docs & Spreadsheets is a powerful program. But even when taken separately from its brother, Google Docs is a useful document-creation and editing program that's entirely digital — meaning that you can access it on the Web, from any Internet connection in the world. And it offers some powerful tools to help you quickly create, edit, share, and publish documents with a minimum of time and effort.

This section will help you get up to speed on working with Google Docs. You'll find information on how to get around in the program and how to use it to create documents that you can collaborate on and share with other people. With this information, you'll become a Google Docs power user in no time.

CHAPTER

3

Welcome to Google Docs

In the 1980s, the world began moving from an industrial-based economy to an information-based one. Since then, data that were previously shared and stored in paper form are now mostly electronic. E-mail has become a daily part of most people's lives, and it's much easier to send a file across the Internet than to print it, fill it out, stick it in an envelope, add a stamp, and mail it. It's a lot faster, too.

Increasingly, even sending documents via e-mail is becoming too slow and cumbersome. If you're working on a document that needs revisions by three people, why take the time to create the document, send it to each individual for editing, and then spend hours consolidating the edits into a cohesive document, when you can all add your contributions to the document at the same time?

If a document is Web-based, it's easy for the authors to create, collaborate, and share in Internet time.

Why Use Google Docs?

Before we get too deep into Google Docs, you may notice that the program is actually called Google Docs & Spreadsheets. That's because two programs are actually combined into one. You have Google Docs, which I address in this section of the book, but there is also Google Spreadsheets, which is a spreadsheet application, much like Microsoft Excel. I cover Google Spreadsheets in Part III of the book.

There will be some overlap in the programs because they are two parts of a whole. Where necessary, I'll repeat information, but if it's not necessary, I'll just refer you back to the section of the book that covered that action or activity. Navigation is a good example. Because the programs are combined, some of the navigational structure is exactly the same. If it is and it's not integral to the directions being given, I'll just point you back to where it was covered the first time.

Now, let's get started with Google Docs. If you already use a document-creation or data-processing application such as Word, StarOffice, or WordPerfect, you may be wondering why you would want to use Google Docs. Here are some of the reasons you may find Google Docs useful, even if you already use another program:

- **Cost:** Owning document-creation software can be expensive. If you purchase Microsoft Word 2003 as a standalone product, you'll pay about $169 for the full version and about $115 for the upgrade from a previous version. And the program is due for an upgrade (to Microsoft Word 2007) before the end of 2006. Each time there's an upgrade, you have to shell out more money. But with Google Docs, there are no licensing fees. No matter how often it's upgraded, the program is always free.
- **Convenience:** Microsoft Word, WordPerfect, and many other document-creation applications are largely computer-based, meaning that if you want to share a document created in one of these programs with someone else, you have to save the file to your hard drive or disk and then attach it to an e-mail and upload the file. With Google Docs, sharing a document is as simple as sending someone an invitation to view the document. It's also a big plus that others don't have to download anything because everyone is worried about security these days.
- **Collaboration:** Collaborating in some of the software-based document-creation utilities is a real pain. You create the document, send it to someone else, and she has to send it back to you. If multiple people are included in the collaboration process, it can quickly become a tedious exercise in frustration. Google Docs enables you to collaborate in real time with up to 50 other people. There's no turn-around time as you wait for the document to make its way through channels. The edits can be done almost simultaneously.
- **Creativity:** One of the big selling features of the upcoming version of Microsoft Word (2007) was to have been the ability to "publish" a document to PDF (Portable Document Format). Adobe, the company responsible for the PDF patents, couldn't come to an agreement with Microsoft, so that feature was thrown out. Google Docs does offer the capability to save a document as a PDF, HTML file, RTF (rich text for-

mat), Word document, or an OpenOffice document. This means you can create a document and then save it in a variety of formats, which gives you countless opportunities for creative publication.

Google Docs just makes sense. Your documents are available when and where you need them, and sharing is nearly effortless. Why would you pay someone for these benefits when you can have them for free?

Signing Up for Google Docs

If you're going to use Google Docs, the first thing to do is sign up for an account. At the time of this writing, Google Docs & Spreadsheets is still in beta testing, and is about 60 percent ready for widespread release. However, it's available to anyone who wants to sign up for it.

Previous versions of Google Docs & Spreadsheets required an invitation to access the program, but that's no longer the case. Now if you have a Google account (which you learned how to get in Chapter 2) you can access Google Docs & Spreadsheets.

To get started using the program, simply surf to the Google Docs & Spreadsheets sign-on page. The URL is `http://docs.google.com`. Be sure you don't use the "www" designation in the URL because it will take you to an error page.

Once you're on the site, simply enter your Google account user name and password in the spaces provided, as shown in Figure 3-1. Then click the Sign In button and you are taken to the default page for the program.

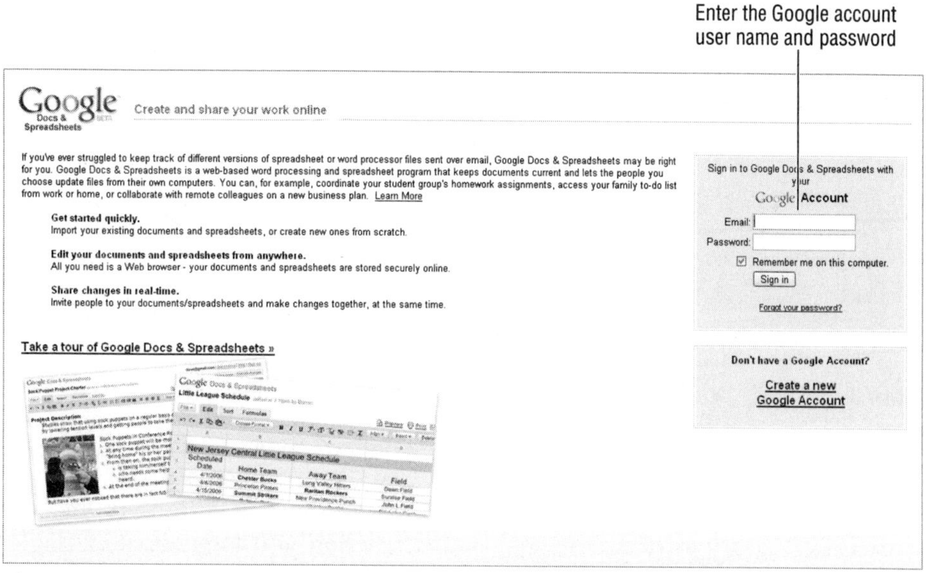

Figure 3-1: Enter your Google account user name and password to sign in.

If you still haven't signed up for a Google account, there's also a link on this page (right below the sign-in box) that will take you to a page where you can create your Google account.

Navigating Google Docs

The first time that you sign into Google Docs & Spreadsheets, you are shown a Welcome page that explains a little about how the program works. Before Google Docs & Spreadsheets, there were two separate programs called Writely and Google Spreadsheets.

If you were a Writely user, you may find that your documents from Writely are not available when you first sign in. This happens when you sign into Google Docs with a different user name than you used with Writely, or if you didn't use Writely in the past. Don't worry; if you're just using a different user name and password now, you can click the Move My Documents button, shown in Figure 3-2, to import your documents from Writely into Google Docs & Spreadsheets. When you use this link, follow the prompts that are provided, including entering your Writely user name and password.

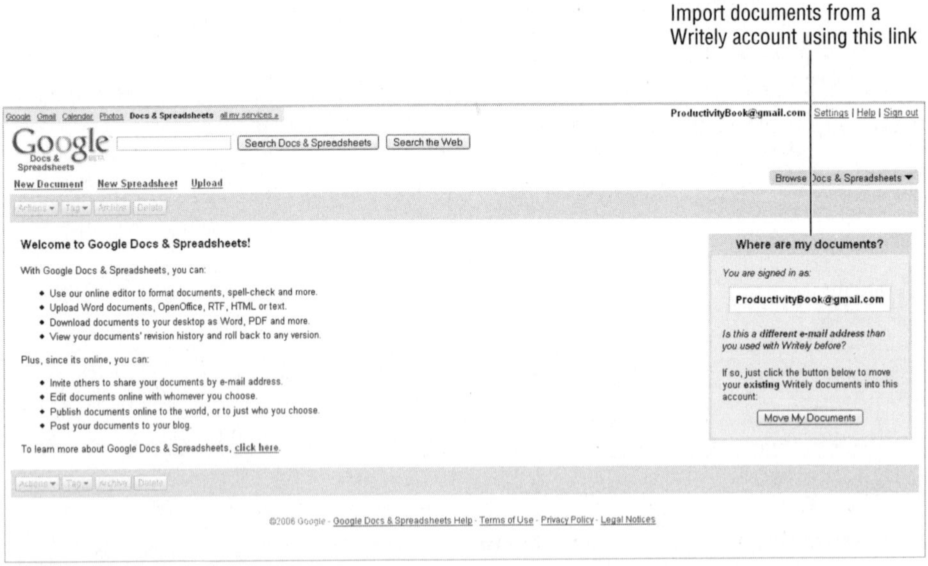

Figure 3-2: Google Docs & Spreadsheets is a little different from its predecessors.

After you've created documents or imported documents into Google Docs, the appearance of the program changes a bit when you first sign on. Instead of the introductory information that you saw when you logged into Google Docs the first time, you'll see that Google Docs is designed with what's called a WYSIWYG (pronounced WHIZZ-y-wig) interface — short for What You See Is What You Get. This means that all the basic functions of the program are right out there in front for you to see.

When you sign into Google Docs & Spreadsheets after you've created documents, you'll see a list of the documents and spreadsheets that you've accessed in the last 30 days, as shown in Figure 3-3. One more thing that you'll notice about this view is that documents and spreadsheets have different icons (also shown in Figure 3-3). This is a quick way to tell which is which in case you have spreadsheets and documents with the same names.

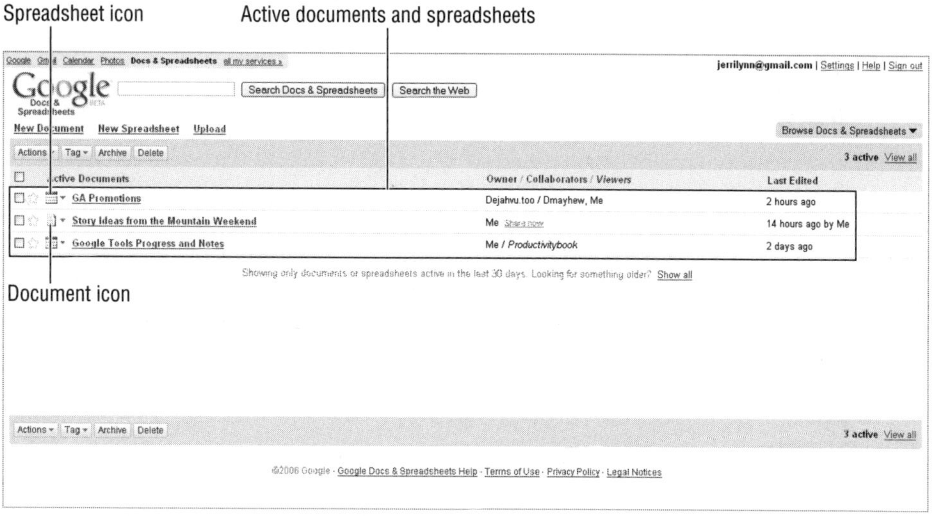

Figure 3-3: Documents accessed within the last 30 days are listed on the front page.

Finding Documents

One thing you won't see when you first log into Google Docs is all of the documents that you've created in the past that are more than 30 days old. These documents are hidden out of view to keep the interface as clean as possible.

NOTE **Google Docs and Google Spreadsheets share a combined navigational system so much of what's covered in the following pages will be exactly the same for the Spreadsheets half of the program. The real difference in navigation will be discussed in future chapters that refer specifically to working with documents or spreadsheets.**

To access your documents that are more than 30 days old, you need to change the view. You can do this in different ways, all of which are labeled in Figure 3-4.

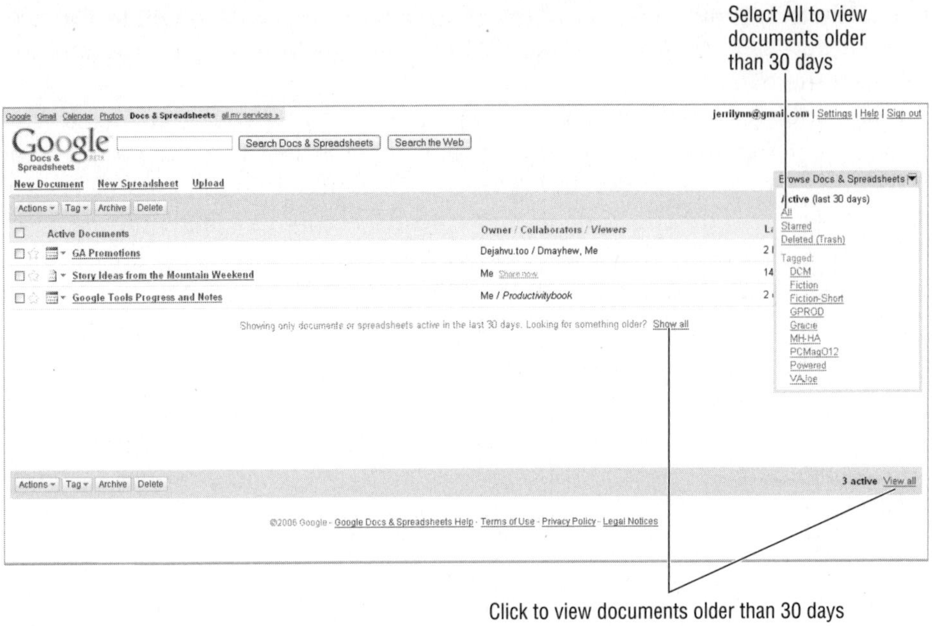

Select All to view documents older than 30 days
Click to view documents older than 30 days

Figure 3-4: There are several ways to access your documents in Google Docs.

The first way to find those older documents is to click the Show All link beneath your document list. This changes your view from only active documents to all documents, including those that haven't been accessed in a while.

Another way to access all of your documents is to click the View all link that you'll find both above and below your document list on the far-right side of the page. In Figure 3-4, the upper link is not shown, but when that menu isn't displayed, you should be able to easily locate it.

Finally, you can use the Browse Docs & Spreadsheets link in the upper-right corner of the screen. As Figure 3-4 shows, when you click this link, a menu appears. Select All from the menu to view all your documents.

In that same menu, there are also commands that allow you to see different views of your documents. These commands include the following:

- **Active Documents:** By default, you're shown the Active Documents tab. This tab lists all of the documents that you've accessed in the past 30 days.
- **All:** This option lists all of the documents that you have created or imported into the Google Docs & Spreadsheets program.
- **Starred Documents:** This option lists only documents that you have starred. Starring a document is as simple as clicking on the star next to the document title.

- **Deleted (Trash):** Here you'll find documents that you've sent to the trash. Documents stay in this folder indefinitely unless you choose to empty the trash folder. But once you've emptied it, the documents are gone forever.
- **Tagged Documents:** Tags are like folders. You can assign any tag to any document. Once you do, the tags will be listed beneath the Tagged Documents option. When you click a tag, you are taken to a list of only the documents labeled with a specific tag.

In addition to the options on this drop-down menu links are also listed at the top of the list view. The links allow you to work with the documents in various ways:

- **Actions:** Gives you options to save in HTML, RTF, Word, OpenOffice, or PDF format. It also lets you copy, delete, star, and unstar a document and remove yourself from a collaboration situation.
- **Tag:** Allows you to apply a new or existing tag to a document.
- **Archive:** Sends selected documents into archive status so they are not shown in your active document view. This is useful if you are finished with a document and don't want it to clutter your screen for the next 30 days.
- **Delete:** Deletes the selected document.

To use any of these commands, place a check mark in the box next to the document name.

One thing you should note about these links is that the titles change depending on the view you're in. If you're in the all-documents view, then a link appears in the upper-left corner that's titled Back to Active documents. When you click this link, you are taken back to your active document view.

Additional Navigation

There's one more toolbar in Google Docs that you need to know about. This one is located at the top of the page and shows links to create a new document, create a new spreadsheet, or upload either a document or spreadsheet. These are quick links that do exactly what they appear to do.

On the right side of the page, there are also links for settings, sign out, and help. These links are associated with your Google Docs & Spreadsheet account, rather than with the documents you create or edit with the program. There's also a search function, which you can use to search your documents should you need to.

Navigating Within a Document

When you create or open a document, the navigational view changes considerably. The navigation system now applies only to the document half of the Google Docs & Spreadsheets program. Here, a tabbed navigation system becomes your top-level navigation, followed by an icon-based tool set, which is used to manipulate your document. These navigation levels are shown in Figure 3-5.

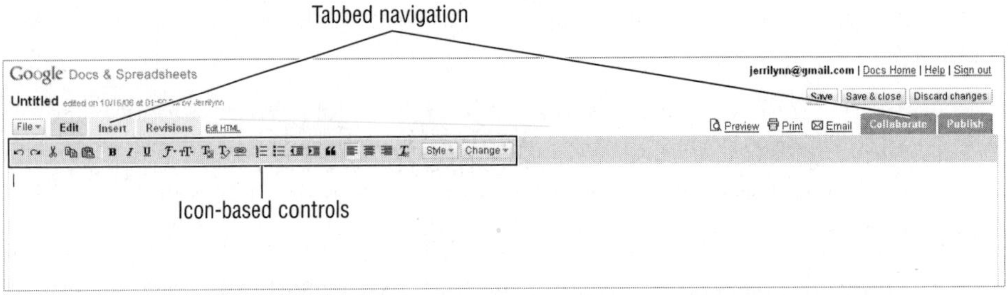

Figure 3-5: The navigational structure is more specific in the document view.

In addition to the tabs and the icons, various buttons and links will help you create, edit, and navigate through your documents.

The tabs within a document allow you to perform various functions. These tabs contain menus with some of the most common commands for working with your documents:

- Edit
- Insert
- Revisions
- Collaborate
- Publish

Each of these functions is covered in more depth in a future chapter, so I won't go into them here. What's important right now is that you understand where the navigational controls are located.

The icon-based controls should be familiar to you if you've used any other word-processing software. These controls are the ones you'll use most often, and they include the following:

- Undo Last Edit
- Redo Last Edit
- Cut

- Copy
- Paste
- Bold
- Italics
- Underline
- Font (18 Styles)
- Text Size (7 Choices)
- Text Color
- Highlight Color
- Link
- Numbered List
- Bulleted List
- Indent Less
- Indent More
- Quote
- Align Left
- Align Center
- Align Right
- Remove Formatting

In addition to these controls, two buttons are also on this list. One is the Style button. Click this button to access paragraph styles, page formatting, and additional text-formatting controls. The other button is labeled Change and it allows you to restore or remove blank lines in your document and create and manage bookmarks within your document.

To the right of the tabs is a link labeled Edit HTML. This link lets you switch to the HTML code view of your document. Farther to the right is a Preview link, which allows you to see how your document will look if you publish it to the Web. This is especially handy if you're creating documents specifically for display on the Internet.

Also in this right corner are links to print and e-mail the document that you're working with, and you'll find (above the tabs) the buttons that enable you to save, save and close, or discard the changes that you've made to the document.

If you make changes in your document that you don't want to keep when you finish, you can click the Discard Changes button and the document is returned to the same state it was in when you first opened it. This is useful because Google Docs automatically saves your work every few minutes to ensure that nothing is lost. In other words, if you happen to be working on a document and your computer crashes, your changes won't be lost.

Finally, in the bottom-right corner you'll find the Check Spelling option. If you click this option, all of the words in your document that have questionable spelling are highlighted. Right-click the highlighted word, and Google makes suggestions about the correct spelling of the intended word. You can also choose to add a word to your dictionary, if it's a word that's not recognized by Google.

Google Docs & Spreadsheets truly is a WYSIWYG document editor. There's not a whole lot to it outside of what you see when you first open the program or a document. Yes, a few commands are buried in the menus of the program, but most of them are intuitive, so it shouldn't take you long at all to become comfortable moving around the program. You can quickly begin using it to create, share, and publish your documents in electronic format or in print.

CHAPTER

4

Working with Documents

Whether you call it a word-processing program or a document-creation, editing, and collaboration program, Google Docs is a tool that makes putting your thoughts into an electronic form easy. With Google Docs, you have the ability to start new documents, import documents you've created in other programs, and even to publish your documents in various formats. With those options available to you, you can share and publish your work with a minimum of effort.

Starting a New Document

It's likely that the first thing you want to do when you begin using Google Docs is to create a document. With Google Docs, creating new documents is easy. Near the top of the active documents page is a New Document link. When you click this link, you're taken to a new blank document. You can immediately begin creating your document by typing into the blank space provided.

Uploading Documents

If you don't have an Internet connection, a time may come when you start a document in another program but want to import it into Google Docs. Or maybe you have documents created previously that you want to import into Google Docs so that you can access them from any Internet connection.

Google Docs allows you to upload documents from other programs such as StarOffice and Microsoft Word. You can even upload plain text documents if that's what you have. Just click the Upload link near the top of the page. When you click the link, you're taken to a page like the one shown in Figure 4-1. Using the Browse button, navigate to the location of the file you want to upload, select the file, and click Open. (You can upload spreadsheets with the same command. More on that later.)

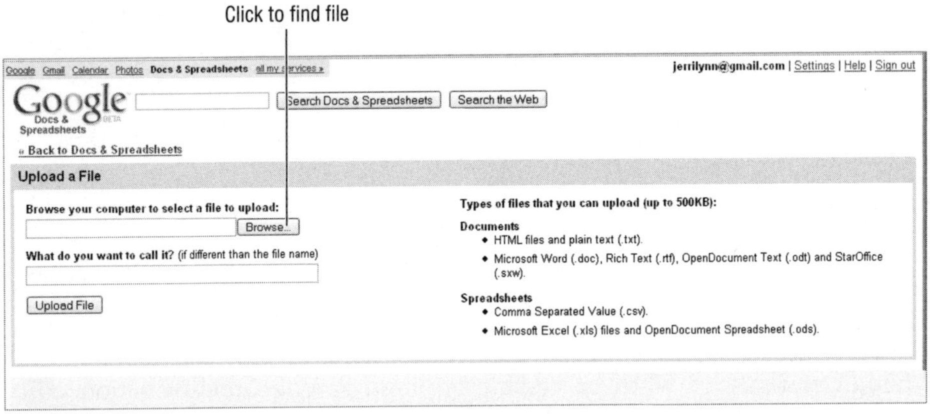

Figure 4-1: Google Docs allows you to upload documents created in other programs.

If you want the file saved to a different name than it already has, enter the new name in the text box under "What do you want to call it?" If you want the file name to remain the same, you can leave the box blank. When you've finished selecting and naming the file, click Upload.

Depending on the speed of your Internet connection, it could take a few minutes for the file to upload. When the upload is complete, the file will be opened in Google Docs for you to work with.

Another option for uploading files to Google Docs is to e-mail them in. Google Docs assigns each user an individual e-mail address, which you can use to send documents to your Google Docs account. On the same page that you use to upload a document, you'll find your Google Docs e-mail address, as shown in Figure 4-2 (part of that address is blacked out to protect me from weirdness). It's a long and difficult e-mail address. The folks at Google Docs created e-mail addresses like this to help keep other people from guessing them and to protect your documents.

That e-mail address is all you need to e-mail documents into your Google Docs account. Create an e-mail addressed to your account, attach the file, and send it. The document is automatically imported into your Google Docs account. There's nothing more you need to do. You can even just enter the text that you want included in your new document in the body of the e-mail and it will be converted for you.

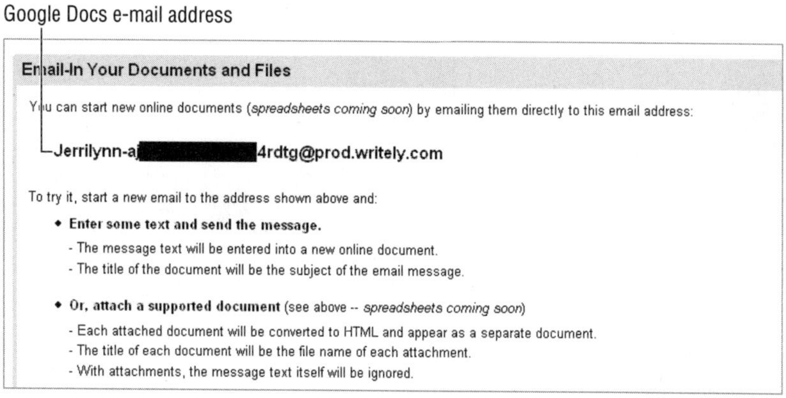

Google Docs e-mail address
Email-In Your Documents and Files
You can start new online documents (spreadsheets coming soon) by emailing them directly to this email address:
Jerrilynn-a[redacted]4rdtg@prod.writely.com
To try it, start a new email to the address shown above and:
Enter some text and send the message.
- The message text will be entered into a new online document.
- The title of the document will be the subject of the email message.
Or, attach a supported document (see above -- spreadsheets coming soon)
- Each attached document will be converted to HTML and appear as a separate document.
- The title of each document will be the file name of each attachment.
- With attachments, the message text itself will be ignored.

Figure 4-2: Your Google Docs e-mail address is a unique way to import documents.

You should receive a confirmation by e-mail when the document has been successfully imported.

If you don't receive a confirmation message, then something went wrong in the process. The most likely problem is that you've changed your nickname in your settings, and the e-mail address that you need to send documents into Google Docs has changed. You can always come back to the import page to make sure you're using the right e-mail address.

Editing and Formatting Documents

Now comes the fun part. You've started your document, uploaded a document, or e-mailed it in, but how do you edit and format the document? It's not too difficult, but before we get started there are some things you should know.

A couple of factors affect the way your document appears when you open it in Google Docs. The first of these is your browser. Some browsers perform differently from others, so when you're viewing uploaded documents, be conscious of the browser that you're using. If you're using Firefox and your document doesn't display as you think it should, try switching to Internet Explorer. This won't always make a difference, but it's worth a try if you're experiencing difficulties.

The other factor to be aware of is the difference in word-processing programs. What you create in one program may not display exactly the same in a different program. So, for example, if you create an invoice in Microsoft Word, when you upload it to Google Docs it might not appear the same (see Figure 4-3). This is especially true if you've created graphics-intense documents in an outside program and imported them into Google Docs.

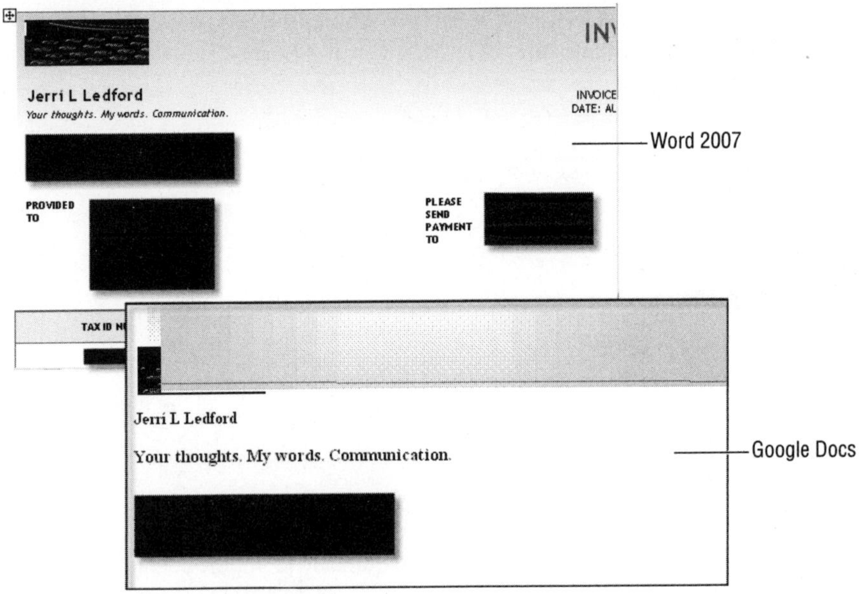

Figure 4-3: Documents created in other programs may look different in Google Docs.

BROWSERS SUPPORTED BY GOOGLE DOCS & SPREADSHEETS

As with most Internet-based programs, the Web browser that you use to access Google Docs plays a big role in how your documents appear. Some browsers aren't supported by Google Docs at all, so it's good to know if your browser is supported. Here's a list of the browsers that Google Docs does and does not support.

Supported browsers:

- Microsoft Internet Explorer version 5.5 and later (for Windows)
- Mozilla version 1.4 and later (for Mac and Windows). The current version is called SeaMonkey.
- Firefox 1.0.6 and later (for Mac and Windows, except for version 1.5b1 on the Mac)

Browsers not supported:

- Microsoft Internet Explorer version 5 for Mac
- Microsoft Internet Explorer version 4 for Windows
- Netscape 4
- Opera
- Safari

In addition to having a supported Web browser, you should also have cookies and JavaScript enabled on your computer. You should be able to enable both of these options from the Options menu in your browser.

Whether you created the document in another application or directly in Google Docs, you'll want to use certain editing commands. The best place to start is with keyboard shortcuts. Google Docs does allow them, although some of the shortcuts may be different from what you've become accustomed to. Here's a list of the keyboard shortcuts that are available in Google Docs:

- **Save:** Ctrl+S
- **Bold:** Ctrl+B
- **Italicize:** Ctrl+I
- **Select All:** Ctrl+A
- **Copy:** Ctrl+C
- **Paste:** Ctrl+V
- **Cut:** Ctrl+X
- **Undo:** Ctrl+Z
- **Redo:** Ctrl+Y
- **Insert Link:** Ctrl+K
- **Insert Comment:** Ctrl+M
- **Go to Top:** Ctrl+Home
- **Go to End:** Ctrl+End
- **Select Next Word:** Ctrl+Alt+right arrow
- **Select Previous Word:** Crtl+Alt+left arrow
- **Single Line Return:** Shift+Enter

Using the Insert Menu

Now, with the keyboard shortcuts out of the way, you can concentrate on using some of the tools that Google Docs provides for creation of and editing in your documents. Some of the neatest tools you'll find in Google Docs are located on the Insert tab. That's where you'll find table tools, image tools, linking capabilities, and several additional commands, as shown in Figure 4-4.

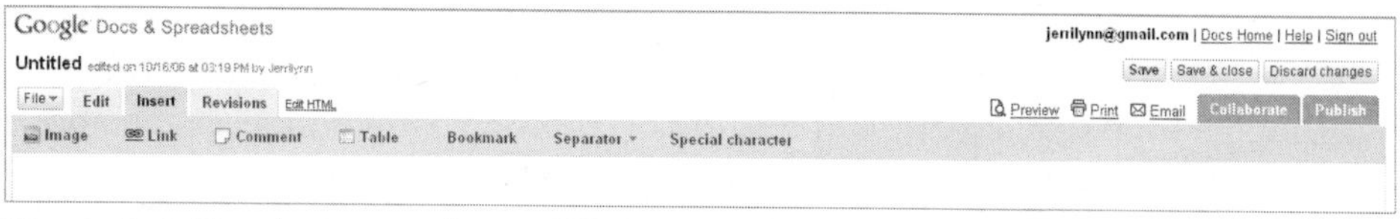

Figure 4-4: Use the Insert tab to add interest to your Google Docs documents.

Insert an Image

Images add interest to documents. The right image can make a statement about the text around it, or it can just add an interesting focal point for the information. With Google Docs, inserting an image into your document is easy. With a few clicks of a button you can add visual appeal and impact to your document.

1. Begin by placing your cursor at the point in the text where you want the image to appear.
2. From the Insert tab, click the Image icon to access the Insert Image dialog box, shown in Figure 4-5.

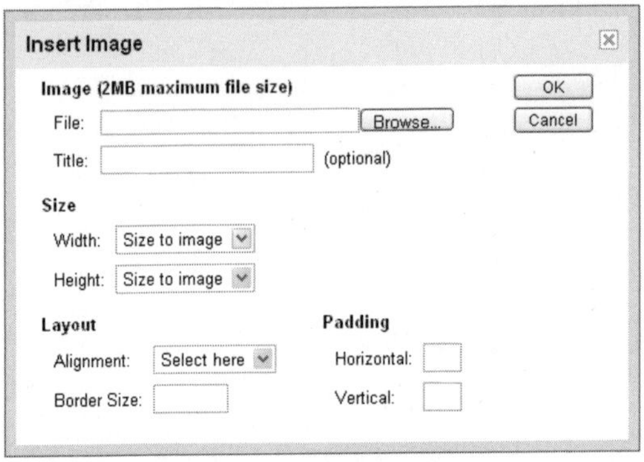

Figure 4-5: The Insert Image dialog box

3. Click the Browse button inside the dialog box, navigate to the location where you have the desired image stored, click the name of the file, and then click Open. You are returned to the Insert Image dialog box, where you can enter a title for the picture if desired, and set the size, layout, border size, and padding (which is the depth of the border around the picture).
4. When you've finished entering the settings for the image, click OK and the file will be uploaded to your document. The speed with which the file is uploaded will be determined by the speed of your Internet connection, so be patient; it could take a few minutes.
5. Once the image is inserted into your document, you can change the image title, size, layout, or padding by right-clicking on the image and selecting Change Image from the menu that appears. The Change Image dialog box appears so you can make the desired changes.

TIP **Changing the size of an image by using the Change Image menu can be frustrating if you don't know the exact pixel dimension you want to switch to. Instead, you can also use the sizing handles around the image. These are the small boxes that you see right at the outer edges of the image after you've clicked on it.**

When working with images in your document, you can't manipulate those images (i.e., changing the color, shape, or format of the image) in Google Docs. That's a function that must be performed in a graphics program.

Once you've inserted an image into a document, you may decide that you prefer not to have it there. Deleting the picture is easy, but in some browsers it requires a keyboard shortcut. Click on the image and then press the keyboard combination Ctrl+X. This cuts the image from the document. Alternatively, you can close your document without saving the changes by clicking the Discard Changes button in the top-right corner. If you use this method, however, be aware that you'll also lose any other changes that you've made in your document during this session.

Insert a Link

In some word-processing programs, activating a hyperlink is as simple as typing the URL — or Web address — into the document and then pressing the space bar. This makes the link active so users need only click the link inside the document to open a Web browser that takes them to the address listed in the link.

Google Docs doesn't have automatic activation of links, so you have to manually activate the link. Don't worry. It's a simple process.

There are two ways to create a hyperlink in Google Docs. The first is to type the URL, highlight it, and then click the Link button on the editing toolbar. The Insert Link dialog box appears. Use this box to select the type of link you're creating and to set the link display properties. Because you highlighted the URL to activate the link, the URL should be automatically entered into the address box, as shown in Figure 4-6.

If instead of a Web address you want to insert a hyperlink that's made up of words, such as "Click here for great deals!" you can do that by placing your cursor at the point in your document where you want the link to appear. Then click the Insert tab and click Link on the toolbar, or click the Link icon on the editing toolbar. The same Insert Link dialog box that you saw before will appear, except now there is no Web site address filling the URL box. Add the URL you want to use, set the display properties to include the words you want to use as a link, and then click OK. As Figure 4-7 shows, the link is created, but the URL isn't visible.

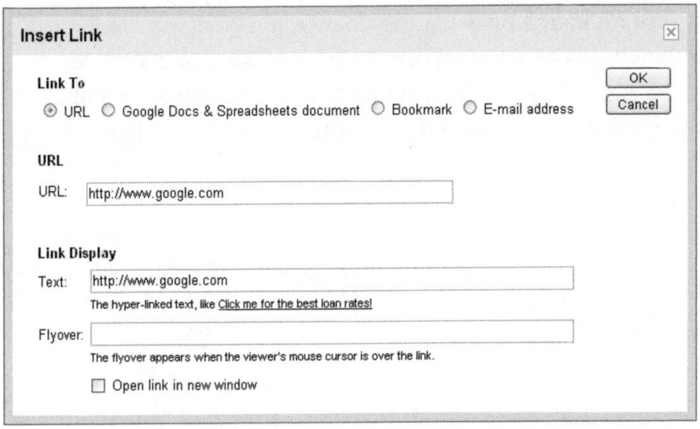

Figure 4-6: Use the Insert Link dialog box to set your link properties.

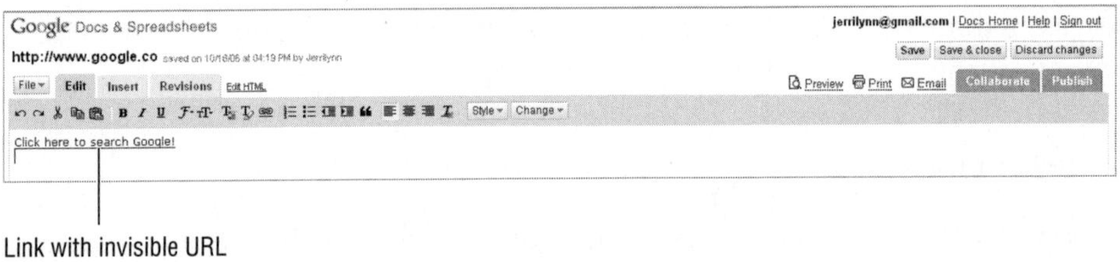

Figure 4-7: Create hyperlinks from text instead of URLs.

Insert Comments

Comments are helpful tools for editing documents. By using an insert-comment function in a word-processing program, you can add notes to other collaborators or to yourself to help you remember information that needs to be added or to make note of facts that you need to check.

Google Docs has a comment function on the Insert menu that makes it easy for you to add and manipulate comments within your documents.

To add a comment, place your cursor in the document in the place you want the comment to appear and then click Insert → Comment. As Figure 4-8 shows, a comment box is inserted into the document at the point of the cursor. Simply type your note or question into the comment box. When you're finished, you need to navigate away from the comment by clicking your cursor elsewhere in the document.

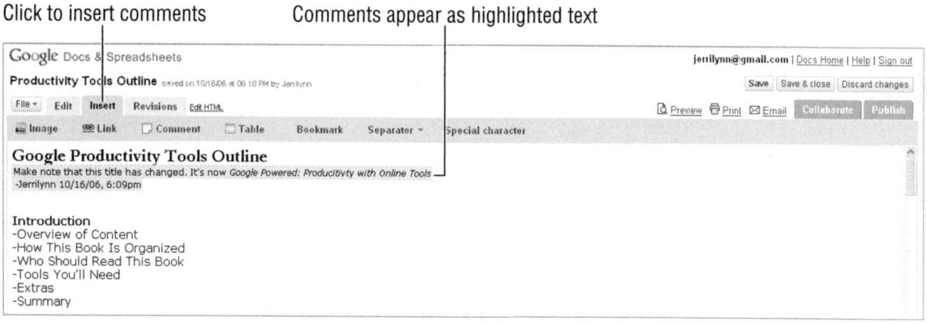

Figure 4-8: Use comments to leave notes for yourself or your collaborators.

If several people are editing your document, each can have a personal color for comments (up to six people, the program's current limit for separate colors). To change the color of your comment, click on your name inside the comment box and select a new color from the menu shown in Figure 4-9.

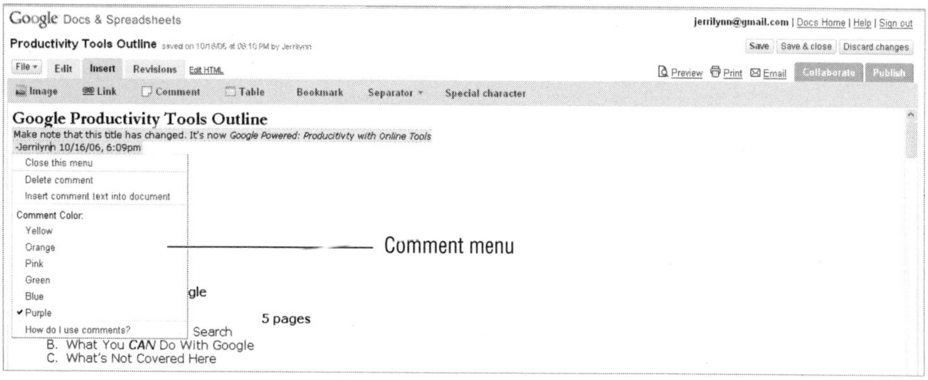

Figure 4-9: Click on your name within the comment box to reveal the comment menu.

One more neat little trick: You can use comments to hold specific pieces of information. For example, if you highlight a segment of text and then click Insert → Comment, you'll be prompted to include the text in the comment. This is handy if there's a specific fact that you want to investigate or that you want someone else to take note of.

You can also add text within a comment directly to the document if you decide you want to. To do this, click inside the comment box and then click the Insert comment text into document link from the menu that appears. *All* of the text within the comment box will then be inserted into that point in your document, including your name and the time and date notation that's included in the comment.

"But what happens with the comments when I publish a document?" you might be wondering. It's simple. Your comments will show on your document only in the editing view. When you preview, publish, or post your document, the comments are invisible to viewers.

Insert a Table

With Google Docs, you can even add tables to your documents. Here's how:

1. Place your cursor in the text where you want the table to appear and click the Table link on the Insert tab.
2. The Insert Table dialog box, shown in Figure 4-10, is displayed. Enter information for the desired size, layout, border, and background color of the table, and then click OK.

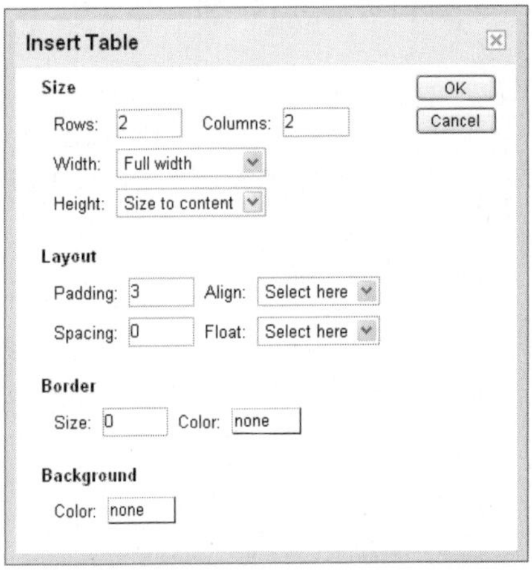

Figure 4-10: Use the Insert Table dialog box to create a table to your specifications.

3. The table is inserted into your document at the point of your cursor. To change the location of the table, highlight the text around it and move the text above or below the table. This moves the table up or down on the page.
4. If you find that you need to change the columns or rows, right-click inside the column or row and use the menu that appears (shown in Figure 4-11) to make those changes.

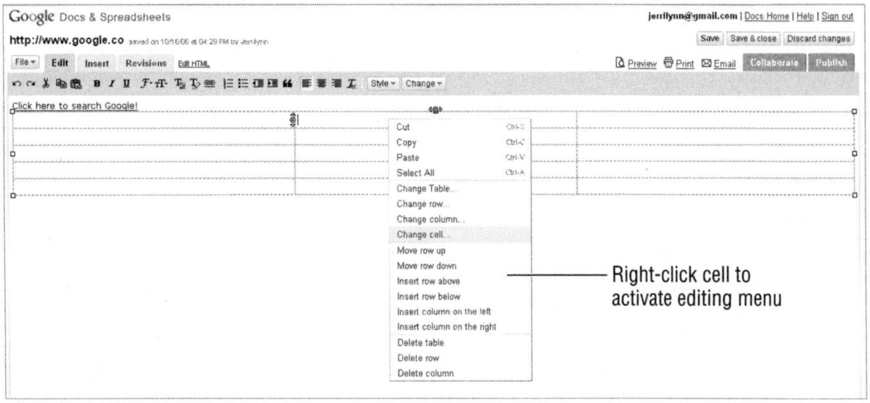

Figure 4-11: Right-click inside a column, row, or cell to access an editing menu.

5. If you need to add rows or columns to your table, click inside a cell, and a small circle with an X in the center and arrows on either side will appear above and beside the cell, as shown in Figure 4-12. The icon above the cell controls columns and the icon beside the cell controls rows. Use the X to remove columns or rows and the arrows to add columns or rows.

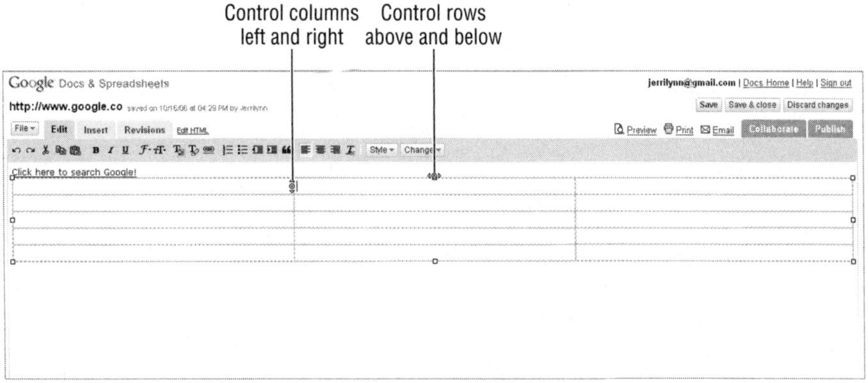

Figure 4-12: Use the icons above and beside the cell to add new rows or columns.

6. When you've finished working with your table, remember to click the Save button in the top-right corner of the page to save your work.

Insert a Bookmark

Bookmarks are useful tools in long or complicated documents. If you're creating a 50-page company report using Google Docs, the ability to link from the table of contents directly to each heading in the book will make it easier for people reading the document electronically to flip back and forth in the report.

Google Docs allows you to set bookmarks using the Insert menu although bookmarks can be a little complicated the first time you use them. Once you get the hang of bookmarking your documents, however, you'll find the feature very useful.

1. Open the document into which you want to insert bookmarks.
2. When creating bookmarks, you have to work backwards, starting with the text within the document. Place your cursor at the point in the document where you want a bookmark to lead, and then click the Insert tab.
3. Select Insert Bookmark and the Insert Bookmark dialog box appears.
4. Enter a name for the bookmark in the New Bookmark text box, or select a bookmark from the list below it (if any have already been created), and then click OK.

   You may think nothing has happened because there will be no evidence that you've set a bookmark, but trust Google Docs. It's on your side.
5. Go back to the place in the document that you want to be able to click to reach the bookmark that you just placed. Highlight the text you would like to have linked, and then click the Link icon.
6. The Insert Link dialog box appears. In the Link to section, select Bookmark.
7. Select the bookmark you want to link to from the drop-down list. Now, if you highlighted text to create this link, the Text entry box will be repopulated, so the only other information you need to enter is the Flyover text, if you want it included. Flyover text is what appears if you place your pointer over a link.
8. When you've finished entering this information, click OK and the link is created. You'll also be returned to the document, but if you try to click the link, it won't appear to be active.
9. To ensure the link is correct, click the Preview button in the upper-right corner above your document. You'll be taken to a document preview, where the link should appear active. When you click it, you should be taken directly to the spot in the document that you intended to be bookmarked.

Bookmarks can be very useful tools when you know how to use them. The first time out, it's a little complicated, but once you get the hang of it, the process is easy. And with bookmarks, your readers don't have to scroll through pages of documents. They can click back and forth. And they'll love you for it.

Using Separators

A separator is an element you'll find useful for adding interest and visual appeal to your document. In Google Docs, separators take two forms: page breaks and lines. A page break literally ends a page and begins a new one. If you're writing a long document with several separate sections or chapters, page breaks make it easier to create specific breaks between sections.

Lines are less dramatic separators. Most of the time, lines are used to break up text that's within a larger section. In long documents, you may want to create these breaks between different topics or sets of instructions.

To insert a separator into your document, place your cursor at the spot you want the separator to appear and then click Insert → Separator. A drop-down menu appears, as shown in Figure 4-13. Select Page break or Horizontal line and the separator is inserted in your text.

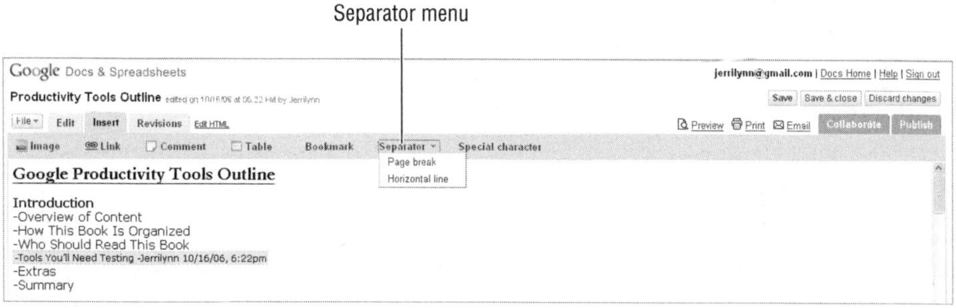

Figure 4-13: Select the type of separator to insert from the drop-down menu.

Using Special Characters

Your last option on the Insert tab is the special-characters function. This function allows you to insert special characters, such as symbols and characters from other languages, into your document.

To insert a special character, place your cursor on the spot in the document where you want the special character to appear and then click Insert → Special Characters. The Insert Character dialog box appears. Click the character that you'd like to insert into your document and the dialog box closes and the character appears on the page where your cursor was located.

If you decide later that you don't want the special character there, just delete it, as you would any other letter that you type into the document (using the Backspace key).

Using the Styles and Fonts

One other important element in creating and editing documents is the Style menu, shown in Figure 4-14. This menu controls your paragraph layout, page spacing, and text formatting.

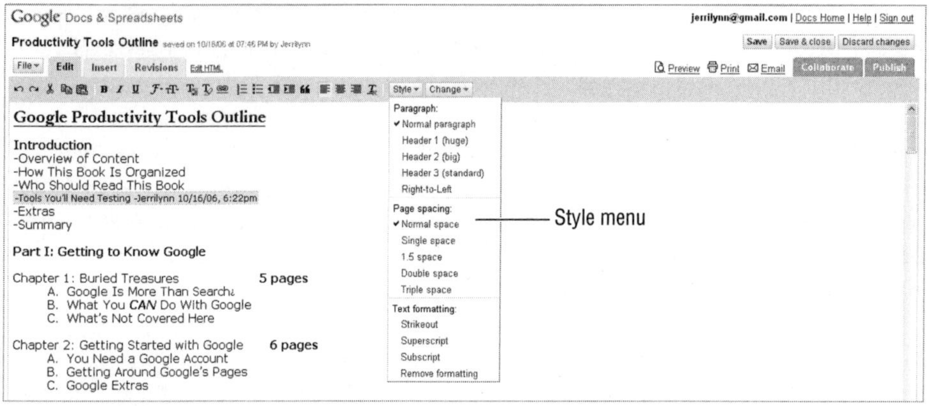

Figure 4-14: The Style menu contains style controls and commands.

To use one of the options on the menu before you type text on a page, place your cursor on the page where you want the style to begin, and then select Style. Click the option that you want, and that option will be applied to your document from that point forward unless you change the style again.

If you have existing text within a document that you want to change, highlight the text, select Style, and then choose the option you want to apply to that text. For example, if you have a paragraph within a document that you would like to have double-spaced, highlight the paragraph and then select Style → Double space. The highlighted text is reformatted into the Double space style.

In addition to the style options, Google Docs also contains 18 fonts in 7 different sizes. You can use fonts to add interest to a document; the fonts available in the Google Docs program can be found under the Font and font-size icons, which are located on the formatting toolbar. To change the font or font size of your text, highlight the text you want changed, and then click the Font or font-size icon. Select the font or font size that you want applied to the text and the changes are made within the document.

Despite the Spartan look of Google Docs, some pretty powerful tools are available for working with your documents. The editing tools covered here are just a portion of those you might like to use. For example, text and background color options are available. You can find these options on the Editing toolbar that is displayed each time you begin or open a document.

Take some time to play with the different editing features of Google Docs. When you come back, I'll show you how to save and delete your documents.

Saving and Deleting Documents

Ah, you're back. Good. So, by now you've played around with the editing controls in Google Docs. There's still more to learn, but before you move on to some of the more interesting features of the program, let's quickly cover how to save and delete documents. It's easy.

If you're working on a document in Google Docs, you'll notice there is an automatic save function. Every so often — about every minute or minute and a half — you'll see a flash near the top-right corner of your page. This is the auto-save feature making a temporary copy of your document. This temporary copy is kept until you close out of the document, save it, or discard the changes you've made to the document.

So, if you're working on a document and lose power to your computer, your document should be current up to the last save when you open it again.

Now, the ability to revert to a previous version of the document is a handy feature of Google Docs. If you find you need to use this feature (and everyone does once in a while), open the document and click the Revisions tab. On the Revisions page, select Compare two revisions to look at two revisions of the same document. Select Browse Revisions to be taken to a view (the default view) of the most recent revision with a drop-down list of available previous revisions. And select Revision History to be taken to a historical list of the revisions that have been made to the document.

If you want to revert to one of those revisions, click the revision to open it, and then from the upper-right corner select Revert to this one. The document will be restored to its previous state, but any changes that you've made since that time will be lost.

When you finish working on a document, click the Save button in the upper-right corner, and your document will be saved and you'll be returned to the Active Document view.

If there's a document that you would like to delete, you can place a check mark next to it in the Active Document view, and then click Delete. You'll be prompted to confirm that you want to delete the document. Click Yes, and the document is sent to the trash.

Every once in a while you may delete a document and then later realize that you didn't really mean to delete it. Not a problem. When you send documents to the trash in Google Docs, they actually go into a kind of limbo where they hang out for a while. In this case, "a while" is until you decide to empty the trash bin.

What this means is that you can recover a document you have deleted. Simply click the Deleted link (in the Browse Docs & Spreadsheets drop-down menu on the Active Document page). You'll be taken to the list of documents in your trash bin. Select the one you want to restore and click Undelete. The document is returned to your Active Document list.

Alternatively, if you're certain that you want to delete all of those documents permanently, click the Empty Trash button. All of the documents in the Deleted (Trash) folder will be completely deleted and cannot be recovered.

Moving On

Using Google Docs is just as easy as it sounds. It does take some getting used to, especially if you've used other word-processing programs in the past. But once you get the hang of the way things work in Google Docs, you'll be creating, editing, and collaborating on documents like a pro.

Once you get the hang of the basics, there are more advanced features in Google Docs that you can take advantage of. Some of the capabilities you learn about in the next chapter include collaborating, blogging, and publishing your Google documents.

CHAPTER

5

Do More with Google Docs

Teachers, students, and many others can use Google Docs to collaborate on documents, notes, reports, or other assignments. That's because Google Docs offers more possibilities than just creating new documents. Using the tools available through Google Docs, you can collaborate on documents and publications, create blog posts and publish those entries, and publish your creations both online and in print. It just takes an understanding of how these features work.

In this chapter, I hope you find that understanding. And I hope that you'll come away with some wonderful ideas about the way you can use Google Docs to collaborate or create.

Collaborating with Google Docs

When you open a document in Google Docs, you might notice the tabs across the top of the page. By default, Google Docs opens a document in the Edit tab. But I've already reviewed editing, so let's talk about collaborating a little.

Why Collaborate?

Why would you want to collaborate with someone else on a document? That's a good question, and there could be lots of answers. Here are a few of the ways that people collaborate:

- As previously mentioned, teachers and students use the program to collaborate on assignments. Google Docs is within a teacher's budget (did I mention it's *free*?). It appeals to students because it's an online venue where students can come together to share their thoughts and questions from the class. For example, a group of students in a continuing-education course might all share their versions of the notes taken at one class. Using collaboration capabilities, the students can add their notes. Then the teacher can review the notes and correct anything that might be incorrect or add thoughts that students seem to have missed.
- Employees can use Google Docs to collaborate on projects. In a marketing environment, this could mean that several team members collaborate on the marketing message they plan to pitch to a client. Or employees can share their documents with supervisors for input. Another way to use Google Docs in the corporate setting is to collaborate on the publication of a corporate newsletter. Whoever is in charge of producing the newsletter can allow employees to collaborate on the articles and information that will be included in the newsletter.
- In the home, parents and children can use Google Docs to come together on schedules, homework assignments, or genealogy projects. One user created a family tree from the information she knew. Then she invited all her computer-using relatives to collaborate on the document. They added information they knew, and now the family tree goes back much farther than she could have imagined.
- Writers can use Google Docs to collaborate with editors and publishers. Most writing/editing relationships require that drafts be passed back and forth numerous times for questions and editing. With Google Docs, there is no passing a document back and forth. The writer can invite the editor to comment, in the Google Docs program, online. This saves a lot of time going back and forth, and when the document is complete the writer can download it in a popular format for submission to the publication. Not only is it easier for the writer, but it makes the editing process much faster and therefore less costly for the publisher.

The ways in which you can use Google Docs to collaborate don't end with these examples. If you can think of other ways to use it for work with another person or team of people, Google Docs's collaboration feature makes it easy.

Invite Collaborators

When you first click the Collaborate tab you are taken to the collaboration page where you'll find two commands that make it easy for you to collaborate on documents with other people: Invite collaborators and Invite viewers.

When you invite someone to collaborate on a document with you, this gives them the ability to change the document formatting, add text to the document, or to perform any other functions that you can perform, except delete the document. When you choose to Invite Viewers, those you invite will be able to view the document, but not to change anything.

After you click the Collaborate tab, you are taken to a page like the one shown in Figure 5-1.

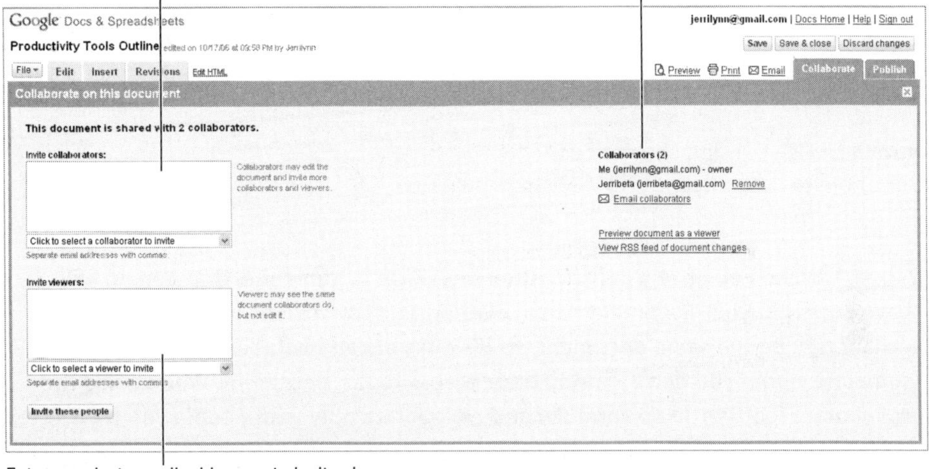

Figure 5-1: The Collaborate page provides tools to invite collaborators and viewers.

To invite a collaborator, enter that person's e-mail address in the Invite Collaborators text box. Additionally, if there are people whom you frequently ask to collaborate, you can select their names from the drop-down list that appears under the text box. You can invite up to 50 people per document to be your collaborators.

If you want to invite viewers, then enter their e-mail addresses in the Invite Viewers text box, or select the e-mail address from the drop-down list below the text box. You can invite as many people as you would like to view your documents. You can also invite a combination of collaborators and viewers.

Once you've chosen the people with whom you want to collaborate or whom you would like to allow to view your document, click the Invite these people button at the bottom of the page. You'll be asked to confirm that you want to send those people an invitation e-mail message. Click OK and you are taken to a very simple e-mail editor (shown in Figure 5-2), which you can use to type a message to the collaborators you're inviting. Type your message and then click OK. Your message is sent to your collaborators and viewers. When they receive the message and accept the invitation, they'll have access to your document.

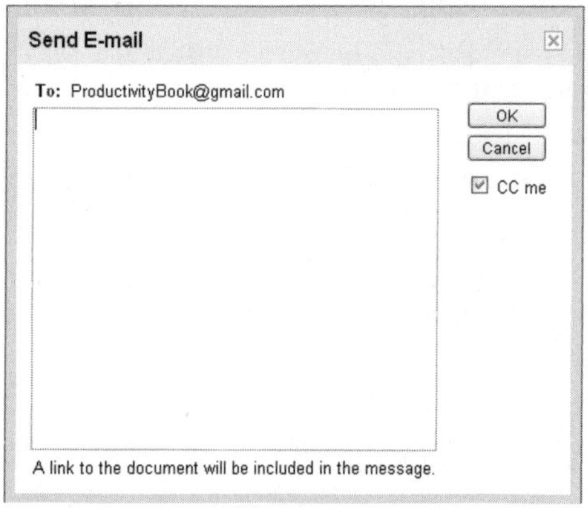

Figure 5-2: Use the simple e-mail editor to send a note to collaborators and viewers.

NOTE **When you send a collaboration invitation to someone, that person will have access to your document. Your collaborators can also invite other people to collaborate on the same document, so it's possible an invitation could go to someone whom you don't want to have access to the document. When using the collaborate feature, do so carefully and collaborate only with people you trust.**

If you prefer, you can also add people to your document as collaborators or viewers without sending them an invitation. To do that, when the confirmation message comes up, click Cancel in the dialog box. The people you've selected will be added, but they won't be notified. You can go back later and click Email Collaborators or Email Viewers to send collaborators a message letting them know they've been given access to your document. These links also work to communicate with collaborators and viewers at any time while they have access to your document.

Two other commands that you'll see on the collaborate page are Preview Document as Viewer and View RSS Feed of Document Changes. The first option allows you to view a preview of your document as viewers will see it.

The View RSS Feed of Document Changes link will take you to an RSS feed that shows a list of the changes that have been made to your document. This is a bit difficult to decipher, however, because it includes much of the code that's required for an RSS feed reader to pick up and interpret the information. However, it doesn't appear that you can currently use an RSS feed reader to access this information. For now, you'll have to read carefully to decipher the changes that are listed.

The RSS feed page is an XML document and it appears that this page may still be under development with the Google Docs & Spreadsheets team. At some point in the future, it may be a more useful, less confusing feature of the program that actually allows you to receive RSS feeds in your favorite reader.

Finally, if you decide that you no longer want collaborators or viewers to have access to your document, removing their permissions is easy. Simply click the Remove link next to that person's name. The user will be immediately removed from your document without any further confirmation. If you later change your mind, you'll have to re-invite your collaborators or viewers. This ability to remove collaborators and viewers is useful if you've reached a completion point in your document and you don't want others to have access to it.

You also have another option for removing yourself from a collaboration situation, even if you're the creator of a collaboration. From the Active Documents view, place a check mark next to the document that you want to stop collaborating on. Then click Actions → Un-collaborate me. You are prompted to confirm that you want to stop collaborating on the document. Click Yes, and you are removed as a collaborator; however, other people collaborating on the document will be unaffected.

If you are the recipient of an invitation to share a document, you'll notice a Remove Me command in the Collaborate menu. You can use the Remove Me command to take yourself out of the collaboration group. When you click Remove Me, you're taken off the list of collaborators for that document; if you need to make changes to it again in the future, you'll have to be invited to collaborate again.

Finally, when you are collaborating with other people on a document, it's easy to see who is editing at the same time you are. In the bottom-left corner of the page is a small dialog box that shows others who are actively editing the document at that moment, as shown in Figure 5-3.

This is an easy way to keep up with who else is working on the document. And if you have questions while you and others are using the document at the same time, you can type your questions directly into the document and highlight them, or use the comment function with your own unique color so comments are distinguishable. You don't need to send an e-mail message.

In fact, this is a clunky form of instant messaging, and it's not what the program was designed for. But it does speed communication during the editing process. And you can delete the comments when you're finished so they don't interfere with the document.

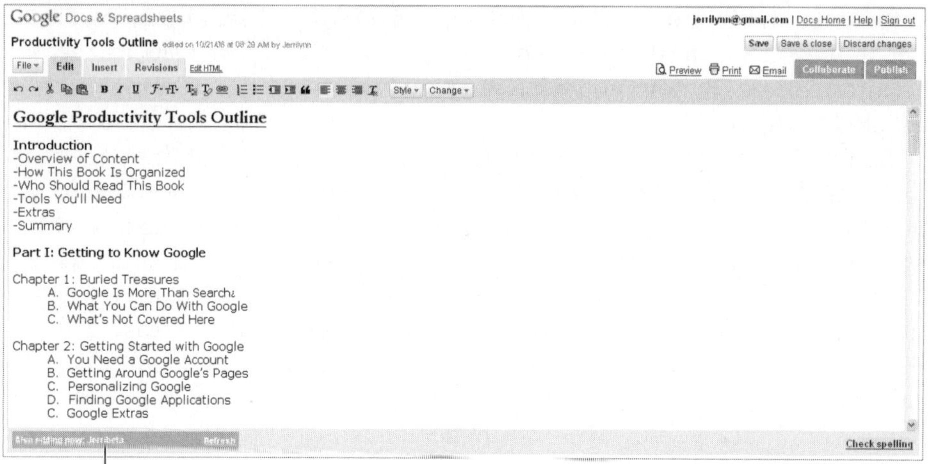

View active collaborators

Figure 5-3: Instantly see who else is collaborating on your documents.

Blogging with Google Docs

One of the neatest features of Google Docs is its ability to turn your documents into blog posts. Such a feature is being added increasingly to word-processing programs, so it's only natural that Google Docs would have it (because the program is, after all, Web-enabled).

The first thing to do if you want to use Google Docs to post your blog entries is to create a blog post. You can start a new document to use as your blog post, or you can open a document you've already created that you want to use for this purpose.

Publishing Blog Posts

With the document open, click the Publish tab in the upper-right corner of the page. You are taken to the Publish this page. Click the Post to blog button, which is at the bottom left, as shown in Figure 5-4.

If you've never posted to your blog with Google Docs, you'll see there is a link just above the Post to blog button that you can click to set your blog site settings. Before you try to post to your blog the first time, you should click this link and fill in the information in the Blog Site Settings dialog box that appears (see Figure 5-5).

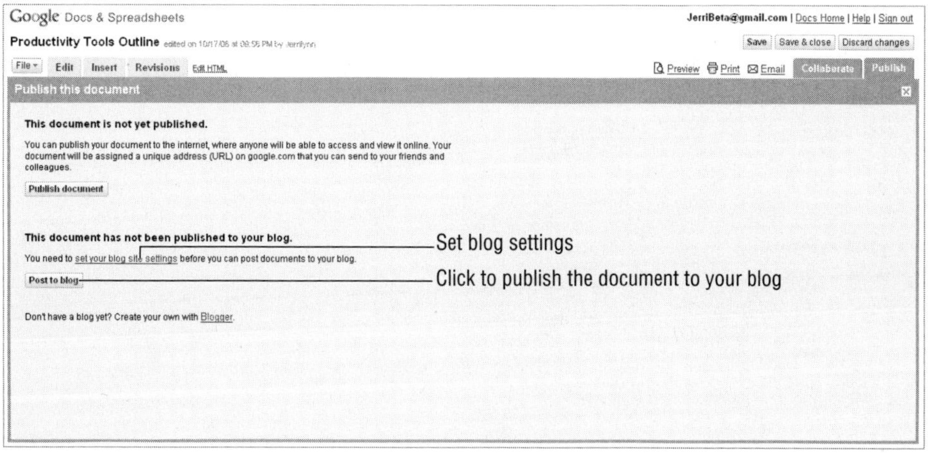

Figure 5-4: Use the Post to blog button to post your document to your blog.

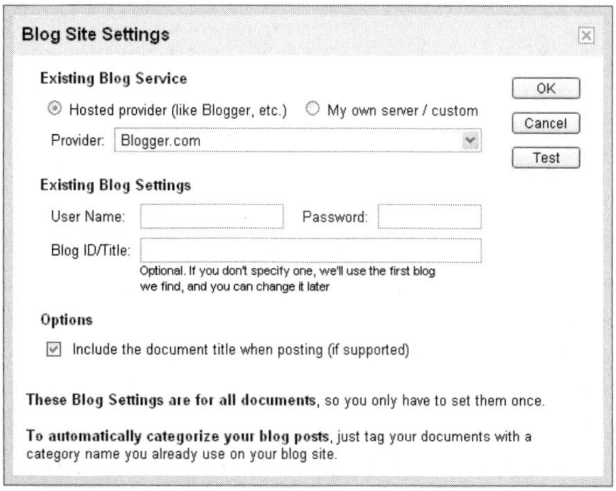

Figure 5-5: Enter the correct settings to post documents to your blog.

The first piece of information that you need to enter is the location of your blog. If you're using a service such as Blogger, WordPress, or LiveJournal, select the service from the drop-down list provided. However, if you host your own blog, or use a different blogging service, then things might get a little skitchy — meaning, hold on to your hats, folks, 'cause it's going to be a fun ride! Instead of just entering information in the form that's provided, click the radio button next to My own server/custom. The dialog box view changes slightly, as shown in Figure 5-6.

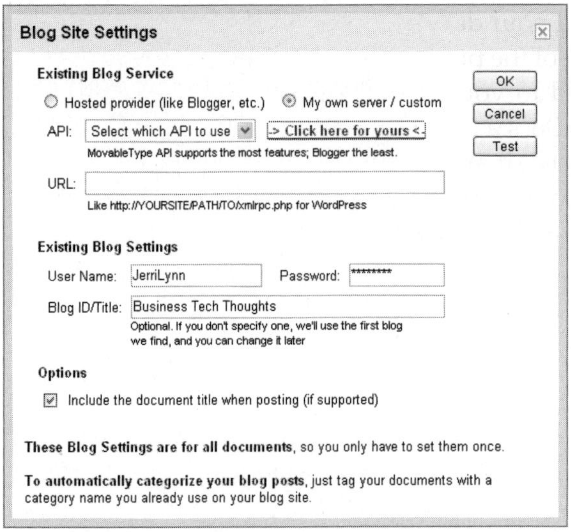

Figure 5-6: Different information is needed when you host your own blog.

If you're hosting your own blog or using a blog that's not listed, you'll need what Google calls an API (Application Programming Interface). A short list of APIs is provided in the Blog Site Settings dialog box in the Provider drop-down menu, but it's more likely that if the correct API for your blog host exists, you'll be able to find it on a separate listing at `www.GoogleDocs.com/View.aspx?docid=afwwtkhg6gn_aj8z6fsv5kx`. (That's a long, complex URL. If you select the radio button next to My own server/custom, you can select the Click here for yours link to access the list, too.)

When you find the correct API, copy the link shown and paste it into the Blog/Ed box. Then enter your user name and password and the title of your blog in the spaces provided and click the Test button. If your settings are correct, you'll receive a confirmation message. If your settings are not correct, you'll receive an error message. Once the settings are all correct, click OK and you are returned to your blog entry, but it will not be published.

From the publish page, click Post to blog to post your document on your blogging site. You are prompted to confirm that's the action you want to take; then your page reloads as the document is being uploaded to your blog. When the process is complete, a message appears above the Post to blog button that says your document was published to your blog.

Any time you change your blog settings, you can click the Change your blog site settings link (below the Post to blog button) to change your blog site settings. At the time of this writing, Google Docs supports six different blogging sites and the ability to create custom sites for those of you who host your own blog on your Web site.

When you're finished posting your document to your blog, simply click the blue X in the upper-right corner of the publish screen to return to the open document screen. You are returned to your previous document view and from there you can navigate Google Docs as usual.

Once a blog has been published, it appears in your documents list with the word "blogged" next to it, as shown in Figure 5-7. This makes it possible for you to tell at a glance if a post has been published or not.

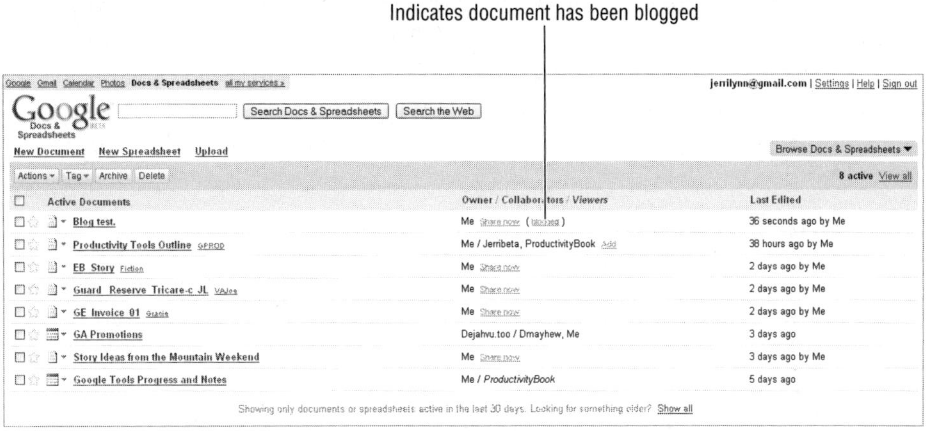

Figure 5-7: Published blog posts are indicated by the word "blogged."

If you click the word 'blogged" next to any document, you are returned to the publish page where you can republish the document to your blog or remove the document from your blog.

Editing Published Posts

At some point, everyone creates a blog post only to find out later there's an error in it. If this happens to you, or if you need to change a published blog post for any reason, you can do that through Google Docs. And it's easy.

To edit your blog post, simply open the original file (this should be the file with the word "blogged" next to it). Make the changes that you need to make to the post, and then click the Publish tab and select Republish post. You'll be prompted to confirm your desire to publish the new version of the post. Click OK and your updated post will replace the old one.

If you prefer to remove the post completely, then from the open document click the Publish tab and select Remove from blog. Again, you are prompted to confirm your decision. Click OK and the post is removed from your blog.

Blogging with Google Docs is easy. It requires only that you know how to use the Google Docs program, that you have a compatible blog (if you don't,

Google recommends Blogger), and that you understand how to use the blogging controls. You have the knowledge, and creating a blog is easy (and usually free), so there's no reason you can't have one.

Publishing with Google Docs

Publishing can mean several different things in today's Internet-driven world. It can mean to print (or have printed) a document in paper format, or it can mean to "print" the document in electronic form. The latter might take the form of a blog post, a Web site, or just an electronic document that other people can view.

Google Docs gives you options to publish in all of these different ways. I've covered blogging already, so let's look at print and electronic publishing.

Publish in Print

When you choose to publish your Google Docs document in print, you have several options. You can print directly from the Google Docs interface using the print link found just above and to the right of the Editing toolbar. Or you can go to File → Print in your Web browser. It behaves the same way.

The one problem that you might have with printing directly from the Google Docs interface is that documents printed from the Web usually have a header and/or footer that includes the URL, the date the document was printed, and possibly the number of pages. If you don't want this information to print, you'll need to make some changes in your browser setup.

You need to clear the header and footer information from your browser to print clean pages. To do this, go to the File menu of your browser and select Page Setup. How the page setup appears will vary according to the browser that you're using, but you should find a listing in the Page Setup dialog box that indicates the settings for your headers and footers.

Change those settings to indicate that the headers and footers of Web pages should be blank, and then click OK. The next time you print a Google Docs document from the Web, you should get clean copy that does not display a URL, date, or page number in either the header or the footer.

Publish to a File

Another way to publish your documents is to publish them to a file that you save on your computer's hard drive or some other storage device. You can then print or share your document electronically.

Google Docs offers several formats for saving your documents to a file. Those file formats include HTML, RTF (Rich Text Format), Word, OpenOffice, and PDF (Portable Document Format).

To save your document to your hard drive or storage device from the open file, click File and then select the file format you want to apply to your document. You should be prompted to open the file or to save it to disk. Select the option that you prefer. If you're saving the document to disk, remember to select the location where you want the document stored and enter a file name that you'll recognize. Then click OK and the file will be downloaded to your hard drive.

Publish Electronically

Finally, you can publish your document in electronic format to the Web. When you click the Publish tab, you are be taken to the publish page where the first button on the page is the Publish document button (you've already dealt with the Post to blog button).

To publish your document to the Web, click the Publish document button. You are prompted to confirm that you want to let anyone on the Internet see the document. Click OK and your page reloads. When the reload is complete, as shown in Figure 5-8, you see confirmation that the document was published to the Web, including the URL for the document's Web site.

As with the blogging capabilities of Google Docs, you can edit your document and republish it or remove it from the Web at any time from this page.

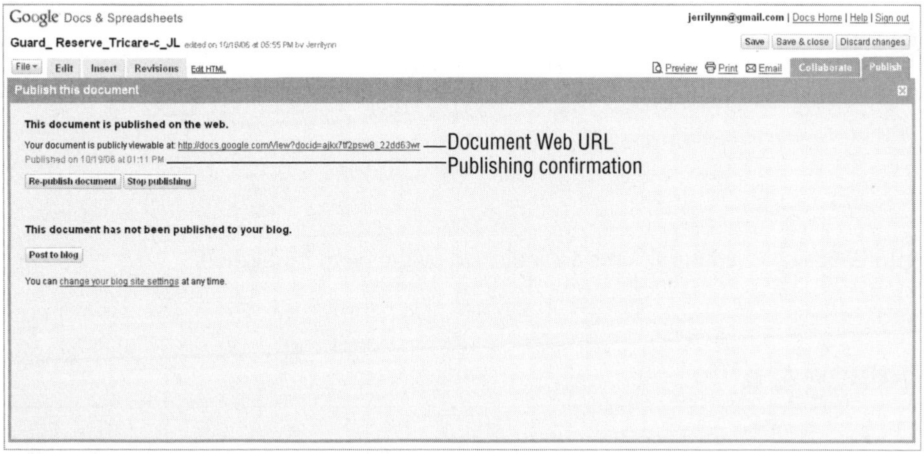

Figure 5-8: Confirmation and controls are displayed after the document is published.

Publishing your documents publicly has few consequences at the time of this writing. That's because Google Docs does not catalog those files (yet) and search engines don't crawl them. So only the people who receive the actual URL of the document are able to see it.

However, there may come a time when making a document public could have dire consequences if you don't really mean for it to be public. There are rumors that at some point there might be a site that catalogs all the public documents created on Google Docs, but that's not confirmed. It may or may not happen. For now, what's important for you to understand is that if you make a document public, you have little if any control over who views it.

The other option you have is to share your document with only the people you choose. To do that, use the collaboration tools that were covered earlier in this chapter.

After you have published a document, it's labeled "published" in much the same manner as a published blog is labeled (see Figure 5-9). This is a quick way to distinguish which of your documents have been published.

Clicking the published link beside any document takes you back to the publish page where you'll have the ability to republish your document or to remove the document from the Web.

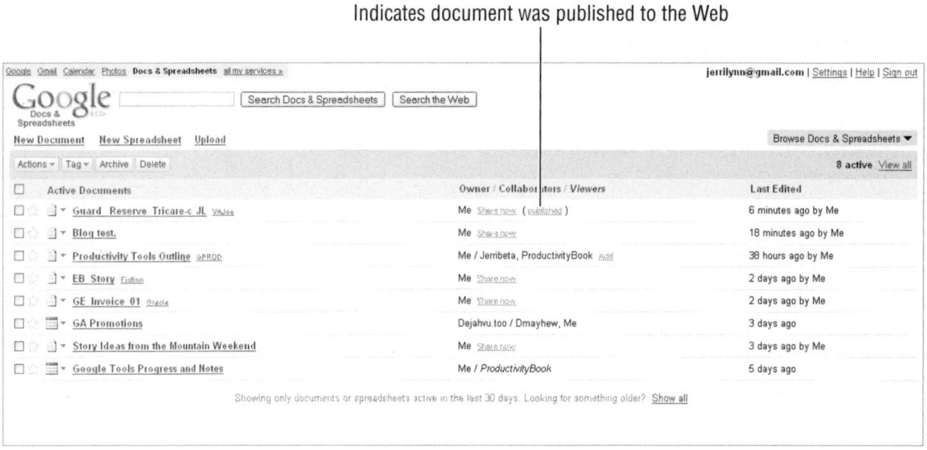

Figure 5-9: Published documents are indicated by the word "published."

Moving On

You have a lot of options for publishing your documents. And all of the publishing methods are easy enough to master. You may have to perform the publishing tasks a time or two before you get used to them, but once you do, you'll be publishing your documents in all kinds of formats. And the ability to publish your documents in a variety of formats will give you more flexibility in how you use those documents. You'll find that you can perform some tasks much more efficiently with Google Docs. This is true even when revisions are involved, which you learn more about in the next chapter.

CHAPTER

6

Revising Documents

Revision. Revision. Revision. This is the key to creating documents that are professional, relay the message that you want to communicate, and appear exactly as you envision them. They're also a royal pain in the hindquarters.

Revisions are a fact of life, however, and there's no way to get around them. A better option is to find a way to make the revision process easier. Have you ever revised a document, only to wish you could go back to an earlier version? Or maybe you've run into a situation where several people are making revisions and you need a document with all of the revisions combined? Not to worry — Google Docs gives you the options you need to handle the revision process with ease.

Google Docs Revision Tools

You got a flying glimpse of the Google Docs revision tools near the end of Chapter 4 when I told you how to revert to an older version of a document and how to compare two documents. This really was just a quick look at those options, so I'll cover them again here. If you think you know enough about using the Google Docs revision tools, you don't necessarily have to read through this section. Just make note of its location so you can flip back here later if you need a refresher.

Anytime you make a change to a document, it's considered a revision. So if you make changes to a document and then save those changes and continue working on the document, when you save again you'll create a newer version of that document. Each version is called a revision.

View Revision History

To find out how many revisions have been made to a document, you first need to open the document in question. Then click the Revisions tab and select Revision History. This takes you to a page like the one shown in Figure 6-1, which includes a list of all the revisions that have been made to the document.

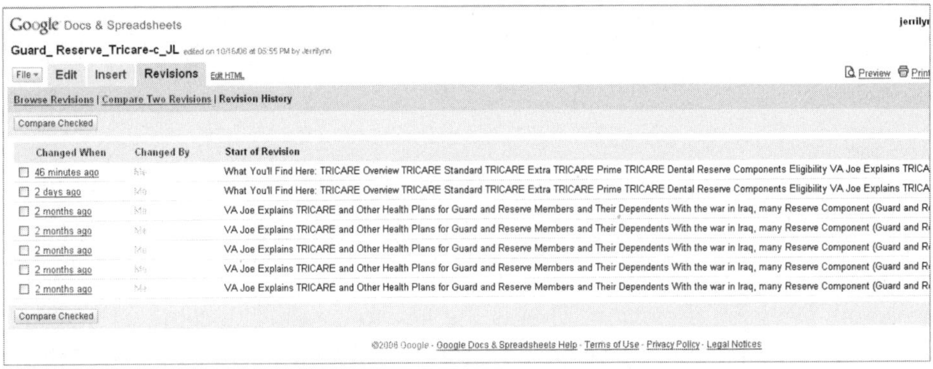

Figure 6-1: View your historical revisions by clicking View Revision History.

When you're looking at the revision history, you see three columns of information:

- **Changed When:** This indicates the time when the document was changed for that revision. Time is measured in hours and days in this view.
- **Changed By:** This column indicates who changed the document during a given revision. This is helpful for identifying document revisions when you're collaborating with others.
- **Start of Revision:** This column represents the beginning of the document at the time of the revision. In most cases, you'll find the first revision blank in this column. The remaining revisions look the same, or similar to each other. This column changes only when the beginning of your document changes.

To open a revision, all you need to do is click the title. The revision is opened, and you can review it or choose to change the document back to that revision. If you don't want to revert to that revision, you have two options: You can click your browser's Back button to return to the revision history view, or you can use the Older and Newer buttons located in the top left (see Figure 6-2) to cycle through older and newer revisions of the document.

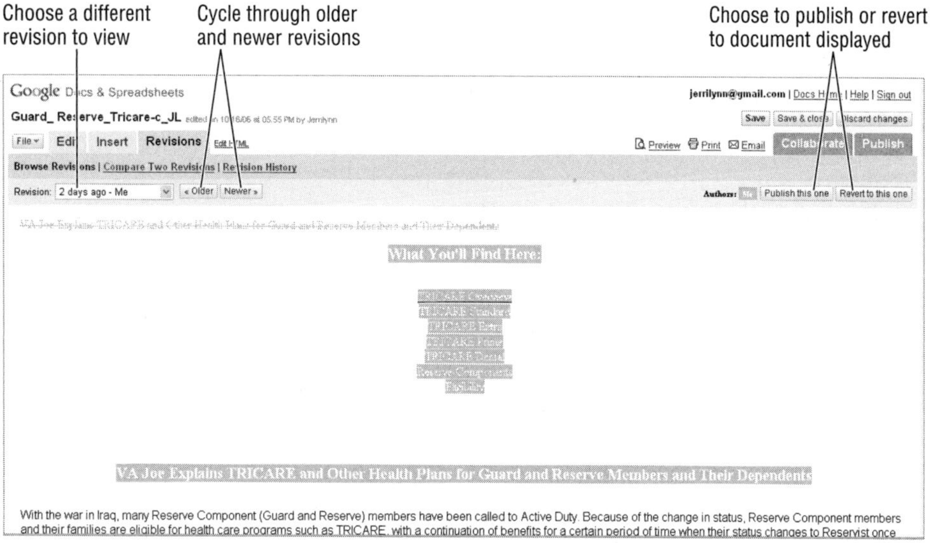

Figure 6-2: Use the Older and Newer buttons to cycle through your revision history.

When you're viewing revisions, you'll notice that each person's revisions are colored differently. This is to help you quickly see the revision and who is responsible for it. If at any time you forget which color corresponds with which collaborator, a legend is in the top-right corner of the page next to the Publish and Revert buttons.

Comparing Revisions

Another useful function of Google Docs is its ability to let you compare two revisions. You might use this to see what's changed in the document since the last time you worked on it, or to see what changes a collaborator has made with regard to the original (or last-saved) version of the document.

To compare revisions, you first need to open the current version of the document. Then, click the Revisions tab and select the Compare Two Revisions link. (If you're in the revisions history view, you can simply place a check mark next to the two documents that you want to compare and select the Compare Checked button above the revisions list.) You are taken to a view of your documents with two drop-down menus near the top. These menus, shown in Figure 6-3, enable you to select the versions of the document that you want to compare.

Figure 6-3: Use the revision-version menus to select the versions to compare.

You may also notice that some text is highlighted while some is not. This is how you tell what's changed from one revision to the next. The highlighted text is the newest text, whereas the text that's not highlighted was already there when the newer version of the document was created.

Viewing revision histories gives you a quick way to see what has changed in a document, and who changed it. If you're collaborating on a document, each person's revisions will be highlighted in color — the same color in which the reviser's name appears in the upper-right corner of the document. This way, you don't have to wonder who changed that paragraph that you liked so well. You'll be able to tell at a glance.

Browse Revisions

One last revision option that you have with Google Docs is to browse through the revisions of any given document. This gives you a way to follow the evolution of a document from start to finish. It's a tool that can be useful for seeing who is the most active during a collaboration situation, or to see where you have made changes, removed changes, or added to a document.

If you want to browse through the revisions in a document, first open that document. Then click the Revisions tab and select Browse Revisions. You are taken to the latest revision of your document.

On the toolbar at the top of the document are some controls for browsing your revisions. The most noticeable tools are the Older and Newer buttons. Use these buttons to cycle back and forth through revisions.

A drop-down menu also lists the various revisions to the document, as shown in Figure 6-4. If you want to view a specific revision, click it in the drop-down menu and you are taken to that version of the document.

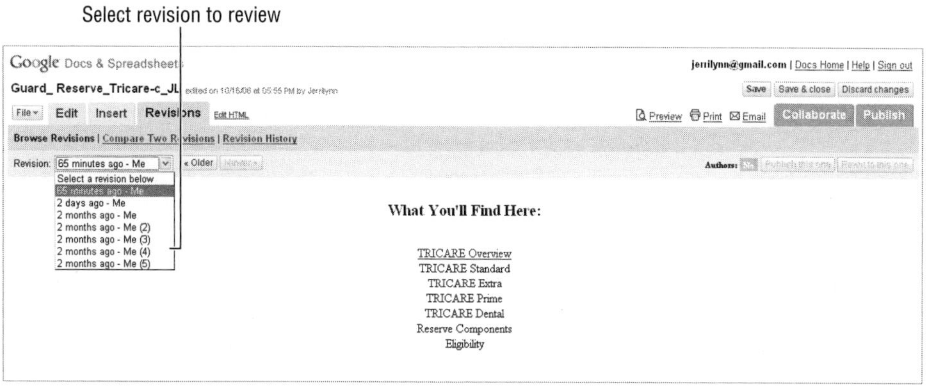

Figure 6-4: Use the toolbar to navigate through the various document revisions.

The revisions features with Google Docs are very useful, especially if you're collaborating on a document. You can compare changes in a document and quickly see who made those changes. Then if you want to revert to or publish an older version of the document, all you have to do is click a button. In other words it takes less time to achieve more efficiency. Pretty cool, eh?

Adding RSS Feeds

Really Simple Syndication. That's what RSS stands for, and you've probably heard about RSS feeds that are basically notifications about new or updated content. Many blogs use RSS feeds to push new blog entries out to readers. But did you know you can use RSS feeds to push document updates out to collaborators? You can even use them for yourself.

Google Docs's RSS feeds aren't terribly difficult to use, but they can be a little confusing the first time or two that you use them. To start, you should be in the active document view of Google Docs (that's the main page you're taken to when you log in).

1. In the upper-right corner of the page, select Settings and then click the RSS Feeds tab. You are taken to the RSS Feeds page, as shown in Figure 6-5.

Figure 6-5: The RSS Feeds page enables you to handle your document RSS feeds.

2. On this page you can choose to make public any changes you've made to your document. There's also a link that allows you to receive changes to the document in your RSS feed reader. This is useful for teachers who are monitoring students or for employers monitoring employees. Then there's an Individual Documents list. This list is used to see the individual documents that have RSS Feeds. Finally, you'll see a list of tagged documents. When you click one of the documents in this list, you are taken to the RSS feed view of the document group, as shown in Figure 6-6. Looks like HTML code, doesn't it?

3. Don't worry about that code; you really don't need it. Just copy the URL that's shown in your browser's address bar.

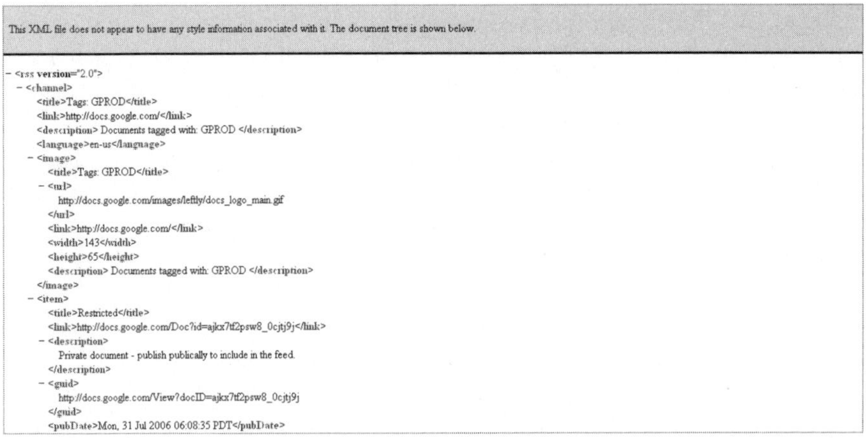

Figure 6-6: You don't need the HTML on this page, just the address of the page.

4. Now, add the URL to the subscription service of your chosen RSS reader, and you're done. The RSS feed is set up, and you're subscribed to it. Now every time a document is updated or added to that tagged group, it'll be pushed out to your RSS feeder.

It's also possible for you to add RSS feeds to all your documents individually as well. To set up feeds for all your Google Docs documents, open each document and click the Collaborate tab. On the Collaborate page, click the link View RSS feed of document changes.

You are taken to a page that looks like HTML code (just like above). Copy the address from your browser's address bar and then paste it into your RSS feed reader, and you're all set.

RSS feeds are most useful when you're working with a group of collaborators, but they can also be helpful if you have a document or group of documents that you want others to be able to read each time you update them. The feeds function much the same way a blog does, but you can limit the number of viewers who can see the documents.

USE GOOGLE READER TO VIEW YOUR RSS FEEDS

There are dozens of different RSS feed readers for you to choose from, but if you're using Google, why not use the Google Reader to capture your RSS feeds? Google Reader is a simple, free program that integrates with your Google Personalized page, and it works just as simply as any other feed reader that you might choose to use.

To access Google Reader, go to `www.google.com/reader`**. It's as easy to use as any other Google program, and you can use the program to share your feeds with others or to discover new time-shifted content on the Web.**

There's no download for the program, either. It's all Web based and you can even access Google Reader from your Web-enabled mobile phone. If you love RSS feeds, this is one useful little tool from Google.

Moving On

For a program that's free, Google Docs still offers some decent features. Various revision views and RSS feeds are just the icing on the cake. And they're not nearly as difficult to use as they might seem on first examination. Having the ability to publish your documents to the Web or to your personal blog also adds value to the program. Give it a shot.

Of course, Google Docs is actually only half of the program. The other half is Google Spreadsheets, and I'm going to cover that in detail in Part III of this book.

PART III

Google Spreadsheets

Managing and organizing financial data, and even some text, is a difficult task. To help keep up with all types of information, many people use spreadsheets. Unfortunately, most of today's spreadsheet applications are designed for about 10 percent of the population — the advanced or expert users. There is far more functionality in these programs than most users need, and that makes using them a frustrating, confusing task.

Google Spreadsheets — the other half of Google Docs & Spreadsheets — is the solution to the confusion. It offers an easy-to-use interface with only the most frequently used functions and capabilities. And if you've been using Google Docs & Spreadsheets for documents, then you're already familiar with the layout of the program. So if what you want is a spreadsheet program that lets you perform only the functions you need and that's available from anywhere, keep reading.

In this part you'll find information about using Google Spreadsheets to create both financial and text-based spreadsheets, and along the way you'll learn all of the neat little usage and formatting tips that make this program indispensable.

CHAPTER

7

Google Spreadsheets

The first time I worked in a corporate office, I was amazed at the number of uses for spreadsheet programs. The office manager (who happened to be my boss) used them to create seating charts to keep up with who was where — a difficult task in an office with more than 150 people. She used them to generate various types of text-based reports, and she also used them to keep up with benefit and training information. She even used them for keeping track of her three daughters' soccer schedules. Until then, I had mistakenly believed spreadsheets were just for keeping track of numbers and accounting information.

I thought the same way many people do who are not Microsoft Excel power users. Spreadsheets are valuable tools, but I don't want to do everything in them. If you're one of those people, then the spreadsheet half of Google Docs & Spreadsheets is the perfect spreadsheet program for you. Google Spreadsheets does not offer as much functionality as some of the premium (and proprietary) spreadsheet applications on the market, but Spreadsheets is more powerful than you might think the first time you see the program, and it's perfectly useful for basic calculations, tracking, and budgeting.

Why Use Google Spreadsheets ?

So, if Google Spreadsheets isn't as powerful as Microsoft Excel or some of the other spreadsheet programs on the market, why *would* you want to use the program? Consider the following reasons:

- **Ease of use:** Many people don't want all of the functionality that's offered by programs such as Excel. It's confusing, and locating the function that you want to access is difficult. If you're a beginning spreadsheet user, or if you simply want a spreadsheet program for basic accounting, bookkeeping, or tracking, Google Spreadsheets gives you everything you need without confusing the matter.
- **Web access:** One thing that most hard drive–based spreadsheets don't offer is Web access. Google Spreadsheets gives you the ability to create, store, and access spreadsheets from anywhere in the world with a computer that has Internet access.
- **Cost savings:** Most spreadsheet applications are relatively expensive, especially if you have several users or computers on which the application needs to be installed. Google Spreadsheets is free, as in zip, nada, zilch — nothing!
- **Collaboration:** With Google Spreadsheets, all of your spreadsheets are stored online, which means you can give others access to them without having to load the file to disk and pass it around. Google Spreadsheets also gives you the ability to have multiple people editing the spreadsheet at the same time. Work gets done in less time, and you don't have to struggle with trying to consolidate multiple versions of a single spreadsheet.
- **Reduced storage space:** The fact that Google's spreadsheets are stored online is also a plus. You don't have to worry about the amount of storage space you have available unless you want to download a spreadsheet, and backup copies of your spreadsheets are always available. You can access them simply by logging into Google Spreadsheets.

As you can see, Google Spreadsheets offers a lot of functionality that's not available in some of the other spreadsheet programs. However, advanced spreadsheet users might find Google lacking in a few areas. There are no pivot tables or charts, and you won't find macros in Google Spreadsheets, either.

Google Spreadsheets offers a clean, uncluttered spreadsheet application. If you're a casual or beginning spreadsheet user, you'll find all of the functionality that you need without any of the clutter. Advanced users might even find Google Spreadsheets useful for sharing or collaborating. Just don't expect advanced or extreme functionality.

Navigating Google Spreadsheets

Initially, Google offered Spreadsheets as a single, invitation-only program. It didn't take the company long to combine the program with Google's word processing program to create Google Docs & Spreadsheets. Now the combined programs are available to the general public, so accessing the Spreadsheets portion is simple.

1. Go to `www.docs.google.com`.
2. Type your Google account name and password (that you created in Chapter 2) into the text boxes provided and click Sign in.

You're there. Signing in really is that easy.

When you sign in to Google Spreadsheets, you're automatically taken to the active document view, which includes both your documents and your spreadsheets. An icon next to the title of the document or spreadsheet indicates what type of file it is. A document icon represents documents, and a grid icon represents spreadsheets. Click the title of the spreadsheet that you want to open, and you are taken to an editing view of that document.

If you want to start a new spreadsheet, all you need to do is click the New Spreadsheet link above the active document list.

Navigational Structure

Have you ever looked at a map and noticed there are several ways to get from one place to another? Google offers the same type of navigation. There are several ways to get around, and a variety of tools for that navigation.

Tabs, Buttons, and Links

Like other Google programs, you'll find a variety of buttons and links in the Spreadsheets program. Most of the spreadsheet-specific navigational features in Google Spreadsheets are found in the open spreadsheet view. Figure 7-1 shows the navigational structure of Spreadsheets. As you can see, there are a variety of ways to work within your spreadsheet.

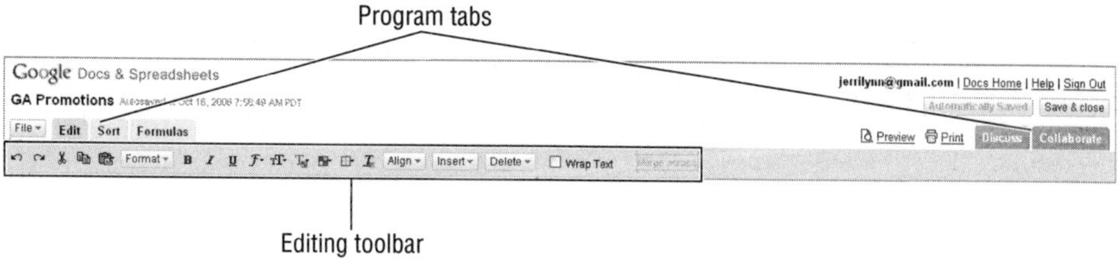

Figure 7-1: Spreadsheets' navigational structure is a system of links and buttons.

These navigation methods fall into three categories: program tabs, buttons, and links. The program tabs allow you to switch between document views, and each tab gives you different capabilities. If you read through the Google Docs section, then you should be familiar with how these tabs work, but these are different from the ones available in a document, so I'll just give you a quick rundown of what each does:

- **Edit:** You'll spend most of your time here. This tab is the default tab that opens when you open or create a new spreadsheet.
- **Sort:** This tab takes you to Google Spreadsheets' sorting capabilities.
- **Formulas:** When you're working with the formulas in your spreadsheet, this is the tab you'll need. You learn more about formulas and how to use them later in this part of the book.

On the far right side of the page are two additional tabs that you'll use frequently:

- **Discuss:** This is a neat feature of Google Spreadsheets. It allows you to chat with others who are collaborating on the spreadsheet with you.
- **Collaborate:** This tab works very much like the Collaborate tab in Google Docs. It's where you manage your collaboration relationships and functions.

Buttons

In addition to the tabs, you'll find four buttons on the Google Spreadsheets screen. These buttons make performing some of the most common tasks in Google Spreadsheets easy.

- **File:** The File button is actually a drop-down menu, as shown in Figure 7-2. When you click this button, the menu opens and you find some of the most commonly used options in the Spreadsheets program.
- **Save/Automatically Saved:** When you first start editing a new spreadsheet, this appears as the Save button. A notification, like the one shown in Figure 7-3, opens prompting you to begin auto-saving your spreadsheet. After you select this option, the button changes to let you know the document has been automatically saved. Once it changes, it doesn't seem to have any functionality at all. It's just there to let you know that the auto-saving feature has been enabled.

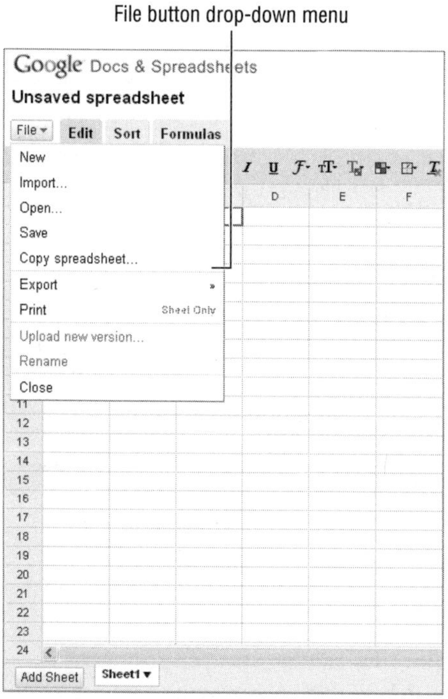

Figure 7-2: The file button opens a drop-down menu that contains common controls.

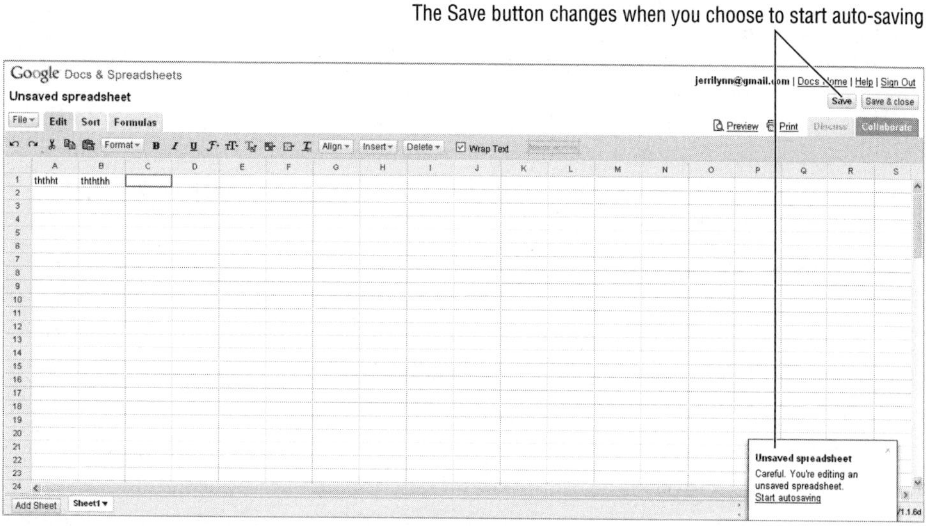

Figure 7-3: The Save button changes once auto-saving has been enabled.

- **Save & Close:** If you enable the automatic saving feature, Google will save your documents periodically. However, it's possible that you can make changes and close the spreadsheet before the auto-save feature saves those changes. So, you have an option to Save & Close your document. When you're finished editing or adding to your spreadsheet, just click this button and the spreadsheet is saved and you're returned to the active documents view of Google Docs & Spreadsheets.
- **Add Sheet:** This button is located on the bottom of the screen, away from all of the other controls. When you click this button, another spreadsheet is added to the workbook that you're working in. If you need several different but related spreadsheets, this button lets you create and keep them all together.

GOOGLE GROUPS

Sometimes the Help section just doesn't have the answers that you're looking for. When that happens, what you really want is some place that you can discuss your problem with other users and maybe even a program representative. Google Groups offers just those benefits.

Google Groups is a discussion forum similar to a mailing list. Thousands of topics are available in Google Groups, to which you can subscribe and where you can participate in discussions. Among those topics are many related to Google programs such as Google Docs & Spreadsheets. These groups give you a way to learn more about the applications and gain feedback from Google team members and from other application users.

To sign up for Google Groups, go to `www.groups.google.com`, and use your Google Account information to sign in to the service. The first time you sign in, you'll be prompted to enter a nickname. This is the name that will appear on any posts that you make to a group.

After you create your nickname, you're taken to a page where you can search for groups on any topic that interests you or browse groups by categories. When you find a group that looks interesting, click the title of the group to learn more about it. For starters, here are the Web addresses of a couple of groups:

- **Google Talk Help Discussion:** `http://groups.google.com/group/Google-Talk-Help-Discuss?lnk=lr&hl=en`
- **Google Docs & Spreadsheets Help Group:** `http://groups.google.com/group/GoogleDocsSpreadsheets?lnk=li&hl=en`

To join a group, click the Join This Group link, provide the information requested and set the frequency of the mailings you would like to receive. Then click Join This Group and you are added to the membership list.

Once you've joined a group, you can post and reply to posts in the group.

Links

So you've got tabs and buttons. The next level of navigation in Google Spreadsheets is links. Again, these links are similar to the ones that you've seen in Google Docs.

You'll find the Preview and Print buttons that you saw in Google Docs. In the top-right corner, the links for Docs Home, Help, and Sign Out are also available. Docs Home takes you back to the active document view of Google Docs and Spreadsheets. Help takes you to Google's Help section. And Sign Out signs you completely out of the Google Docs & Spreadsheets program.

Toolbars

Each of the tabs shown in Google Spreadsheets also has its own toolbar. These toolbars differ considerably by tab. For example, the Format tab contains the most populated toolbar, as shown in Figure 7-4, whereas the Sort toolbar (shown in Figure 7-5) shows only one drop-down menu and two buttons.

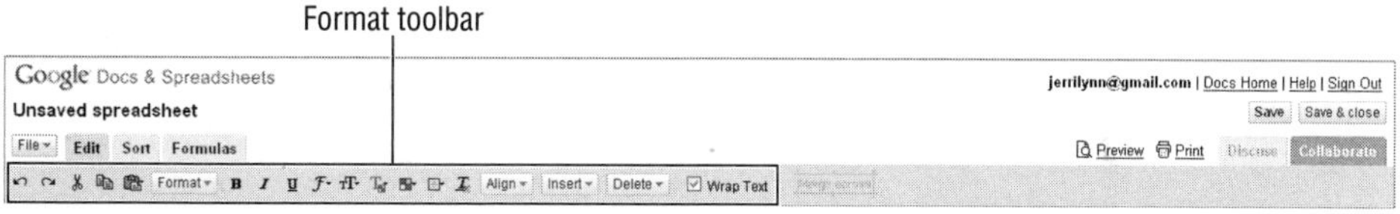

Figure 7-4: The Format tab contains the most options for working with spreadsheets.

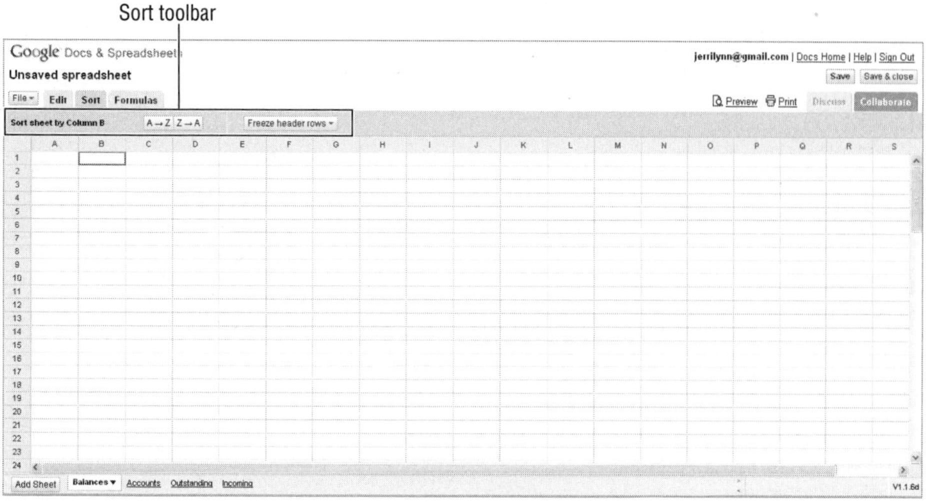

Figure 7-5: The Sort tab contains only a few commands.

The functions in each of these tabs will be covered more completely in the remaining chapters in this section, but for now familiarize yourself with where each tab is and locate the toolbars for each tab. Then when you begin using them in the coming chapters, you'll be able to quickly find the commands needed.

Sheet Navigation

One last navigational toolbar that you'll want to be aware of is the sheet navigation toolbar, shown in Figure 7-6. This toolbar is located just beneath your spreadsheet (you caught a glimpse of it previously when you saw how to add sheets to a workbook), and it contains the controls that you'll need for adding, naming, moving, and deleting sheets within a workbook.

TIP **Within a spreadsheet application, worksheets are the spreadsheet pages that you create. A workbook, on the other hand, is a collection of worksheets. You define how many worksheets are in a workbook, up to the maximum number allowed by the spreadsheet application.**

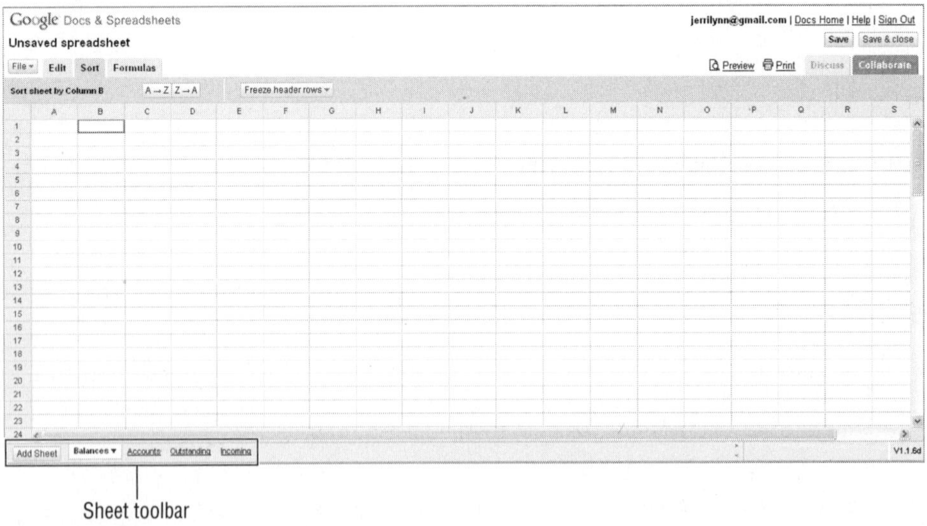

Figure 7-6: The sheet navigation toolbar is located below the active spreadsheet.

When you start a new spreadsheet, the worksheet is named Sheet 1 by default. But if you look at the tab that displays that name, you'll see there is a small downward arrow next to the sheet name. This indicates that there is a sheet menu there, as shown in Figure 7-7. To access this menu, simply click the sheet name. This works only on the sheet that you're currently viewing, so if you want to see the sheet menu on a different sheet, you'll need to switch to the view of that sheet by clicking the sheet name. Then click the sheet name a second time to see the sheet menu.

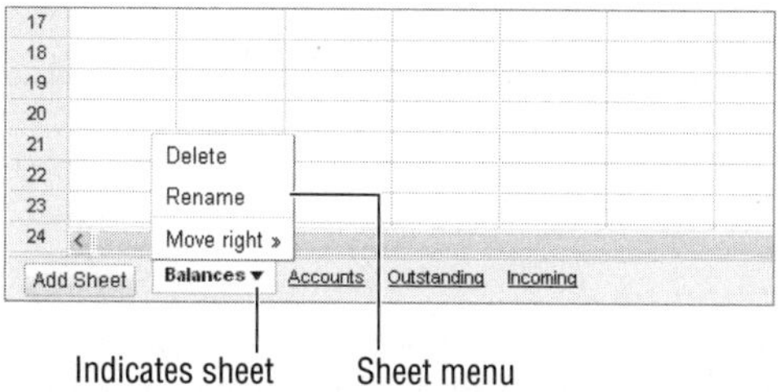

Figure 7-7: The Sheet menu contains options to rename or move a specific sheet.

TIP **Google allows you to create workbooks with up to 20 worksheets that consist of 50,000 cells, 256 columns, or 10,000 rows. However, should you reach any one of those limits, you'll be automatically prevented from adding any further worksheets, cells, columns, or rows to your workbook.**

Getting around Google Spreadsheets is pretty easy. In fact, that's one of the most appealing elements of it because your workspace isn't cluttered with unnecessary functions or commands. What you need is at your finger tips, and nothing more. So, what more could you want?

Keyboard Navigation

About the only thing you could ask for now is keyboard navigation, and with Google Spreadsheets, you've got it. Chapter 8 covers the keyboard shortcuts for editing commands, but Table 7-1 provides keyboard navigation shortcuts that you can use to move around quickly in Spreadsheets.

Table 7-1: Navigational Keyboard Shortcuts

SHORTCUT	FUNCTION
Arrow Up	Move up one cell
Arrow Down	Move down one cell
Arrow Right	Move right one cell
Arrow Left	Move left one cell
Tab	Move right one cell
Shift+Tab	Move left one cell
Ctrl+Home	Move to cell A1
Ctrl+End	Move to the last cell in the last column
Page Down	Move down one screen
Page Up	Move up one screen

Moving On

Moving around in your spreadsheet is simple once you get the hang of it, and if you've used any type of spreadsheet application in the past, there probably won't be much of a learning curve in Google Spreadsheets. In fact, any experience with different spreadsheet applications will put you ahead of the game in Google Spreadsheets because many of the commands and buttons are very similar.

In upcoming chapters in this section you learn more detailed information about putting Google Spreadsheets to work for you. Before you know it, you'll be using Spreadsheets to keep track of budgets, schedules, inventory lists, and anything else you can think to do with it.

CHAPTER

8

New Spreadsheets

Google Spreadsheets is a Web-based program that enables you to perform many of the functions of a full-featured spreadsheet program. No, you won't be able to create a pivot table or charts from your data, but most people don't use those functions anyway. In fact, the majority of people who use any kind of office application use only about 10 percent of the functionality that's available in that program.

Typically, the most basic functions are those that are used most often, such as creating and editing documents or spreadsheets. With Google Spreadsheets, all of the functionality that's available to you is useful. There's nothing so complicated that you can't get your mind around it, and yet there's enough functionality in these spreadsheets that you can perform almost any task you choose.

All the basics of Google Spreadsheets are covered in this chapter. From creating and editing documents to saving and deleting them, you should feel very comfortable using Spreadsheets by the time you finish reading the following pages.

Starting a New Spreadsheet

If you've accessed Google Spreadsheets in the past, you know that when you log in to Google Docs & Spreadsheets you're automatically taken to the active document view. To start a new spreadsheet, click the New Spreadsheet button above the active documents list.

Suppose you're working in a spreadsheet and then decide you want to start a new one. How do you get to a new spreadsheet? It's not difficult at all.

As shown in Figure 8-1, on the very top of the page is a File button. Click the button and select New. You are taken to a new, blank spreadsheet. Which Internet browser you're using will determine how the new spreadsheet behaves. For example, if you open a new spreadsheet in the Firefox browser, the new spreadsheet may appear in a different tab. Using these tabs, you can very quickly flip back and forth between spreadsheets.

Click to start a new spreadsheet

Figure 8-1: Click the New link to start a new spreadsheet.

If you open a new spreadsheet from within Internet Explorer, the new spreadsheet opens in a new window. You can still flip back and forth between the open spreadsheet and the new one, but you'll have two separate windows open.

NOTE **At the time of this writing, Google Spreadsheets supported only four browsers: Internet Explorer 6 or higher; Firefox 1.07, 1.5+, or higher; Mozilla 1.7.12 or higher; and Netscape 7.2 or higher. At some point in the future, additional browser support may be added, but for now if you plan to use Google Spreadsheets you must use one of these browsers.**

Opening Existing Spreadsheets

When you log into Google Docs & Spreadsheets, opening the spreadsheet that you want is as simple as clicking on the title of the spreadsheet. But what if you're working in a spreadsheet and want or need to open a different one? It's easy. Click the File button, and select Open.

The Open a spreadsheet dialog box shown in Figure 8-2 appears. Click the name of the spreadsheet you want to open. The dialog box will close and the spreadsheet will open in the same window or tab in which you are currently working, if you started with a blank spreadsheet. If you were working in a spreadsheet that was saved in the past, then the new spreadsheet will open in a different tab or window.

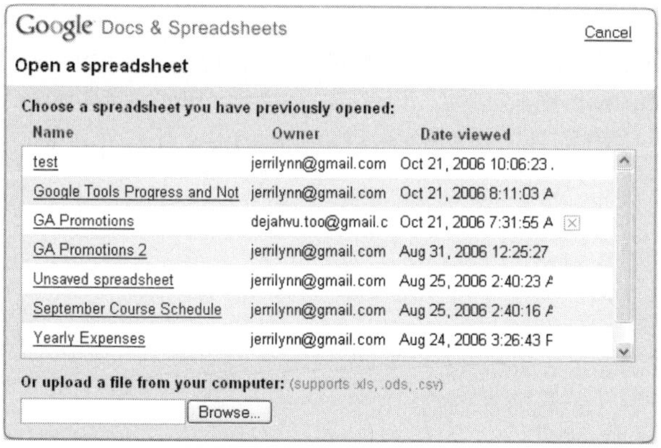

Figure 8-2: Use the dialog box that appears to select a spreadsheet to open.

Uploading Existing Spreadsheets

One of the really great features of Google Spreadsheets is that you can also upload existing spreadsheets that were created in other spreadsheet programs. Google allows you to upload spreadsheets in both XLS and CSV formats.

A NOTE ABOUT SPREADSHEET FORMATS

Currently, most spreadsheets are in one of the two formats that Google Spreadsheets supports. XLS is a Microsoft Excel binary file format and CSV (comma separate value) is a more universal format.

However, times are changing. Today, more and more spreadsheet programs are going to XML-based file formats because they're more flexible in our digital lifestyle. In fact, with the release of Microsoft Office 2007, the new file format for Microsoft Excel will be .XLSX, indicating the format of the file is XML compatible.

At this time, Google Spreadsheets doesn't support XML-capable formats, but that's likely to change in the near future. For now, if you have an existing spreadsheet in XML format that you want to upload to Google Spreadsheets, you can save the file as either an XLS or CSV file and then upload it.

To upload a file to Google Spreadsheets, follow these steps:

1. From inside an open spreadsheet, click the File button and select Open.
2. The Open a spreadsheet dialog box that you saw in Figure 8-2 appears. In the bottom-left corner of the dialog box is a text box and a Browse button. Click Browse.
3. The File Upload dialog box appears. Choose the file you'd like to upload and click Open.
4. The file should upload. When the upload is complete, you'll see a message next to the Browse button that says, "File imported successfully. Open now" (shown in Figure 8-3). Click Open now and the file opens.

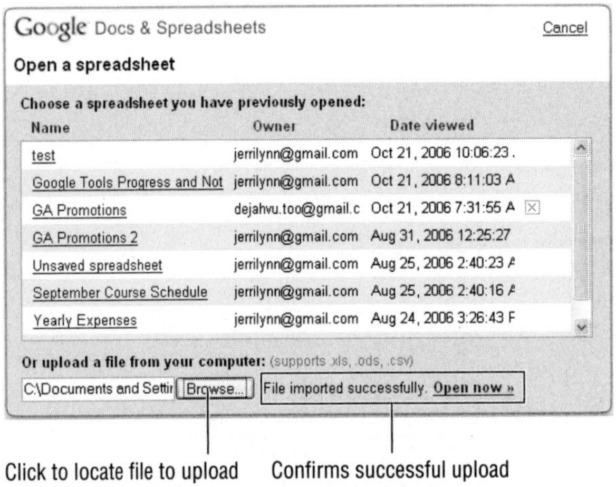

Figure 8-3: Message shows file was imported successfully.

5. If the file you're trying to upload is not a recognized file format, Spreadsheets won't be able to open it and you'll receive an error message, like the one shown in Figure 8-4.

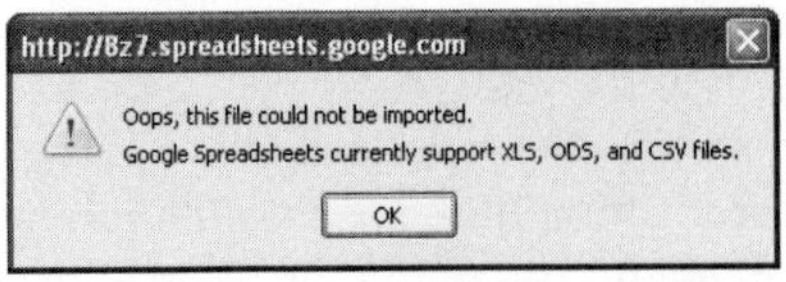

Figure 8-4: Incompatible files will generate an error message.

An alternative way to upload spreadsheets into Google Docs & Spreadsheets is to start in the active document view. There, click the Upload button and you're taken to the same form that you used to upload documents in

Google Docs, shown in Figure 8-5. It works the same way, and you can upload spreadsheets or documents.

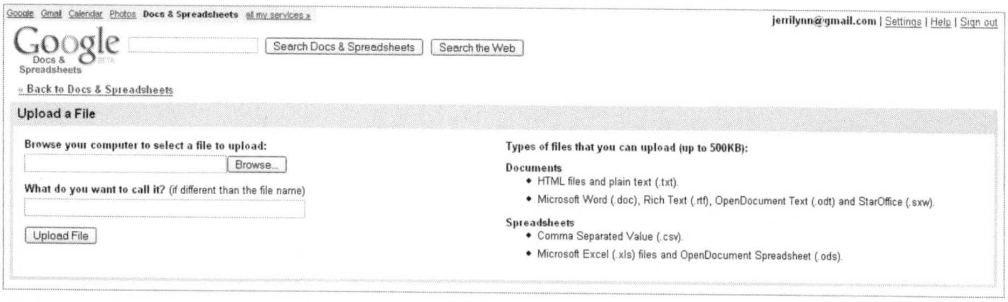

Figure 8-5: Use the upload page to upload spreadsheets or documents.

The one feature you won't find in Spreadsheets — and it's a nice feature in Google Docs — is the ability to e-mail spreadsheets into the program. Remember that with Google Docs you can e-mail a document into your account, but at the time of this writing, the only way to add spreadsheets created outside Google Spreadsheets is to upload them.

The good news is that there's a note on the upload page (just above your e-mail address for e-mailing documents into Google Docs) that states the feature will be coming for spreadsheets, too, so it's just a matter of time before you can e-mail spreadsheets into the program, just as you do documents.

Editing and Formatting Spreadsheets

So you've opened or uploaded a spreadsheet — now what can you do with it? More than you might think. Most of the same editing capabilities that you'll find in other spreadsheet programs exist in Google Spreadsheets, too.

Adding Data to Cells

The first thing that you're likely to do is enter data into cells on your spreadsheet. But how? In Microsoft Excel you can either type directly into the cell or into the text bar at the top of the worksheet. That text bar doesn't appear in Google Spreadsheets. To type text into a cell, just click the cell and start typing.

If you want to change the data that's in the cell, you do the same thing. Click inside the cell and start typing. Any text or numbers that were in the cell to start with will be replaced by the new data that you type. But that also means that you cannot use that method to change just a portion of the data in cell. For example, if you typed a date into a cell and you just want to change the year, when you click inside the cell to edit it, you have to retype the date completely.

If you want to edit only a portion of the data that's in a cell, there *is* a way to do it. It's just not as simple as clicking in the cell and moving the cursor around. Instead, click inside the cell and then press the F2 key on your keyboard. This opens the cell for editing, as shown in Figure 8-6, and then you *can* edit just a portion of the data within a cell.

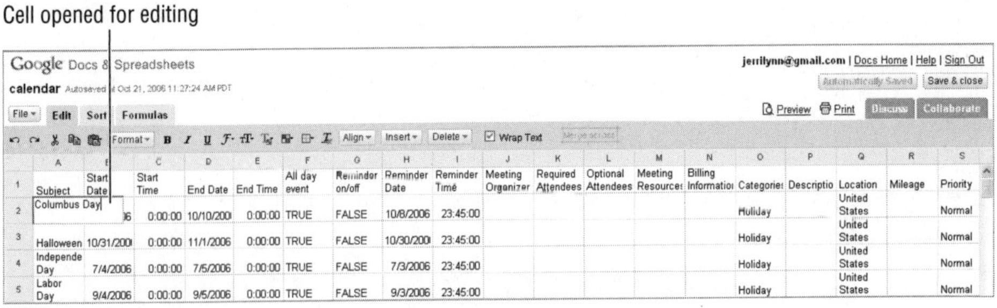

Figure 8-6: The F2 key is used for editing data within a cell.

When you've finished entering data into a cell, you can take one of two actions to accept the data and move on. You can either press the Enter key on your keyboard — this accepts the data and moves you to the next cell in a column — or you can press the Tab key. Pressing the Tab key accepts the data and moves you to the next cell in the row.

Auto-Formatting

When you enter data into a cell, the type of data you enter determines how it will be formatted. For example, entering a number results in a number, but if you put a dollar sign in front of the number, then Spreadsheets reformats it to currency. Any letters that are entered are formatted as text. And if you use the dash (—) or forward slash (/), then your data will be formatted as a date. Using the colon (:) triggers time formatting.

Using Formulas

Formulas are a little different than other types of data. A formula tells the spreadsheet to perform calculations with the data in other cells and to put the answer in the current cell. The spreadsheet needs a way to recognize that the data entered in the current cell is a formula — and the indicator is the equal (=) sign. Use the equal sign before any formula to tell the program that what follows is a formula. So if you're entering the sum formula into a cell, the formula would look something like this: =Sum(C2:C5).

FORMULAS IN GOOGLE SPREADSHEETS

When you begin using Google Spreadsheets, click the Formulas tab. Only six formulas are shown on the page. However, next to the formulas is a link for More. This link leads you to a list of the 200+ formulas that are available in Spreadsheets. And if the formula you're looking for isn't in that list, then you can always write your own.

Writing your own formulas is an art form, however. If you've never written a formula for a spreadsheet, then you might want to find a good book to help you learn how. Any book that contains a chapter or two on writing formulas should do just fine.

With the formulas that are available in Google Spreadsheets, you usually just need to select the formula and then select the range — or group of adjacent cells — to which you want the formula to apply. There are two ways to select a range in Spreadsheets. Either click in the cell where you want the range to begin and then drag your mouse to the cell where you want the range to end, or you can place your cursor in the first cell of the range and then press and hold the Shift key while using the arrow buttons to select the cells you want included in the range.

A faster way to select a range of cells is to click inside the first cell in a range, then press and hold the Shift key, and then click inside the cell at the end of the range. This will select all of the cells between the first one and the last one.

Changing and Merging Cells

I'm a very visual person. That means I like a lot of color and visual appeal in everything I do. Spreadsheets and numbers? Well, they're not really my favorite things in the world. But I've discovered a way to make them more interesting. I add a lot of elements to my spreadsheets, such as merged cells or rows and columns that vary in size.

In Spreadsheets, you have some options for functions such as merging cells and changing the size of rows and columns. And these functions are easy to execute, which makes them all the more appealing to those of us who happen to be visually motivated but not completely technical.

Changing the Size of Cells and Columns

Aside from the need for visual appeal, you might find many reasons for making the size of a row or column larger than the default setting in Spreadsheets. For example, if your spreadsheet contains both text and numbers, the text portion (or the number portion) may be larger than the space provided. If that's the case, you can adjust the size of your rows or columns by placing your cursor over the dividing line (shown in Figure 8-7) and then clicking and dragging the cursor until the height of the row or the width of the column is the desired size.

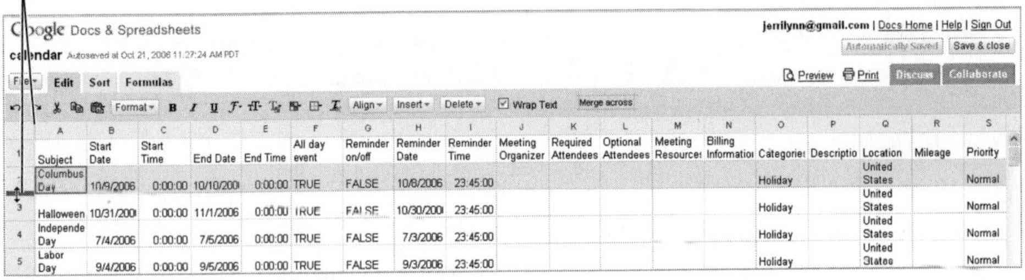
Click and drag to change the size of a row or column

Figure 8-7: Increase row height and column width with a mouse click.

Rows change in height when you press Enter if the data you type is more than will fit in the allotted size. However, columns will not automatically get wider.

Merging Cells

Another function you may find useful is the ability to merge cells across a row. Merging cells is basically the ability to take a number of adjacent cells and make a single large cell out of them. You can merge cells in rows, but you can't merge cells in columns.

To merge any number of cells in a row, click in the first cell and then drag your pointer to the last cell that you want included in the merge, as shown in Figure 8-8. Then click the Merge across link to merge the cells.

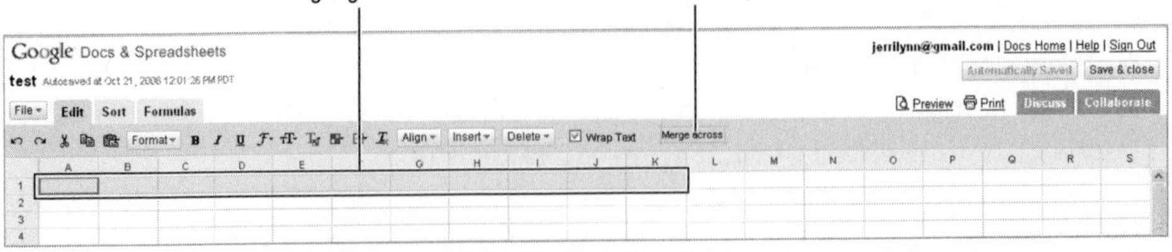
Highlight cells
Click to merge

Figure 8-8: Click and drag to highlight cells for merging.

Once you've merged a group of cells, the Merge across link will change to Break apart. So, if you decide later that you don't want the cells merged, you can un-merge them by placing your cursor in the cell and clicking the Break apart link.

Adding Visual Effects

One more formatting capability that you might appreciate is the ability to add visual effects, such as color, bold, italics, borders, and special alignments. All of these options are available on the Format toolbar.

To add an effect to a cell, row, or column, highlight it and then select the desired option.

Spreadsheets don't have to be just about numbers. You can use a spreadsheet to create an invoice, a schedule, a budget, or just about any other type of document that you can think of. And with the tools that are available through Google Spreadsheets, you can add visual appeal and functionality to any spreadsheet you create.

Saving and Deleting Spreadsheets

When you're finished working with your spreadsheet, you'll probably want to save it. You can either save the spreadsheet to the Google Spreadsheets program, which means it will be saved online so that you can access it from anywhere. Or you can save it to your hard drive in XLS or CSV format.

Saving a Spreadsheet

Google Spreadsheets automatically saves your spreadsheet when you update it. The auto-save cycle is about every 60 to 90 seconds when you're editing a spreadsheet, a little longer when the spreadsheet is inactive. But if you want to ensure that the latest data has been saved when you close out of a spreadsheet, you can click Save & close, in the upper-right corner of the page.

The spreadsheet will be saved and you'll be returned to the active document view of Google Docs & Spreadsheets.

You can also save a copy of your spreadsheet under a different name. From the open spreadsheet view, click the File button and then select Copy Spreadsheet. A dialog box like the one shown in Figure 8-9 opens. Enter a new name for your spreadsheet and then click OK.

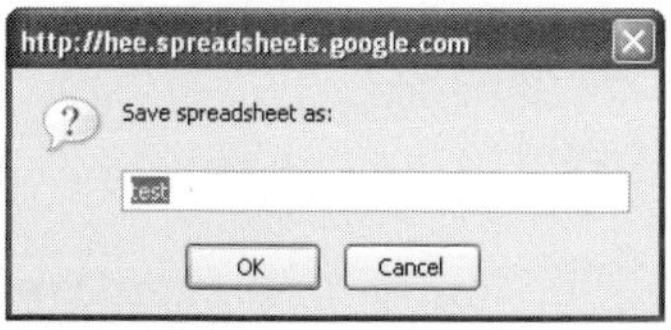

Figure 8-9: Use the Copy Spreadsheet dialog box to rename your spreadsheet copy.

When you're creating copies of your spreadsheets, it's possible to save more than one copy with the same name. Instead of changing the name when the Copy Spreadsheet dialog box appears, leave the name the same and click OK. A second copy of the spreadsheet will appear in your active document list with the same name. Just be aware that this can be confusing if you're accessing one of these files regularly.

Downloading a Spreadsheet

If you want to work on a spreadsheet when you don't have an Internet connection, you can download a copy of your spreadsheet in XLS or CSV format. From the open spreadsheet, click File and then highlight the Export option. A pop-out menu appears from which you can select the format in which you'd like to save the file, as shown in Figure 8-10.

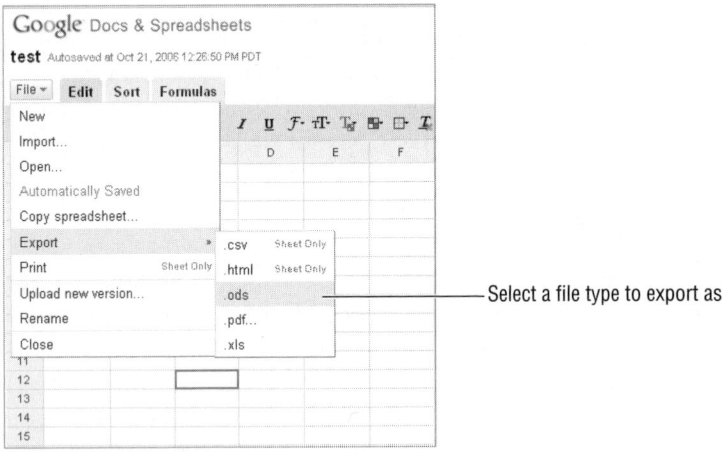

Figure 8-10: Select the type of file you want to download.

You'll be prompted to select a location to save the file to. Navigate to the desired folder and then click Save.

NOTE **Downloading files can be useful, but you should know that you can download only a single worksheet in CSV, which doesn't support multiple-page downloads. If you need to download an entire workbook (multiple worksheets), you can download the files in XLS format only.**

Don't worry. When you're ready to upload a new version of a file, you can go to File → Upload new version and then select your file from your hard drive. The copy on Google Spreadsheets will be replaced with the file that you're uploading.

Moving On

Google Spreadsheets offers some great tools for creating and working with spreadsheets. You're not limited to creating only spreadsheets full of numbers, either. Using the editing tools in Spreadsheets, you can add visual appeal and interest to even text-based files.

In fact, you can do all kinds of things with Google Spreadsheets. But that's a topic for another chapter, so keep reading.

CHAPTER

9

Do More with Spreadsheets

Spreadsheets are useful for two types of data: numbers and text. You can use numbers in spreadsheets to create budgets, track sales, or even track hours worked on a specific project. Text in spreadsheets is best suited to list-type data, where columns and rows are most useful. Inventory lists, human-resources data, and even schedules are good examples of the types of text-based spreadsheets you might find useful.

In this chapter you look a little closer at what you can do with Google Spreadsheets and how to use some of the more advanced features of the program.

Creating Financial Spreadsheets

Are you familiar with the ABCs of finance? **A**ccounting, **B**udgeting, and **C**heckbooks are three words that many people simply don't want to hear. Setting up a budget, balancing a checkbook, and accounting in general are just not activities that most people want to think about, much less do. So, many people avoid spreadsheets because they're associated with these types of activities.

But there is so much more that you can do with financial spreadsheets. It doesn't have to be all about how much money you don't have. Instead you can use spreadsheets to show you how much you do have. Rather than writing your savings deposits into a passbook that you probably have to search for every time you need it, why not just create a spreadsheet into which you can enter the deposit and then let the spreadsheet do all your figuring?

Budgeting, tracking sales, keeping track of financial donations, and even calculating the interest on a loan are also tasks you can complete with a spreadsheet.

It all starts with a blank spreadsheet, although you can upload some templates from other programs. The problem with a template, however, is that you often lose some of the functionality you had when the template was in the original program. In some cases, you lose a lot of formatting, too, so you need to be cautious when uploading templates.

What you can do, however, is use a template that you like in another program to give you ideas for designing your own templates. This is useful for formulas, too. If you're not the best when it comes to creating formulas, you can always find a spreadsheet template that has the function you need and copy that formula for your spreadsheet.

It's not a completely foolproof system. You'll still have to make some changes to the formula because it's likely that your new spreadsheet won't be exactly the same as the one from which you're copying the formula. You need to understand the basics of formulas and how to use them.

More About Formulas

Besides formulas, you'll also see references to functions, which are preprogrammed formulas telling the spreadsheet what to do. These all can seem like mystical entities that don't make sense to ordinary humans. Unless you've been taught how to write them, they may look like a jumble of uninteresting numbers. But the truth is there's a logic to those numbers, and if you can wrap your mind around it, putting together formulas will be child's play.

Formulas (or functions) are basically a group of indicators that work together to perform a mathematical equation. The indicators fall into three categories: numbers, operators, and references. Numbers ... well, you know what those are. Operators — which may also be called formulas — are the mathematical symbols or indicators that help you find the answers you're looking for. And the references are the cells on which you want the operation performed. Also, remember that every function starts with the equal sign (=), which indicates that what follows is a function, which includes a formula.

Confused yet? Figure 9-1 shows a labeled function that might make it a little clearer for you.

Now, there's still a very subtle line between formulas and functions. Functions are the commands that tell your program to execute a formula. And the formula is the actual computation that the program is to perform. So, in the Average example shown in Figure 9-1, the function shown indicates that the formula for averaging should be used on cells A1–A15. The spreadsheet is pre-programmed to understand that the formula for "average" is X+X+X/3, so it carries out those calculations for you. Clear as mud isn't it?

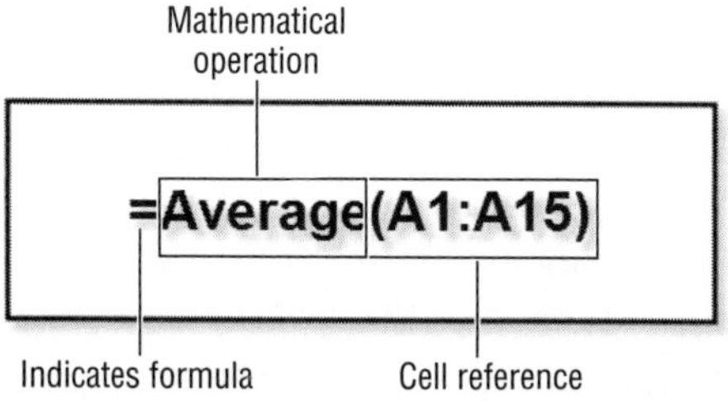

Figure 9-1: The function to average cells A1 through A15

Suffice it to say that I'm going to try to make this as easy for you as possible by referring, from this point forward, to both functions and formulas as just formulas. All you really need to know is that together the two of them perform the calculations, so you don't need to drag out the calculator.

Select a Formula

In Spreadsheets, there are two ways to enter a formula into a cell. The first is to place your cursor in the cell and then, from the Formula tab, select the formula that you want to use. The formula will be entered into the cell, as shown in Figure 9-2, but you still have to fill in the cell range that you want calculated.

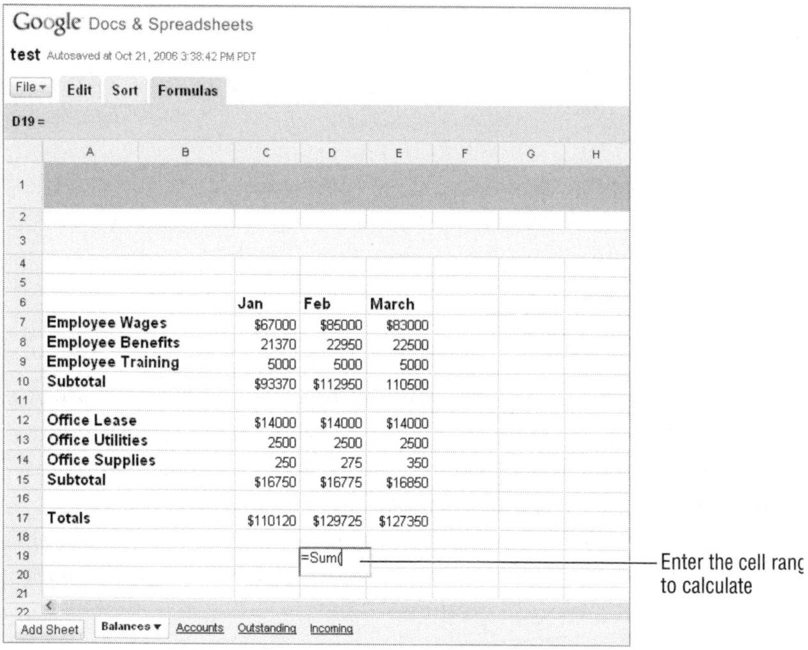

Google Docs & Spreadsheets
test Autosaved at Oct 21, 2006 3:38:42 PM PDT
File Edit Sort Formulas
D19 =
Jan Feb March
Employee Wages $67000 $85000 $83000
Employee Benefits 21370 22950 22500
Employee Training 5000 5000 5000
Subtotal $93370 $112950 110500
Office Lease $14000 $14000 $14000
Office Utilities 2500 2500 2500
Office Supplies 250 275 350
Subtotal $16750 $16775 $16850
Totals $110120 $129725 $127350
=Sum(
Add Sheet Balances Accounts Outstanding Incoming
Enter the cell ranç
to calculate

Figure 9-2: Complete the formula and then press Enter or Tab to accept.

When you enter the cell range to be calculated, you also need to close the parentheses around the cell range. In the formula shown in Figure 9-2, you could enter a cell range of B7:B15 (think of the colon as "to"), but you need to enter the end parenthesis after it. When the formula is complete it will look like this: =Sum(B7:B15).

Another way of entering a range of cells in a formula is to click-and-drag from the first cell in the range to be calculated to the last cell in the range, as shown in Figure 9-3. When you've selected the range of cells you want to calculate, enter the closing parenthesis to complete the formula.

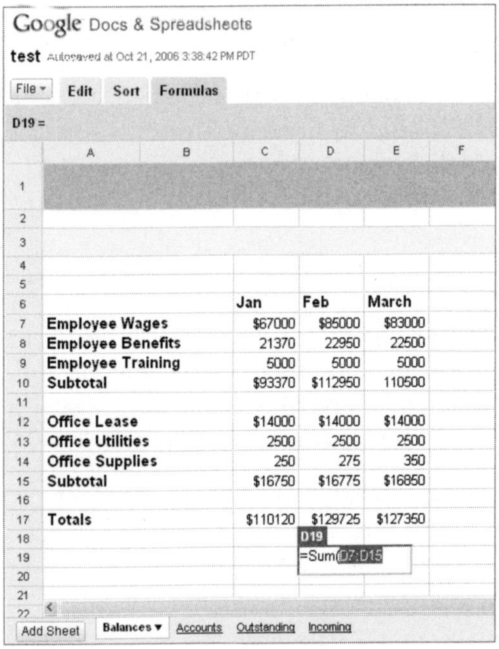

Figure 9-3: Click-and-drag from the first cell to the last to include a range in the formula.

Type a Formula

The second way to enter a formula in a cell is to type the formula. The most important thing to remember when using this method is that you must use the equal sign (=) as the first character in the formula to indicate that a formula follows. This ensures that the action you want taken is actually taken.

For example, you can create a formula to add two cells by typing =B1+B2 into a blank cell. Simply use the cell range and the mathematical operators that you would use for any mathematical equation.

If you're familiar with nested functions in spreadsheets, then you'll probably use this option regularly. A nested function occurs when you have more than one mathematical operation taking place in a given formula. I'm not going to delve any deeper into them in this book. If you need those kinds of functions but aren't familiar with them, you can pick up a good book on creating spreadsheets, or just search the Web for the information. You'll find everything you need to know.

TIP **After you enter a formula into a cell it disappears and the answer to the equation appears in the cell in place of it. If you want to see what the formula in a given cell is, click inside the cell and then look at the lower-right corner of your screen. There you'll find a reference area where the formula name will appear.**

Formatting Numbers

Not every number that you enter in your spreadsheet will be a whole number or a dollar amount. Decimals, dates, and percentages are also commonly used in financial spreadsheets. And you can enter them, just as you would any other number.

You can also change the formatting of a number (or row or column of numbers) by highlighting it, and then selecting the Format button on the editing toolbar. From the menu that appears (shown in Figure 9-4), select the form you want the numbers to take and everything you highlighted will be changed.

You have two other options when formatting numbers with the Format menu. You can round to the nearest whole number or change the format of a number to indicate a date or time.

Sorting and Freezing

One last function you may want to be aware of is the ability to sort rows or columns of data. Sorting is useful if you want to sort your data from highest to lowest amounts, by dollar value, or even by date. And with Google Spreadsheets, you can sort numerically or alphabetically, so you have plenty of options.

When you first start using Spreadsheet's sorting functions, it can be a little confusing because sorting also involves a function called *freezing*. When you freeze, you select a row of data that should not be sorted. For example, you may choose to freeze your column headers, sorting only the rows that contain numerical data.

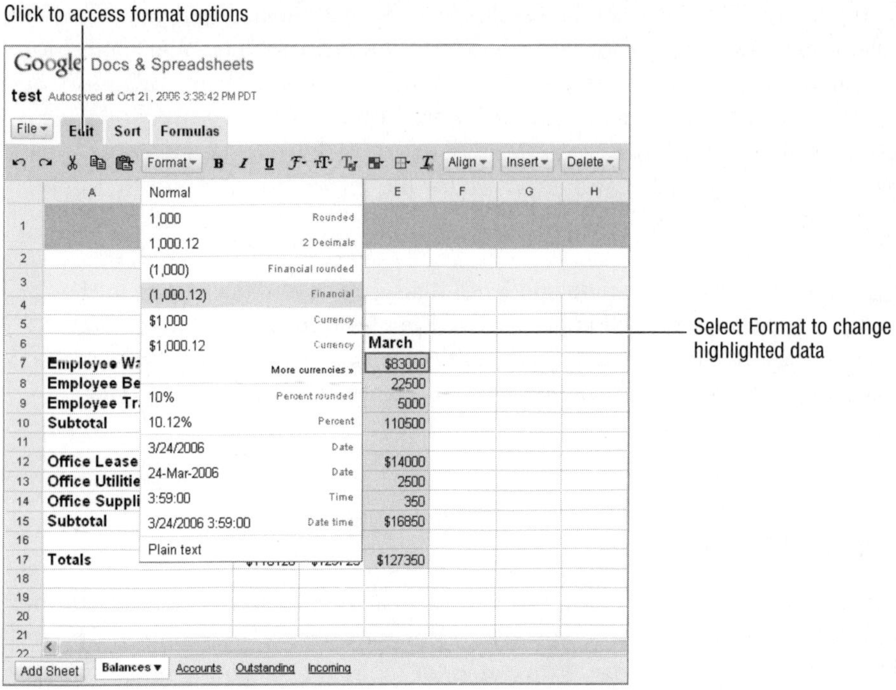

Figure 9-4: Select different number formats from the Format menu.

To freeze one to five rows in your spreadsheet, select the Sort tab and then click the Freeze rows button. From the menu that appears, select the number of rows that you want to freeze, and those rows (from row one to row five) will be frozen. This works only on the top rows in your spreadsheet. You can't freeze rows farther down in the spreadsheet.

This has a useful application outside of sorting your data. If you are working in a spreadsheet that has a large number of rows, freezing the header rows makes it possible for you to keep track of the header for each column. You can scroll through rows below the headers (which you've frozen) and the headers stay in place. This makes it easy to know what each column of data is, even if you're 150 lines deep in your spreadsheet.

Once you've selected the rows that you want to freeze, then you can sort your spreadsheet by any other column in the spreadsheet. Decide on the column that you want to sort, place your cursor in any cell in that column, and then select (from the Sort tab) whether you want to sort the cells by descending (A–Z) or ascending (Z–A) order.

On a financial spreadsheet, A–Z sorts from the lowest number to the highest and Z–A sorts from the highest number to the lowest.

CAUTION **Be careful when sorting spreadsheets that have multiple formulas embedded in them. The Sort function may cause the formulas to malfunction, so the data in the cell will appear as an error.**

Creating Text Spreadsheets

Spreadsheets are valuable for more than just manipulating numbers. Writers use them to track submissions, human-resources managers use them to track benefits and training, and teachers use them to track assignments, grades, and student participation. And there are dozens of other ways to use text-based spreadsheets.

With Google Spreadsheets, you can create text-based spreadsheets in much the same way that you create a numbers-based spreadsheet. Figure 9-5 shows a text-based spreadsheet. As you can see in the figure, the columns and rows work in essentially the same way as on a financial spreadsheet.

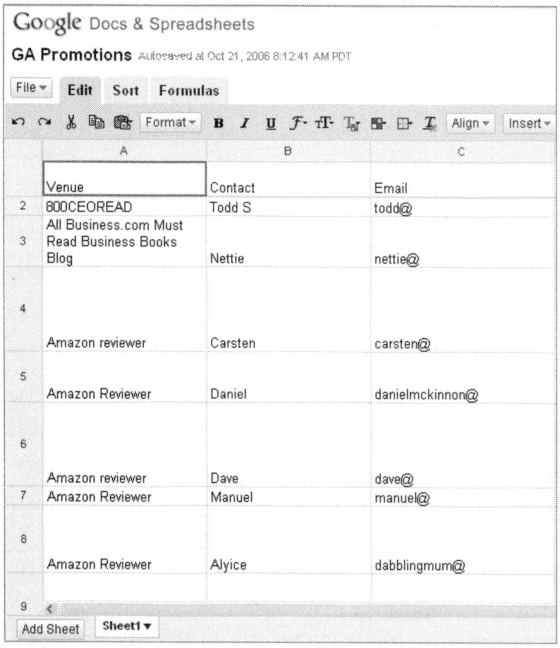

Figure 9-5: Use Google Spreadsheets to create text-based spreadsheets, too.

All the functions that you can use with financial spreadsheets, including formatting and some formulas, are also available in text-based spreadsheets. The only real differences are the information that's included in the spreadsheet and the ways in which text-based spreadsheets are used. You'll even find a few text-based formulas in the formula list that you can access by clicking more on the Formulas tab.

Next to each function shown in the Insert a Function dialog box is also a more link, as shown in Figure 9-6. When you click this link, you're taken to a help page with a description of each function.

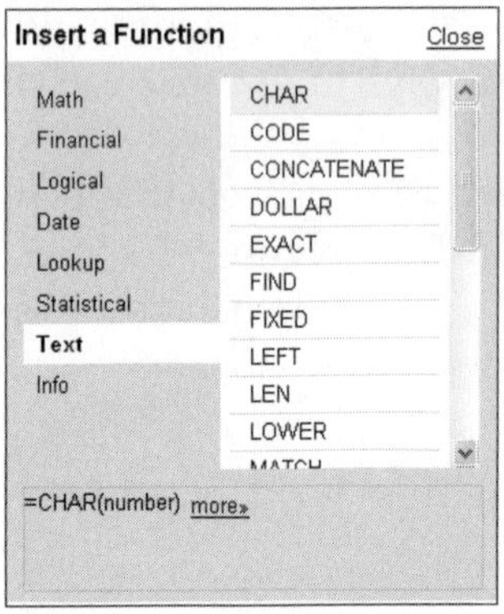

Figure 9-6: Formulas for text-based functions are found in the Insert a Function list.

Moving On

Google Spreadsheets looks deceptively simple. When you first open the program, there doesn't appear to be a lot of functionality built into it. But when you begin to use it, you'll find most of the functionality that exists in other programs. The benefit of Google Spreadsheets is that it's a Web-based program, so you can access your spreadsheets from anywhere.

Once you have access to them, you can manipulate them, add to them, or even create new spreadsheets using the simple interface. If you're new to spreadsheets or you find other programs confusing, then you'll be very pleased with the usability of Google Spreadsheets.

CHAPTER

10

Collaborating and Sharing

One aspect of Google Spreadsheets that makes it different from most other spreadsheet programs is its collaborating and sharing capabilities. Not only is the program available to you online, but you can also make it available to other users, who can then collaborate on a spreadsheet with you at the same time you're editing the document.

You also have printing capabilities with Spreadsheets, and if you need to work on a spreadsheet when you have no Internet connection, you can export spreadsheets to your hard drive. And in this chapter, you learn how to do it all.

Sharing Spreadsheets

Anyone who has ever worked with a spreadsheet knows that at times you need the ability to share a spreadsheet with other people. Maybe you've put together a soccer schedule that you want the coach to approve before you send it out. Or it could be that you've created a sales tracking spreadsheet and want to share it with your salespeople.

In some other programs, when you want to share a spreadsheet you have to find a way to pass the file from one person to another. Maybe you'll upload the file to an e-mail or download it to disk and pass it around. Either option is not very convenient. It requires the people with whom you want to share the spreadsheet to download or upload the file.

There's an easier way. In Google Spreadsheets, sharing a spreadsheet is as easy as inviting someone to view it. You'll find the option to share on the Collaborate tab on the right side of the page, as shown in Figure 10-1.

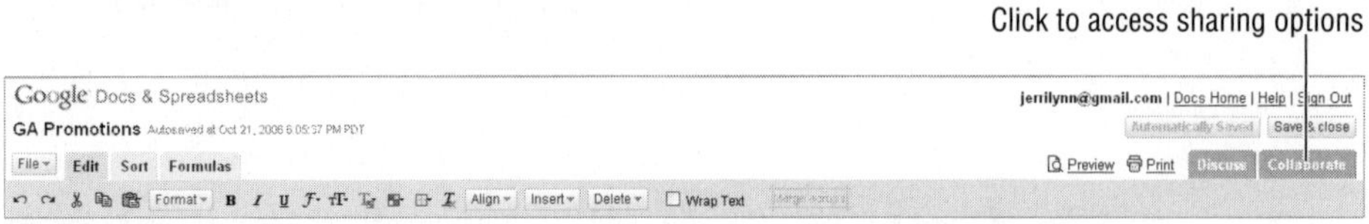

Figure 10-1: Use the Collaborate tab to share your spreadsheet with others.

Clicking the Collaborate tab will cause a column to appear on the right side of the page, as shown in Figure 10-2. This column gives you two options for sharing: Invite collaborators and Invite viewers.

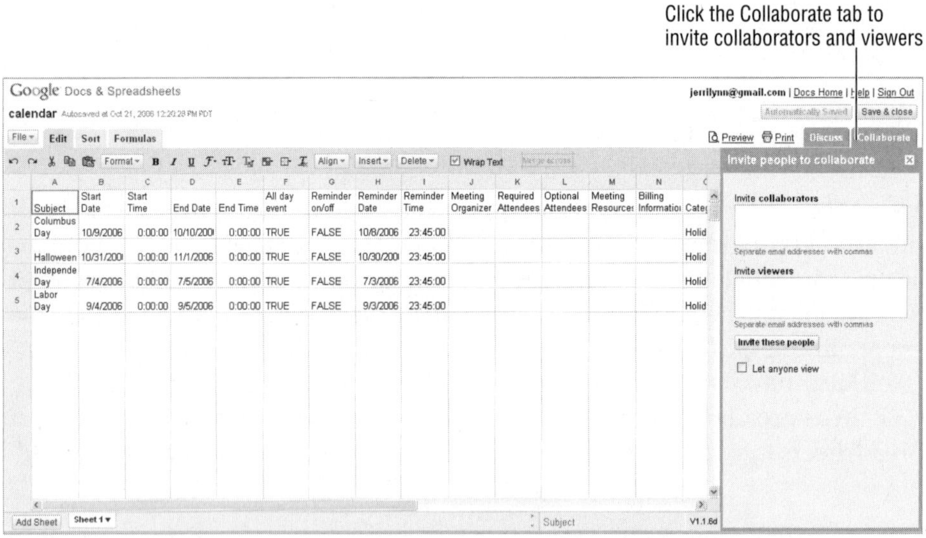

Figure 10-2: Sharing options allow others to view or edit your spreadsheet.

These collaboration tools work the same as they worked in the Docs part of Google Docs & Spreadsheets so you should be familiar with using them by now. I won't go into detail here about how to use these controls. If you didn't read Part II, you can flip back to Chapter 5 and review the instructions on how to use them.

There are no limits on the number of people with whom you can share a spreadsheet. Invite anyone you want to. Just remember that these people have access to all of the information in the spreadsheet, so you may want to make sure there's no sensitive information available to them.

Removing Viewers

At some point, you may decide that you want to remove a viewer (or collaborator) from a spreadsheet that you've invited her to access. For example, perhaps you've asked someone to preview preliminary figures but want to keep the final figures under wraps until the release date.

To remove a person's viewing or editing abilities on your spreadsheet, go to the Collaborate tab and then click the Remove link next to the viewer's name. The name will be removed from the list and access to the document will be ended. However, if you decide at a later time that you want to allow that person to view the spreadsheet again, you'll have to go through the invitation process a second time.

Real-Time Editing and Collaboration

One of the truly unique features of Google Spreadsheets is the ability to edit your spreadsheets in real time with other people. This reduces the amount of time it takes to pass a spreadsheet around for approval and editing, and it makes it unnecessary to struggle to combine multiple versions of the spreadsheet.

To invite other people to edit your spreadsheets, click the Collaborate tab and then, in the text box below Invite collaborators, type the person's e-mail address, and click Invite these people.

The Invitation dialog box, which you saw in Chapter 5, appears again but with a slightly different message. Type any personal message that you would like to include with the invitation into the text box provided, and then click Send Invitation.

After you've sent invitations to viewers and editors, those people's e-mail addresses will appear below the invitation boxes on the right side of the collaborate page, as shown in Figure 10-3.

Chat with Viewers and Editors

Once you've offered to share your spreadsheet with someone and he has accepted the invitation, then you have another, surprising option that you'll probably find very useful. It's the ability to chat with others who are editing or viewing the spreadsheet.

You'll find the option to chat with other users in the Discuss tab, shown in Figure 10-4.

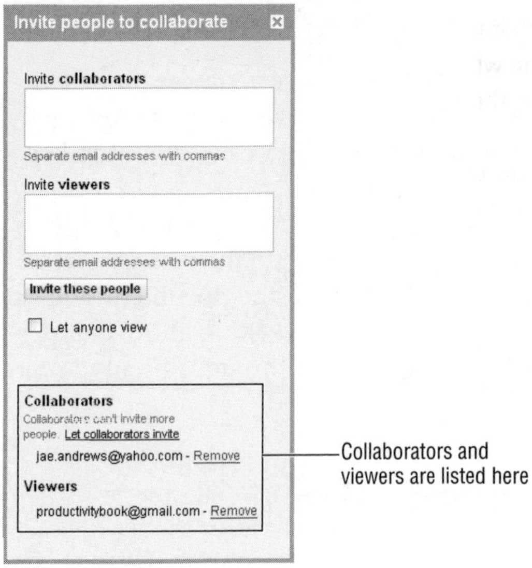

Figure 10-3: Editors and viewers are listed on the page for easy reference.

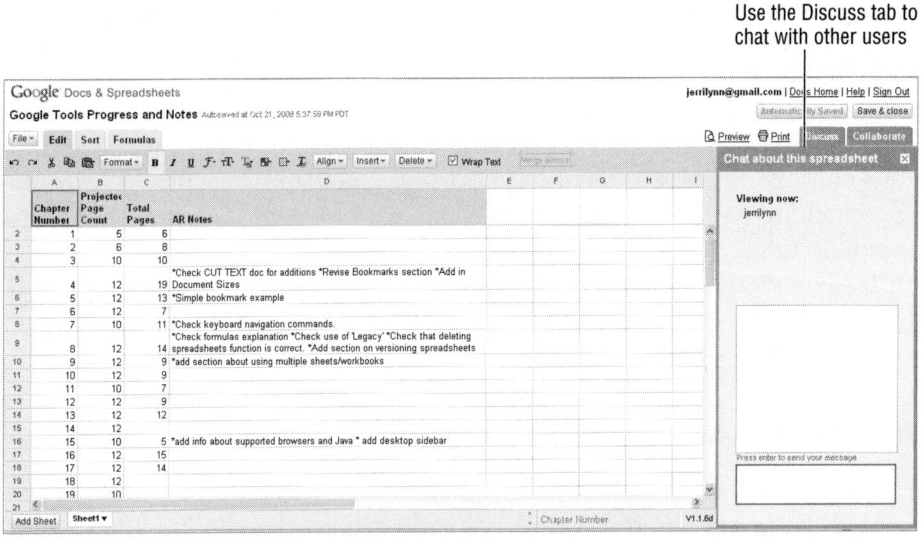

Figure 10-4: The chat option appears only if others are logged in to Spreadsheets.

When the Discuss tab opens, you'll see a list of the people who are also editing your document. There is also a window in which you can view the chat, and a window that allows you to send your messages to all the collaborators who are online. Type your message into this window (it's the bottom one) and press Enter on your computer keyboard and the message is sent.

CAUTION **When you choose to chat with editors and viewers who are online, be cautious, because everyone who is online and has access to your document can view and participate in the chat.**

When you're finished chatting, you can hide the chat controls by selecting the blue X at the top of the chat controls box.

Real-Time Editing

In addition to chatting, you can make changes to your spreadsheet at the same time as someone else. All you (or your collaborator) need to do is enter the numbers or text that is to be added or changed. These are updated instantly on each user's screen.

If you plan to use this option for editing spreadsheets with someone else, it might be wise for each of you to pick a different color font to use during the editing process. This will help each of you to identify quickly the changes that have been made to a spreadsheet.

When the editing process is complete, it's easy to convert all the text back to black. Just click-and-drag from the first row to the last to highlight all the text, and then select the Text Color icon and choose the color you would like the text to have.

TIP **Don't worry over what might happen if you and another person happen to be editing a cell at the same time. The text that will appear in the cell is the last that was entered and accepted by the system. This is one of the times when it's useful to have each person using a different color text.**

Simultaneous editing capability, or even just shared capability, comes with its own set of issues. For example, when you're sharing your spreadsheet with others for editing, they have the ability to delete the spreadsheet from your system as well as from their own. To prevent an accidental deletion of a spreadsheet that you can't afford to lose, always save a copy of it under a different name in your list. This ensures that even if someone else deletes it, you'll have a copy.

Another concern when you're sharing editing capabilities with others is that those you invite to share a spreadsheet could create their own copy of the sheet and then share it with others. This could potentially create a breach of confidentiality if you're sharing sensitive information. Always use caution when sharing spreadsheets and ensure that nothing sensitive is included in them.

Unsharing a Spreadsheet

When you were a kid and decided to stop sharing a toy, chances are someone accused you of giving something and then taking it back. As a youngster, you probably didn't want to hear this. But as an adult (especially one sharing spreadsheets that may contain sensitive information), taking back a gift isn't always a terrible thing.

In fact, Google Spreadsheets gives you the ability to share, but it also gives you the ability to "unshare." To stop anyone whom you've granted access to your spreadsheets from accessing them in the future, click the Collaborate tab and then click the Remove link next to the name of the person you want to stop sharing with. Yes, it's taking back a gift, but sometimes you just have to.

However, be aware that you will not be asked to confirm your unsharing. The editor or viewer that you've previously added will simply be removed and will no longer have access to the document. Should you change your mind about allowing this person to access the spreadsheet, you'll have to go through the invitation process again from the beginning.

Printing Spreadsheets

Another way that you might choose to share your spreadsheet with someone else is to print it. After all, we may be a digital society these days, but we still shuffle tons of paper around. So, naturally, you would expect Google Spreadsheets to have a print option; it does, but you could spend days looking for it.

The Print link is right above your spreadsheet on the right. And you use it just as you used the Print link in Google Docs. Just click it, choose the printer you want to use, and click OK.

The one drawback with printing your spreadsheet from the Web is that your browser settings may affect the way the printout appears. For example, most Web browsers are set to print the date and the address of Web pages. You can change that in some Web browsers. Refer to your Web browser's help section for directions on removing the header and footers.

In addition to the ability to print spreadsheets, you can also preview how they might appear to collaborators or viewers. Next to the Print link is a Preview link. Click that link to be taken to a preview of your spreadsheet.

Moving On

Google Spreadsheets is no Microsoft Excel. But many people don't want Microsoft Excel. It can be confusing and complicated to use. Google Spreadsheets is straightforward and easy to use, *and* it offers some collaboration and editing options that no other spreadsheet program offers.

With Google Spreadsheets, you can collaborate in real time or allow other people to view your spreadsheet online without the need to download a file. And you can chat with your viewers or editors when they're signed into Google Spreadsheets at the same time you are. You can even print from Google Spreadsheets if you know the secret (and you do now).

Ultimately, Google Spreadsheets is the program for the ordinary user of spreadsheets. You won't find some of the functions that you find in other spreadsheet programs, but you will find an interface that's easy to use and has enough functionality to enable you to perform most of the spreadsheet functions you need. And the best part of the program? It's free, so all of these capabilities and features (even sharing and collaboration) won't cost you a single penny.

PART

IV

Google Page Creator

Did you know nearly 93 million Web sites are on the Internet? Is one of them yours? If you don't have a Web site yet, it's time to get one. After all, everyone else has one.

Maybe the reason you don't have a site is that you don't want to think about the complexities of finding a domain, a hosting service, and the right software to create the perfect site. What's more, it's pretty expensive, so it's understandable that you just might not be ready to face the creations of your own Web site.

Well, it *was* understandable. But now there's Google Page Creator. All the hard work is done for you. Google figured out the complexities, so all you have to do is use the Page Creator software — which incidentally is Web-based — to create the site. The program is easy to use and Google handles everything else for you. And do you want to know the best part? Like all of the other Google programs, it's completely free!

What are you waiting for? Keep reading to learn how to use this software and you'll (finally) have your own Web site in no time.

CHAPTER
11

Welcome to Page Creator

Web sites have many purposes. For businesses, they can serve as tools to sell goods or services or to provide information about upcoming events. And personal uses for Web sites include sharing family information and photos or hobbies. You can even use a Web site to share your views on specific topics with the world or to help certain groups of people.

In the wake of natural disasters, Web sites spring up before the clouds even clear. And during an election year, there are more political Web sites than there are politicians. Web sites have simply become one of the most frequently used methods of communicating messages and providing products.

One of the problems with Web sites, however, is that they're not easy to create. Or at least they didn't used to be easy. You had to have Web-design software (such as FrontPage), or you needed to understand markup languages such as HTML to create a Web site from scratch. Design programs are expensive, and languages such as HTML can be difficult (and time-consuming) to learn.

Even if you do have a design program, understanding how to use it is like understanding a completely new language. It takes lots of practice to become fluent. And then there's the issue of where to put the Web site.

Web sites exist on servers that are connected to the Web. In order for others to be able to view and interact with your Web site, you have to have a name for it that belongs exclusively to you, and you need a place on a server for the Web site to reside. The name is commonly referred to as a domain name and providing a "home" for the site is referred to as *hosting*.

It's a confusing jumble of terms that creates frustration for people who aren't propeller heads. What's more, buying a domain name and paying for hosting — both recurrent costs — can become expensive, especially if you don't know what you're looking for or where to find the best prices.

So, many people avoid creating a Web site altogether. Oh sure, you'd love to have a site, but who wants to deal with all of the complexities and expenses of getting one? Well, you do, actually. And it's not nearly as frustrating as you might think. Google's Page Creator is the answer that you've been looking for.

Why Use Page Creator?

I referred to it before, but now let me say it right out. Google Page Creator takes all of the hassle out of creating and publishing your Web site. Of course, there are more reasons to use it than just because Google created it, so let's look at those.

For starters, Google Page Creator has the usual appealing price point — it's free. Like all the other applications covered in this book, the program is made available to users at no cost. At some time in the future, that could change, but I doubt that it will. What's more likely is that Google will add small, unobtrusive advertisements to your pages. They'll be far less distracting than the advertisements that you find on some services, and because they'll use Google's proprietary technology, the ads will reflect the content on your Web site.

In addition to the really great price break on Google Page Creator, many users are drawn to it because the domain name and hosting are provided. When you create a Web page with Google Page Creator, your domain name is tied to your Google account user name, and Google hosts the pages for you for free — up to 100MB. That's a whole lot of storage. My personal Web site at about 15 pages takes up less than 5MB on the Web.

Finally, Google Page Creator is a WYSIWYG editor — What You See Is What You Get. This just means that it's easy to use and you won't spend weeks trying to figure out how to get the program to perform the way you want. All of the controls are easy to locate and use. Keep reading, you'll see.

Navigating Page Creator

To get started with Google Page Creator, you need to have a Google account. If you don't have one, flip back to Chapter 2 to learn how to sign up for one. When you're finished, come back here and follow these instructions for creating a Page Creator account.

With your brand-new Google account user name and password, log on to `www.pages.google.com`. You'll be taken to a welcome page that includes some basic information about the capabilities of Google Page Creator.

In the top-right corner of the page is a link that reads, I'm ready to create my pages. If you click this link you are taken to the bottom of the page where you're prompted to read the user agreement, agree to it, and then click another button (which appears when you agree to the user agreement). This one reads I'm ready to create my pages.

Do actually read through the user agreement. It's an important and legally binding document, so you want to understand it when you agree to it. When you're finished, click the I'm ready to create my pages link and you are taken to the Google Page Creator Edit Page.

The Edit Page is where you begin creating your first Web site. After that, each time you log into Google Page Creator you're taken to a page-manager area, from which you'll navigate to the other capabilities of Google Page Creator.

When the Edit Page appears, you are automatically taken to a blank template. The navigation tools are in the borders around the template, as shown in Figure 11-1.

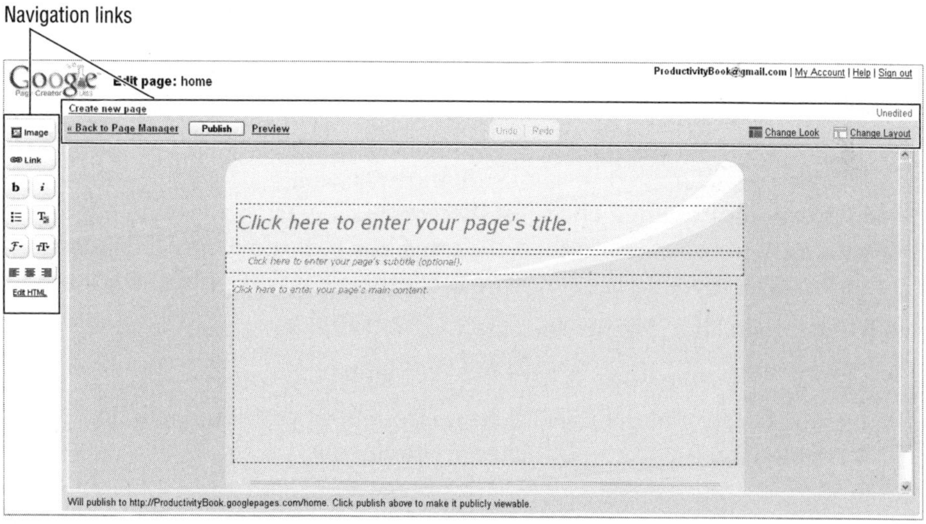

Figure 11-1: Navigation tools surround the page-creation area.

On the left side of the page are the links you'll use to design your Web site. You learn more about these links in Chapter 12.

Across the top of the page are the management, publishing, and layout links. Publishing links are covered in depth in Chapter 14, and layout links in Chapters 12 and 13. So, let's look at the management link.

If you click the Back to Page Manager link, the page you're working on will be saved and you are taken to the Page Manager, shown in Figure 11-2.

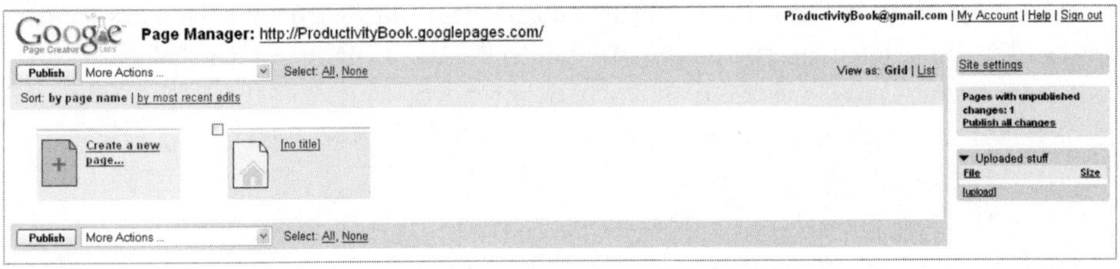

Figure 11-2: The Page Manager is where you control Web site publishing activities.

On the Page Manager page, you have some options for working with pages that you've already created. The first thing you'll notice on this page is the Web link next to the Page Manager title. This is the link to your page, and if you click the link, you are taken to a preview of your site.

Beneath that title is a Publish button and a drop-down menu. The Publish button is used to publish your site to the Web. You look at it more closely in Chapter 14.

The drop-down menu, shown in Figure 11-3, contains action commands:

- **Tell your friends:** Place a check mark in the box next to the page that you want to share with your friends and then click this option. An e-mail window appears that you can use to send an invitation to your friends to view your site.
- **Discard unpublished changes:** Place a check mark next to the page you want to change, and then click this link to remove any changes that you've made to the site since the last time it was published.
- **Unpublish:** Unpublishes the selected Web site.
- **Duplicate:** Duplicates the selected Web site.
- **Delete:** Deletes the selected Web site from both your Web-site list and from the Web if you've published it previously.

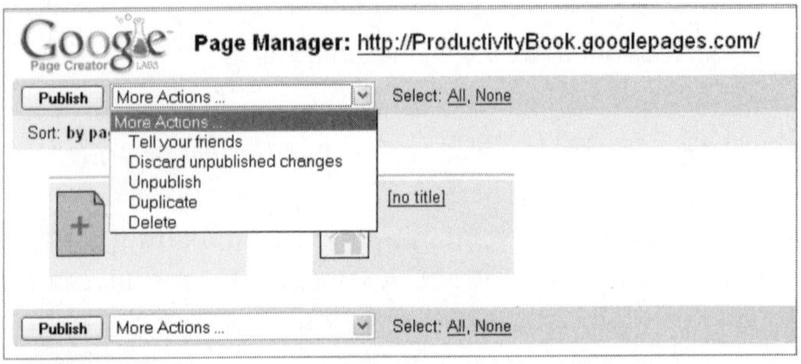

Figure 11-3: Use the drop-down menu to work with your Web site.

You may notice a duplicate toolbar beneath the list of your pages. This toolbar performs the same functions as the one I've just discussed. But it's handy to have if you have multiple pages that you've created or published.

On the right side of the page are some additional navigation links, as shown in Figure 11-4. These links lead to tools that will help you navigate the Edit Page as well as links to help you manage your Web pages and settings, and upload files.

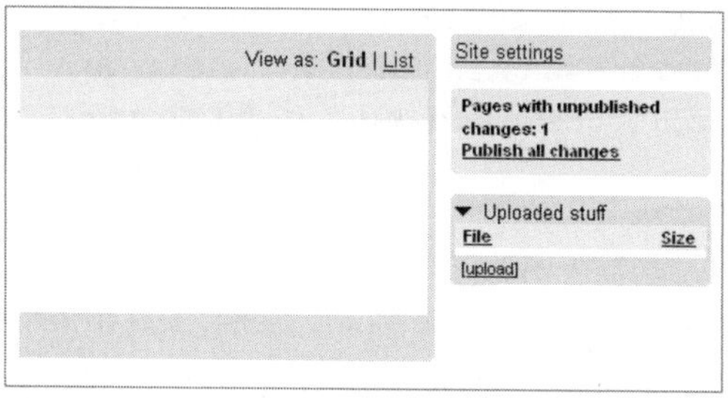
View as: Grid | List
Site settings
Pages with unpublished changes: 1
Publish all changes
Uploaded stuff
File
Size
[upload]

Figure 11-4: Additional navigation links and functions are on the right side of the page.

If you click the List link, the pages that are displayed in the Page Edit view will change from icons to a list. This takes up less space, so if you have multiple pages, it should be easier to find the one you're looking for.

Another option you might be interested in is the Site Settings link. Click this link and you are taken to a page like the one shown in Figure 11-5.

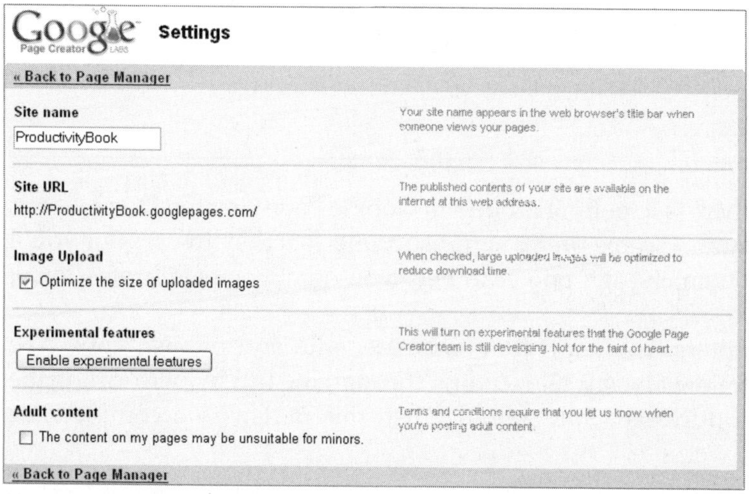
Google Page Creator LABS
Settings
« Back to Page Manager
Site name
ProductivityBook
Your site name appears in the web browser's title bar when someone views your pages.
Site URL
http://ProductivityBook.googlepages.com/
The published contents of your site are available on the internet at this web address.
Image Upload
Optimize the size of uploaded images
When checked, large uploaded images will be optimized to reduce download time.
Experimental features
Enable experimental features
This will turn on experimental features that the Google Page Creator team is still developing. Not for the faint of heart.
Adult content
The content on my pages may be unsuitable for minors.
Terms and conditions require that you let us know when you're posting adult content.
« Back to Page Manager

Figure 11-5: The Site Settings page lets you adjust how your page performs.

On the Site Settings page, you can change the name that appears in the title bar of your site, view your site URL (this does not change), adjust image uploading settings, select experimental functions, or set your site as adult content.

The Experimental Features link leads you to a disclaimer where you must choose if you want to allow these features on your site or not. If you click No, you are returned to the Site Settings page. If you click Yes you are taken to an information page where you can confirm you selection.

CAUTION **Use caution when selecting Experimental Features. The features that are included in this set are brand new and not well tested. That means you could experience technical difficulties with your site as a result of choosing this option.**

If you do choose to use the Experimental Features, when you confirm your selection you are taken to the Site Settings page where you'll see a red notice beneath Experimental Features that indicates they are enabled. Also, the button associated with these features changes to allow you to turn them off should you decide in the future that you don't want to use them.

When you're finished with your Site Settings page, click the Back to Page Manager link to return to the Page Manager.

The last option you have on this page is to upload stuff. This link lets you upload graphics and other files that you want to include on your Web site. To upload a file, click the Upload link and then click Browse to navigate to the place on your hard drive where the desired file is stored.

When you're done uploading your files, they will appear listed below the Uploaded Stuff title. Next to the title there's a small arrow. If you click this arrow, you can show or hide the files that you've uploaded.

Moving On

That's really all there is to getting around in Google Page Creator. Don't worry, though. This program seems pretty simplistic, and it *is* easy to use. But you'll find it has more than enough power to help you quickly create professional, eye-catching Web sites.

In coming chapters, you learn how to create, edit, and publish your Web site. And if you follow along while reading through the text by performing the actions that are addressed, you should finish this part with a complete, or nearly complete, Web site.

CHAPTER

12

Creating a Web Site

Since people began creating Web pages, there has been a gap between what can be done and what is done with those pages. The problem is that most people just don't possess the technical knowledge to create a Web page, or at least one with any degree of complexity.

In the beginning, you had to create Web pages by writing the code that was the base for those pages. If you weren't well versed in the code, you could learn it, but it took a lot of time and effort to learn it well enough to create great pages.

Later, programs such as Microsoft Publisher and FrontPage began hitting store shelves. These programs helped you create Web pages but were still not the easiest software to use.

You still have both these methods to create pages, but services also are available that provide a WYSIWYG (What You See Is What You Get) Web-page creator. They also provide space on the Web to put the page, which is another element that can make Web-page creation daunting. These services are usually point-and-click simple, and require very little time to learn. Google Page Creator and Google Pages are just such services.

Creating a Web Site

When you first log in to your Google Page Creator account, you'll see a list of the Web sites that you've created, if you have created any at all. This is the Page Manager screen, and it's where you'll always begin your work in Page Creator.

Creating a Web site with Page Creator starts with a blank page. From the Page Manager screen, click Create a new page. As Figure 12-1 shows, the link changes to a text box where you should enter the name for your page. Select a name that reflects the title you plan to use on your page. And then click Create and Edit.

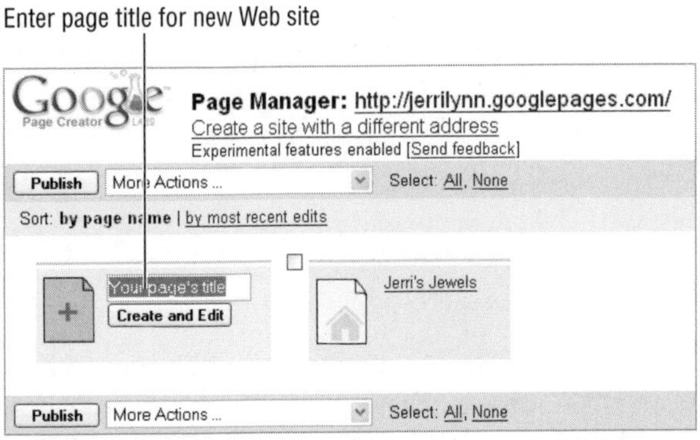

Figure 12-1: Enter a name for your site that reflects the site's title.

You are taken to a predesigned Web site with the title that you entered at the top of the page. The design of the page will be either the Google default page or the same design that you used in a previous Web site.

Choosing a Layout

If you don't like the default layout that is generated for your new Web site, changing it is as simple as clicking a few buttons. First, click the Change Layout link on the right side of the page. Your existing page will save, and then you are taken to the Choose Layout screen shown in Figure 12-2.

Don't get worried about the page saving before you're ready to save. You'll have the option to change the design of the page, even after it has been saved. For now, select the layout you would like to use. You'll see that the page saves again, and then you are returned to your work in progress with the new layout in place.

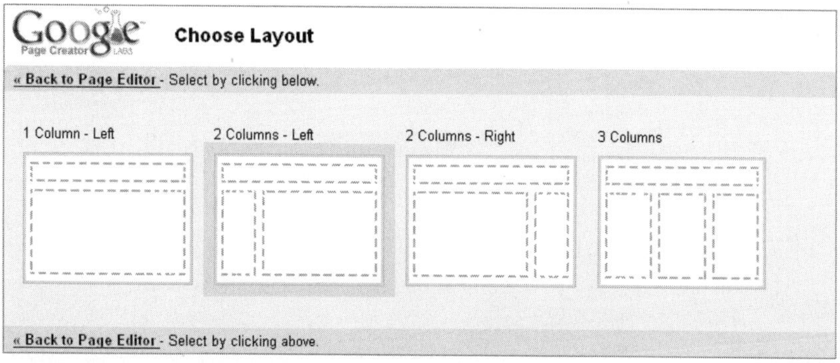

Figure 12-2: You select the layout for your site on the Choose Layout screen.

Another part of page layout is the design of the page that you're creating, and everyone has different design tastes. Google's Page Creator includes page layout options for most tastes. And all you have to do is choose the one you like.

To change the design of your page, click the Change Look link. It's located on the right side of the page, next to the Change Layout link. Again, you'll see that your page saves, and then you are taken to the Choose Look screen, shown in Figure 12-3.

You can preview any of the designs shown by clicking the Preview link below the thumbnail of the page. This will take you to another tab or window where you can see what the site looks like.

When you find a design you like, click directly on the thumbnail. You go through the page saving again, and then you are taken to the new site that has both the layout and the look that you selected.

One nice feature of Google Page Creator is the ability to edit some elements of the HTML on your own. If you happen to know HTML, then you can change your page in any way that can be manipulated by HTML. If you don't know HTML, there are many great tutorials on the Web that will tell you just about everything you need to know in a few minutes.

To edit the HTML for your Web site, you first have to choose a section in which you want to edit the HTML. Place your cursor inside any of the boxes on a page, and then click the Edit HTML link in the lower-right corner of the page.

The Edit HTML page appears. In the text box on the Edit HTML page, enter, change, or add HTML code to design that section as desired.

When you're finished, you can preview the results of your work by clicking the Preview tab. When you're satisfied with the results, click Save Changes and your HTML will be saved to the final page. If you decide you don't want to make changes to the HTML for that section, click Cancel and you are returned to the design view of your Web site.

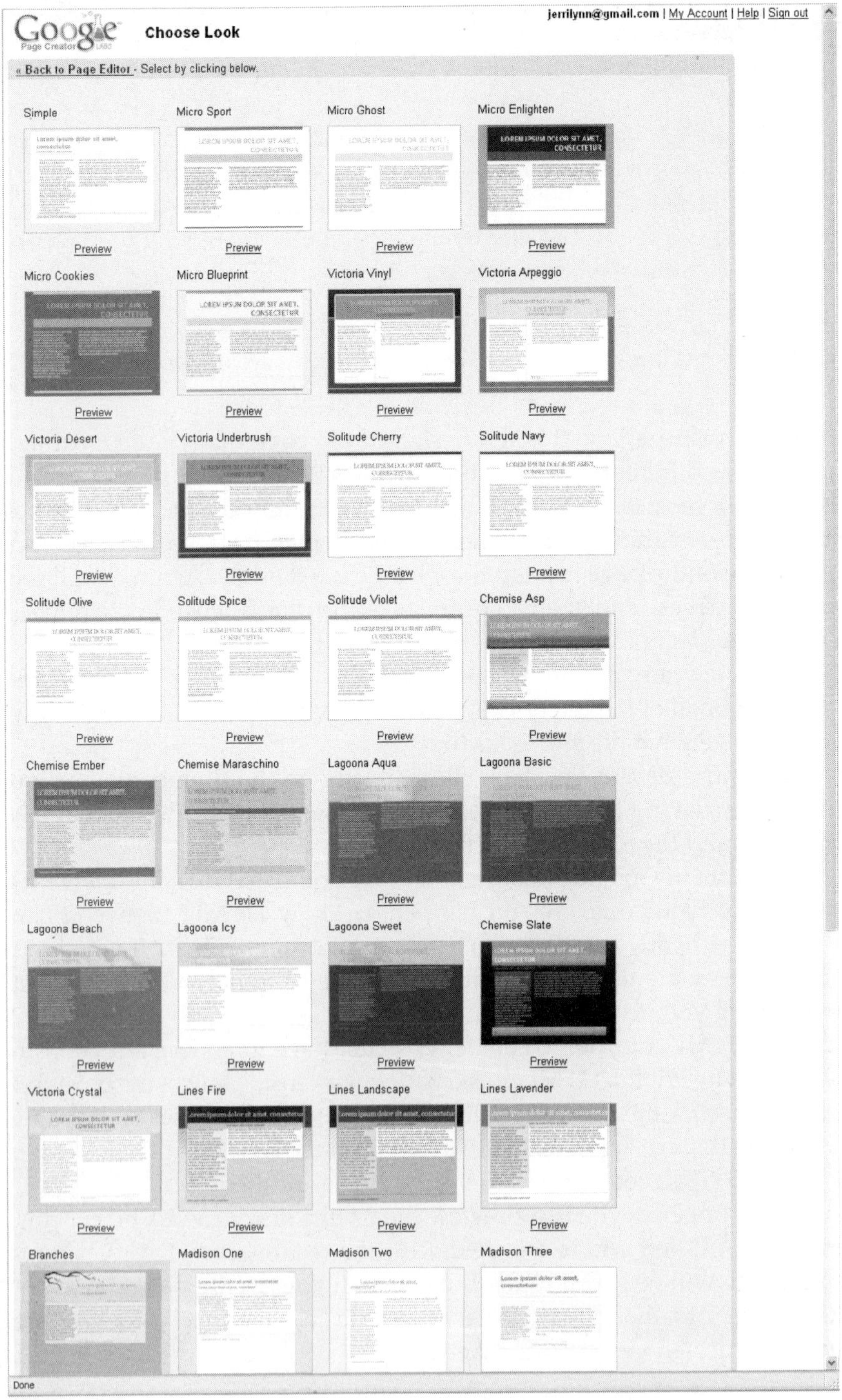

Figure 12-3: Google gives you 41 different designs to choose from.

Adding Pages

Here's where things get a little hinky when it comes to creating your Web site with Google Page Creator. You could search for hours for a way to add pages to your site and probably would never figure it out. But there's a reason for that.

To create a multi-page Web site with Google Page Creator, you actually need to create separate pages and link them together. That is, you designate a word or words that, when clicked, will take the user to a different page. It's a bit cumbersome, but it works.

Before you do anything you need to create the first page for your site. The preceding instructions should get you through that without too much trouble. Once you have the page created, highlight the word or words that you want to use as a link for your page.

When you're creating the first page in your Web site, choose a column layout for it; then you can use one of the columns to list the links to other pages in the site. You can also just include the links throughout the text on your page, as described previously. But this tip is just a little niftier way for users to navigate.

After you've highlighted the text you want to use as a link, click the Link button, as shown in Figure 12-4.

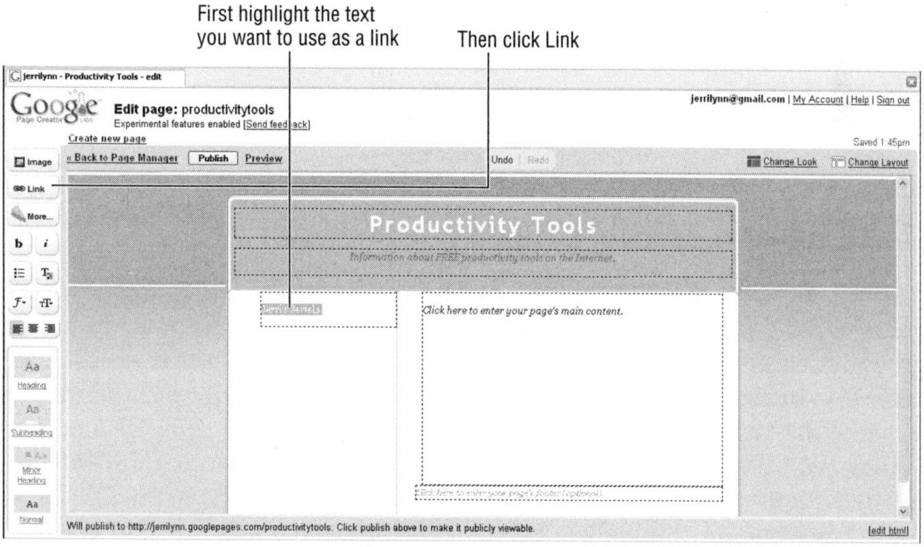

Figure 12-4: Use the buttons on the left to add links and other elements to your page.

When you click the Link button, an Edit Link dialog box appears (shown in Figure 12-5). In the dialog box, enter a name for the page (hint: make it the same name you are using for the link) and then click the Add Page button.

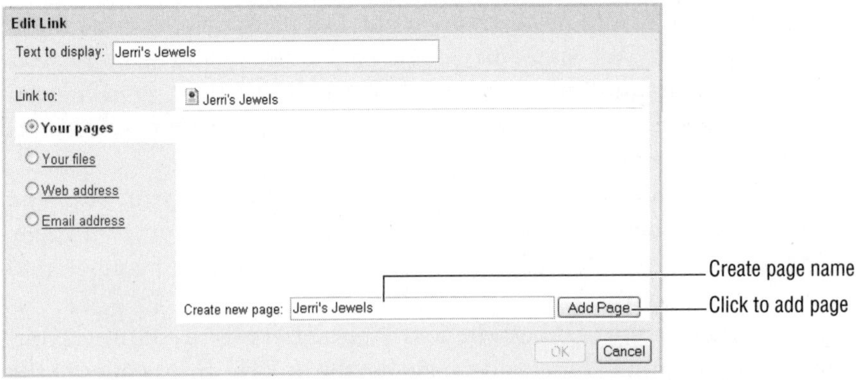

Figure 12-5: Use the Edit Link dialog box to create new pages for your site.

The new page will be added to the list of pages shown in the dialog box. You can repeat this process as many times as you need to in order to create the number of pages you'd like in your Web site. But remember that the last page you create will be the page link displayed on your Web site. When you're finished adding pages, click OK to return to your Web site.

Once you're back on your page, you can add the additional pages that you created by adding the link text, highlighting it, clicking Link, and then selecting the page that you want the text to link to.

Changing and Editing Links

Creating Web sites is somewhat of a dynamic activity. The site changes, sometimes before you even publish it for the first time. And instead of jumping through hoops to change something, you would always prefer the easiest way possible to make the changes, right? Google gives you some simple options for changing the links on your page if you want or need to.

After your link has been created, click it and the Link toolbar appears, as shown in Figure 12-6. This toolbar contains links that lead you to the Edit Link dialog box (change), to the page to edit it (edit page), or to a preview site that lets you see how the link works (test link).

You can also delete a link by clicking the Remove Link button on the toolbar. Be careful when you select this option, however, because it will delete both the link and the text that is used for the link. The link will also be removed completely from the Edit Link dialog box, so if you decide you want to add it back, you'll have to recreate the link completely.

Click a link to access the Link toolbar

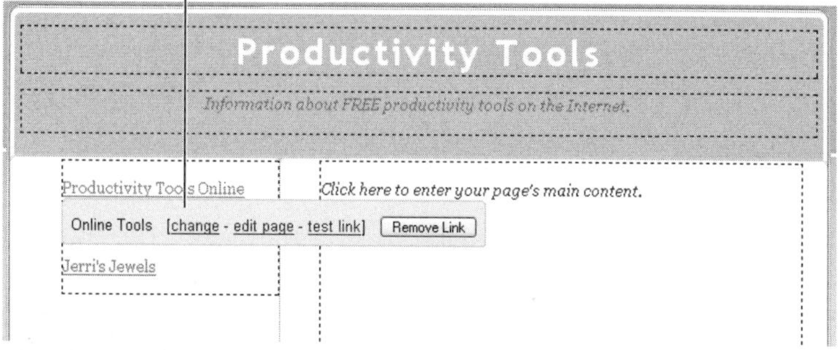

Figure 12-6: Use the Link toolbar to edit links or pages, or to test and preview pages.

Adding Graphic Links

Not everyone likes to use text as the basis for links. If you prefer to use graphics or pictures for your links, you can use those as well. All you need to do is add the picture, click it, and then click the link button. Then follow the same steps that are listed previously for adding the link and you're in business.

If you're not sure how to add pictures or graphics to your site, don't stress. You learn how to do that in Chapter 13.

Saving Your Pages

Once you have your page layout, design, and links, you may want to save your page. The good news is that Google Page Creator has a great auto-save feature that should protect you in the event that you accidentally close out of the Web site or your computer crashes.

Google Page Creator also saves your pages automatically when you change an element of the page (such as the layout or design). And it will automatically prompt you to save when you close out intentionally before the auto-save feature has protected your page.

Still, maybe you've just added an element and want to be certain you don't lose it. Saving is easy. Just click the link on the upper-right side of the page that reads save now, as shown in Figure 12-7. If you don't see that link, then you probably will see a green or blue bit of text that says Saved and has a time after it. This indicates when the page was last saved.

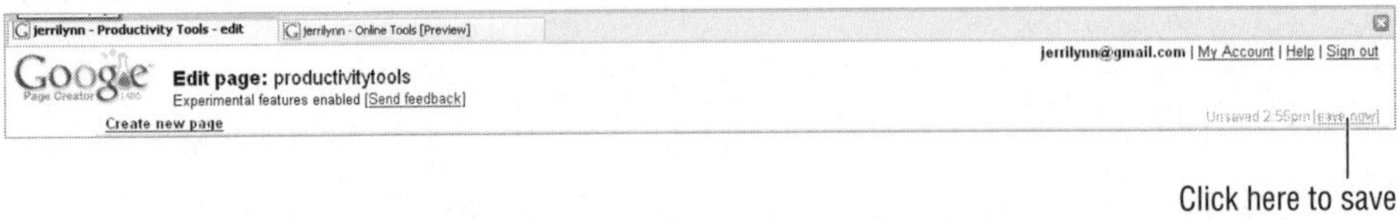

Figure 12-7: If your Web page hasn't been saved, you can tell (and save) at a glance.

That's really all there is to it. Saving is mostly taken care of for you, but if a new element hasn't been saved, Google does everything it can to get it saved quickly so nothing is lost if something goes wrong.

OPTIMIZING YOUR SITE FOR GOOGLE SEARCH

If you're creating a Web site, it's a pretty good bet that you're doing so because you want people to see your site. And people can find your site in two ways: either you send them a link to it, or they find it through a search engine.

With Google Page Creator you've got a jump on many of the other Web sites out there because within a few hours of creation your pages will be crawled by the Google spider and included in Google's catalog of sites.

However, it doesn't do a whole lot of good to have your site crawled if the information on it isn't relevant to the searches that will find the site. For example, if you've created an informational site about hairless cats but don't include the words "hairless cats" near the top of the page (or even in the title of the page), then the chance that the site will turn up in a search for hairless cats is pretty slim.

It's important that the key words you want to be used to find your page are as close to the top of the page as possible. It's also helpful if you use the terms more than one time on any given page. So, if your hairless-cats page has a sub-page that includes information about purchasing hairless cats, then you want to use that phrase near the top of the page and then two or three times throughout the text of the page to ensure that someone searching Google and using the search string "purchasing hairless cats" will see your page as one of the results returned.

One more thing about your site and search engines. Be sure to use alternative text for graphics or include captions for all the pictures on your site. This also helps with your page ranking, and it might even land you in the Google Images search engine, which is just that much more exposure.

Dozens of books are available about search engine optimization, and even specific titles about getting ranked high in the Google search engine. These are just basic tips for how to get your pages seen by other people. If you really want to learn more about it, take some time to read a few of those books. You can find every title you'll need at Amazon.com.

Moving On

As you can see, starting a Web site, even one with many different elements and pages, isn't difficult at all with Google Page Creator. The program really is point-and-click easy. But so far, you've seen only the very beginning of the program.

There's much more to creating Web pages, so you're not done yet. In the next chapter, you learn everything you need to know about editing your Web site. This includes adding text and graphics, and even changing the color scheme or effects that you're using for the page.

CHAPTER

13

Editing Your Web Site

By now you've probably played with Google Page Creator some, and you may even have created a whole Web site. But even if you haven't, you need to know how to edit your Web site, which you'll do dozens of times during the creation process, not to mention the number of times that you'll do it once the page has been published if you update it regularly.

The point-and-click ease of Google Page Creator extends into the editing features of the program, too. Which means it's easy for you to make changes to your site whether it's before you publish the site or after.

Changing Your Site Layout

If you've lived in one house for any length of time, you've probably gotten tired more than once of the furniture arrangement. Every year or two you get up in the morning and just know it's time to move everything around.

Web sites can work the same way. After you've had one up for a while, you'll stop by to add something to the page or update an existing element, and you'll just know that it's time to liven things up a bit. No worries. It's a lot easier than rearranging the furniture in your living room.

To start, sign in to the Page Manager at Google Page Creator, and open the page you want to rearrange. Once the page is displayed, click the Change

Layout button on the right. You are taken to the Choose Layout screen that you saw when you first created the layout for your page.

Now all you need to do is select the layout you want to switch to. The page goes through a save cycle, and then you are taken back to your page, with the new layout in place.

Here's where it gets a little skitchy. The layout for your page will be changed only on the page that you have open. For consistency, you'll have to navigate to each page in your site and go through the process of changing the layout on each one.

It's cumbersome, but according to every study that's been done on Web-site navigation, users are more comfortable with a consistent look and feel from page to page. When the layout or design of a Web site changes from one page to another, users get confused and frustrated and are more likely to exit the page and not come back.

So the layout of each page will need to be changed. And unfortunately, the only way to do that is to actually change the layout of each one. When it's done, your page will be more user-friendly for the effort.

Adding and Editing Text

One of the nice features of Google Page Creator — although it can also be one of the drawbacks of the program — is that once you select a layout for your site, all the necessary text boxes will automatically be included and formatted. All you have to do is add the text.

But what if you're not happy with the font or the size of the text? It's easy enough to change them. First, highlight the text that you want to change. Then, from the toolbar on the left side of the page, select the font button or the size button, as shown in Figure 13-1.

When you click one of these buttons, a drop-down menu appears. Select the change you would like to make from the menu, and the text you have highlighted changes according to your choice.

Like changing the layout of the page, however, this is effective only on a single page. So, if you want to change all the text on every page of your site to a different font, you need to highlight and change the text in each text box on every page. It's a pain, but for consistency's sake, you should make sure that the text is consistent in appearance and size throughout your site.

If users are expecting titles to appear a certain way on each page and they're different, the users won't surf as freely as if everything is consistent. What's important to remember in Web-site design is that consistency makes for a no-thought-required experience for users. If they have to stop and think about the pages they're visiting and how they'll navigate through them, then they're more likely to leave your site and go somewhere else on the Web that's easier on their minds.

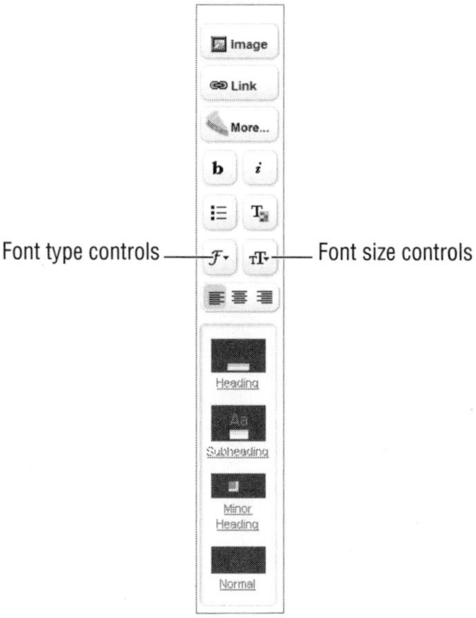

Figure 13-1: Select the font or size buttons to change how text looks on your page.

Headings and Text Structure

Most documents have some type of text structure that aids in the reading of the text. Think about a book, for example. When you pick up a book, you can tell immediately that chapter titles will be in a specific size and type of font throughout. Depending on the book, different types of text may mean different things — italicized text may mean there's a quote you should pay special attention to, whereas bold, left-aligned text may identify sections and help you see quickly what the text following will be about.

This is all text structure, and just about every document has some kind of structure, even if it's not a good one. For its part, Google Page Creator gives you some textual structure controls to help you create — and readers to read — the text for your Web site.

These controls are on the left side of the page, also, as shown in Figure 13-2.

These controls are used for functions such as creating a heading, subheading, or minor heading, or for switching back to normal text after creating one of those other elements.

How you use the controls is entirely up to you. But remember that when creating a Web site you should keep the end user in mind. Design your site in such a way that it's easy to read and is consistent throughout. You might want to take some time to surf around the Net and look at how sites similar to yours

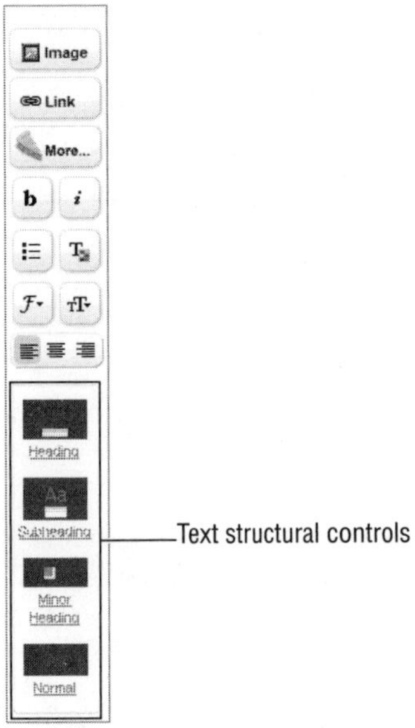

Figure 13-2: Use the structural text controls to create even more site consistency.

are designed. If you can find several that you're pretty sure reach a wide audience, those are the best ones to examine — they probably have paid teams of Web-site designers who draw on the knowledge that's been gained about Web-site navigation since the Internet came into being.

Text can be an interesting and even a vital part of your Web site. Take some time with your text to ensure that your headings are consistent and that the type and size of the text are consistent throughout your pages. Also keep in mind that some fonts are easier to read than others. The designers who created Google Page Creator templates have already set up a textual structure for you. Unless you really hate it, don't change it except to add things such as headings and subheadings to the text.

Adding Color and Effects

One aspect nearly everyone enjoys when designing a Web site is playing with the different colors and effects that are possible with whatever program you're using. However, this is one area where Google Page Creator is a little lacking.

If you want to change the color of your Web site, you have only two choices. The first is to change the design of the site completely. That's the only way to change the background colors of your site (or page). But, if you are happy with your background colors and what you really want to do is change your text colors, then you're in luck, because you do have that option.

You'll find the button for text color on the toolbar on the left side of the page. To use it, highlight the text that you want to change, and then click the button. As shown in Figure 13-3, the color pallet opens, and from it you can select the color you want to use.

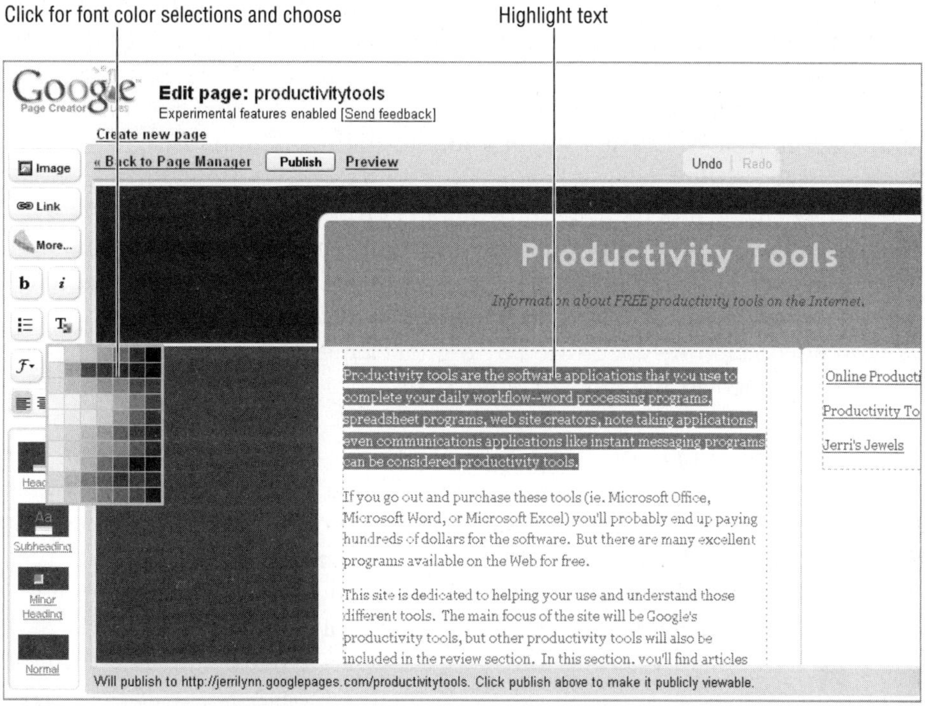

Figure 13-3: Click the font color button to select a different color for highlighted text.

There are also some text effects on that same left-side menu. You can add bold, italics, and bulleting, and even change the alignment of your text using the buttons on this menu. But if you're looking for WordArt, or if you want to customize the colors of your background, you have only one choice — code it in HTML. You can edit the HTML of a page, so it's possible to make any changes that you want to make through the HTML.

However, changing the HTML does require knowledge of it. As I discussed previously, you can find many great books on the subject if that's how you want to approach building your Web site with Google Page Creator.

Google Page Creator isn't designed to be as powerful as some of the other Web-site creation software packages that you can buy. But then Google Page Creator is a free, Web-based tool that allows you to throw together an attractive, but simple, Web page. If you want something more extensive than that, you should consider learning HTML or purchasing a more powerful Web-design package and the domain name and hosting that go along with it.

Adding Graphics to Your Web Site

One final design element that's available is the ability to insert pictures into your Web pages. Graphics add a lot to a Web site when they're used properly.

One thing not to do when putting graphics into your Web site is to use huge files. High-resolution photos are excellent for printing, but they're a nightmare for uploading in a Web page. When you add high-resolution photos to your Web site, pages load more slowly and users who want everything to appear as soon as they click a link to or within your site grow frustrated.

So, when you're putting photos on your site, remember to keep them at a lower resolution. Usually around 150 dpi (dots per inch) or less is adequate. Don't get scared away by that dpi abbreviation — it simply indicates the density with which pictures are created by digital elements called pixels. The term "dots" was coined in the days of dot-matrix printers, and it's stuck around ever since.

Back to the resolution of your photos. 150 dpi or less should show all the detail that's necessary for display on a computer or laptop screen, and yet the pictures are still small enough to load quickly. If your pictures have a higher resolution than 150 dpi, you should consider using a graphics manipulation program to change the resolution. If you're downloading pictures from your digital camera, you may even have an appropriate software program that came with the camera. If not, Photoshop, although expensive, is an excellent resource.

When your pictures are ready, inserting them into your Web site is easy. All you need do is place your cursor in the page where you want to the photo to appear. Then, click the Image button on the left toolbar. An Add an image dialog box, like the one shown in Figure 13-4, appears.

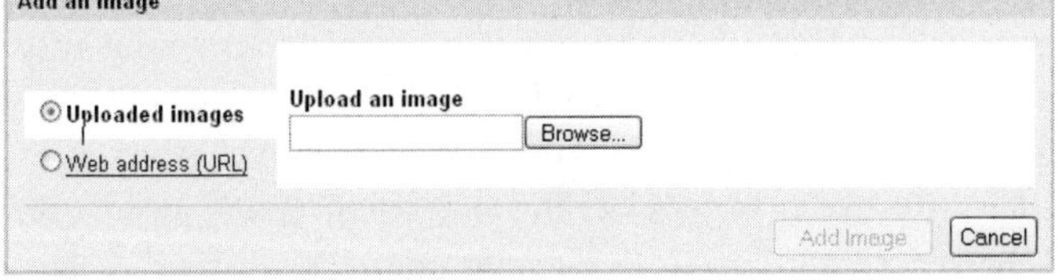

Figure 13-4: Use this dialog box to select the image you want to add to your page.

Click Browse to locate the place on your hard drive where the picture is stored. The File Upload dialog box, shown in Figure 13-5, appears.

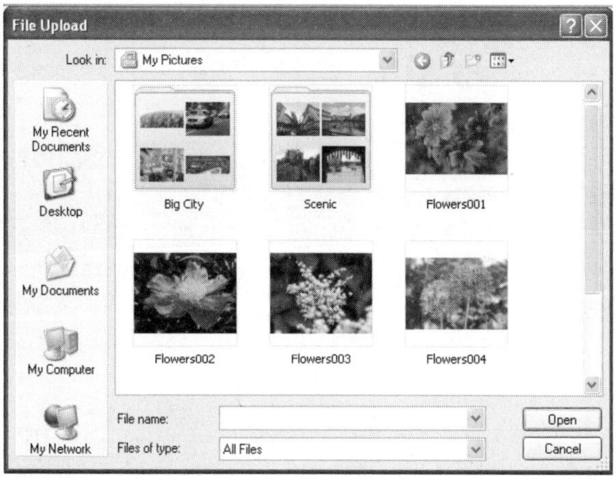

Figure 13-5: Select the location and the file that you want to upload to your site.

Navigate to the file location, select the image that you want to upload to your Web page, and click Open. You are taken back to the Add an image dialog box where a preview of your picture is available, as shown in Figure 13-6.

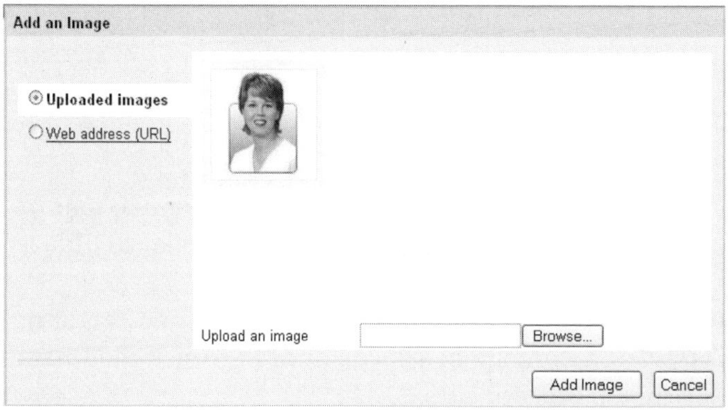

Figure 13-6: Preview the pictures that you plan to upload to your Web site.

If you want to add additional pictures, you can repeat the process until you've selected all of your pictures. When you're finished, click Add Image and the picture or pictures that you've chosen are inserted into your Web site at the point where your cursor was located.

When the picture has finished uploading, you are returned to the editing view of your Web page, and a toolbar, like the one shown in Figure 13-7, appears beneath your photo.

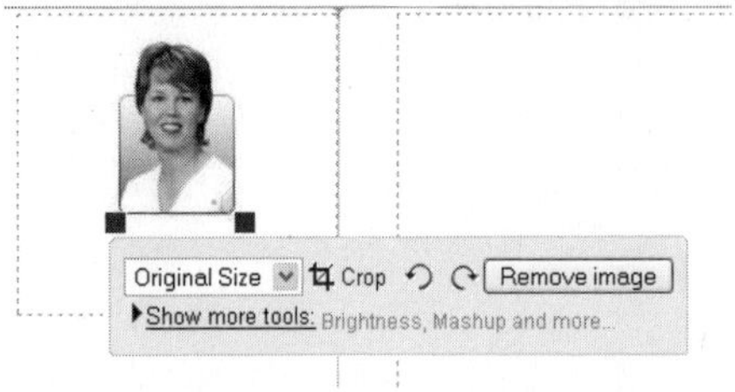

Figure 13-7: Use the photo toolbar to manipulate and change your pictures.

You can use this toolbar to change the size, crop, or rotate your picture. There's also a Show more tools link on the toolbar. If you click this link, a drop-down menu and controls for Brightness, Mash-Up, Enhance, Reduce Colors, Sharpen, and Revert Edits appear, as shown in Figure 13-8.

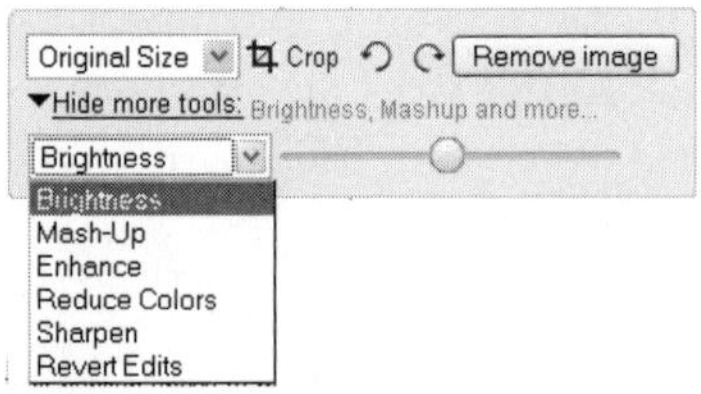

Figure 13-8: The Show more tools option leads you to additional photo controls.

Each option changes the controls on the toolbar slightly. Use them to manipulate your photo, and when you're finished click outside the toolbar to hide it. It's really that simple.

You can also add an image from a Web site. To do that, place your cursor on your Web page where you want the image to appear, and then click the Image button. The Add an image dialog box appears.

Next, click the radio button next to Web Address (URL). As shown in Figure 13-9, the dialog box changes, and you are taken to a page where you can enter the URL or Web site address of the picture that you want to add to your page.

When you enter the URL of the image you want to add to your site into the text box provided, the image should appear in preview mode in the dialog box, as shown in Figure 13-10.

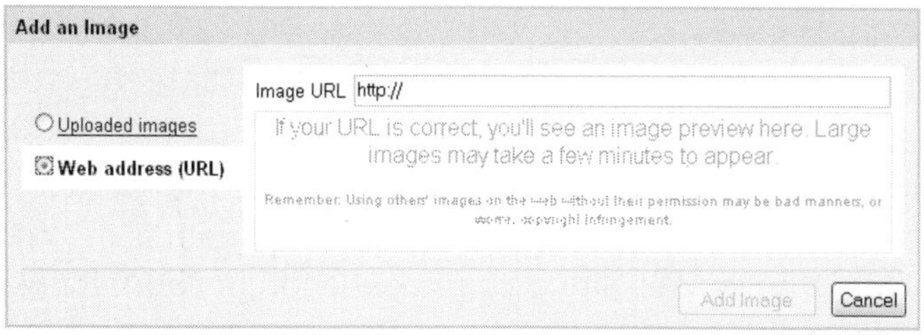

Figure 13-9: Add a picture from a Web site using the Web Address option for uploads.

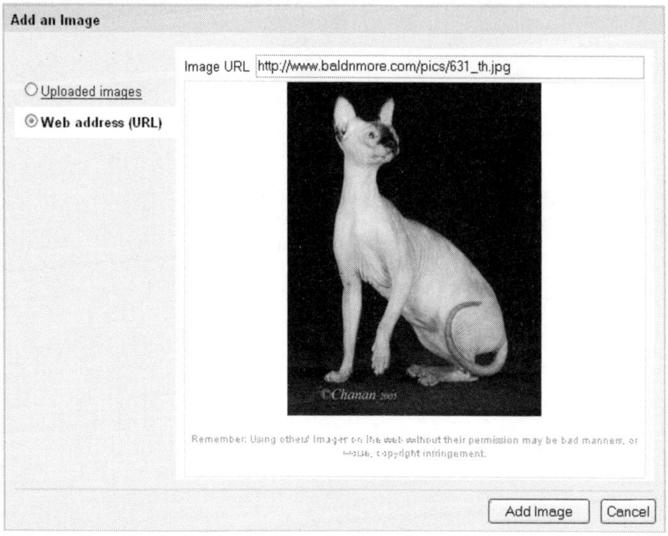

Figure 13-10: When you enter the image URL, a preview should appear.

If the image doesn't appear, either you've typed the URL incorrectly, or you've entered a URL that has too many images for Google to choose from. To accurately pull an image from another Web site, you have to have the exact URL of that image, including its location on the page. Often, you can find this URL by right-clicking on an image and selecting the View Image option from the dialog box that appears.

When you've entered the correct URL and you see the image preview, then click the Add Image button to add the image to the site. The image will be uploaded and again, the image editing toolbar will appear.

CAUTION **Use caution when uploading images from other Web sites to your own. Often these images are protected by copyright. If you upload an image from another Web site to your own, make sure you have the proper permissions from the image owner. Otherwise, there could be legal ramifications.**

Moving On

Google Page Creator may not be as powerful as some of the other Web-page creation software packages available, but its tools are easy to use, and the price can't be beat. You can change your images and layout, add your own text, and even manipulate the HTML of your Web site if you know enough about it.

The editing controls in Google Page Creator are relatively easy to use, too. You may occasionally run into a control or element that's a little confusing, but for the most part, the program is extremely easy. You can even publish your site. But that's a topic for the next chapter, so keep reading.

CHAPTER

14

Publishing Your Web Site

When you're starting Google Page Creator, you'll probably find the program easy to use. You may also find that it's not as feature-rich as some other Web-design programs, but the ease of use makes up for anything that's missing.

Here's another bonus with Google Page Creator. Google also includes the real estate you need to publish your site. That's technically a place called Google Pages, but it's not at all what you might think of when you ponder that name.

Readers may remember AngelFire and some of the Web-based page creation tools of the late 1990s and the early 2000s. In some cases, those pages were arranged in something that was designed to resemble a neighborhood. That's because your Web page is your "home" on the Web. It's a representation of you and your life, just as your home is in your real-world neighborhood.

Google Pages is arranged less like a neighborhood. In fact, you won't find any kind of front page that leads to the pages that are published on Google Pages, and you'll have to have a specific URL to get to the sites that are published there.

To find that address (for your site), click Site Settings on the upper-right side of the Page Manager page when you log in to Google Page Creator. There you'll find the URL for your site. Of course, that's not a useful URL unless you've actually published your Web site, so let's look at how you can do that.

Space Limitations

Before I get too deep into all the particulars of Google Pages, let's talk for a minute about your space limitations. Although it may seem as if the Internet goes on forever — there are billions of pages on it — in reality, there are limits. And some of those limits apply to the size of the Web site that you're trying to upload.

For that reason, Google put some restrictions on the size of the Web sites that you're uploading to Google Pages. Specifically, you're limited to 100MB of data and uploaded files for your Web site. Now, before you begin to feel restricted, that's *a lot* of space.

The average Web site is not more than a few megabytes in size. Only if you'll be creating a site that's entertainment-intense (such as a music or video site, or even some picture sites) should you really need to worry about the space that you have available on the site. With the space that's provided by Google, you should have more than enough room to do whatever you want to do with your site.

That said, definitely stay in touch with the files that you put online, and if you find that your space limits are becoming restrictive, remove some of the old content on your site. Removing the content doesn't mean deleting the page, just unpublishing it so you have room for other stuff.

Publishing Your Site

I once worked with a Web-design software program that required virtually an Act of Congress, signed and endorsed in triplicate, before the site could be published to the Web. I had to first design the site, and then make sure that all of the proper databases were in place, and then make sure the right extensions were included with both the hosting service and the software. Then I had to log into the site and make sure that first this and then that were working.

It was a pain. What could have taken 2 or 3 minutes to do was a drawn-out process that took more like 15 minutes, and this was after I had spent hours putting the site together. To top it all off, even if I had everything right when I published the site, there was always the possibility that something would render differently once it was published to the Web.

This is the nightmare of publishing your own Web site that frightens many people away from it altogether. However, things are much different with Google Page Creator; publishing your own site is really just as simple as designing the pages and then clicking a button to begin the publishing process.

When you're ready to publish your site, you have several options. You can go to the Page Manager and place a check mark in the small box next to the page (or pages) that you want to publish.

Then, from the toolbar just above and to the left of the page, click the Publish button. The page will load momentarily and then your page or pages are finished publishing. That's really all there is to it.

Another option is to publish from within a page that you've opened for editing. When you finish working on your page, click the Publish button near the top of the page, as shown in Figure 14-1.

Figure 14-1: You can publish your Web site from within the editing interface.

When you're publishing your page from within the page editor, you'll see a new toolbar appear. This toolbar, shown in Figure 14-2, gives you options to see your published site or to share it with friends.

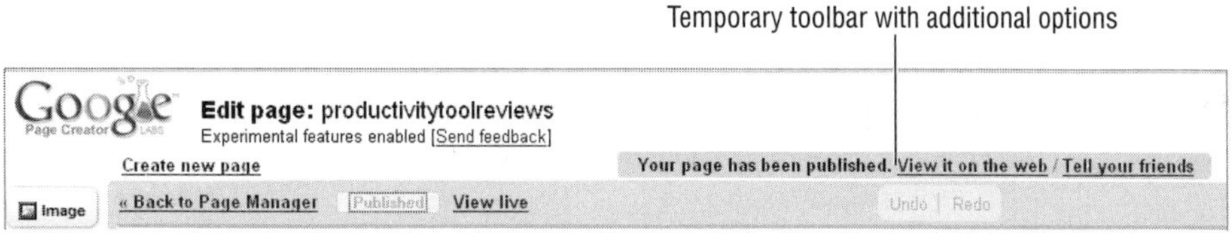

Figure 14-2: Use this temporary toolbar to view and share your Web page.

When you click the option to see your page live, you are taken to your Web site. When you click the option to share with friends, an e-mail with the link included automatically opens. All you have to do is address it and click Send.

Finally, you can also publish your site right from the Page Manager, *as long as it has not been published before or has changes that have not been published.* If these conditions apply, you'll see a link on the right side of the page, as shown in Figure 14-3.

One other neat feature, which is also shown in Figure 14-3, is that pages with unpublished content will be shown with a different color than pages that have current, published content. This allows you to see quickly which pages have been published or updated and which have not.

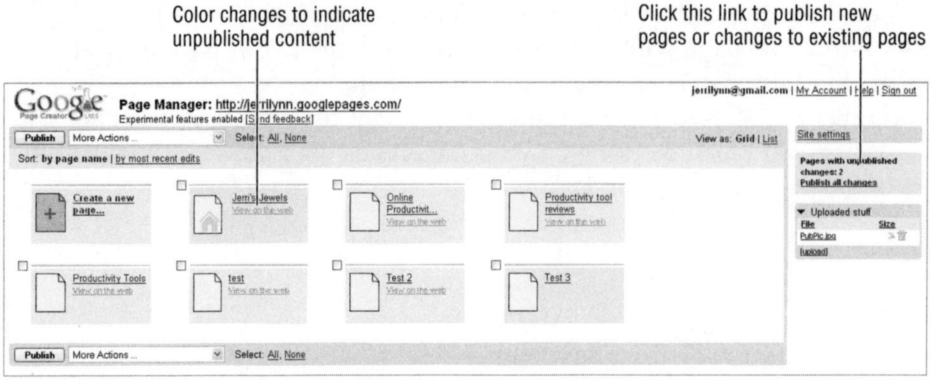
Color changes to indicate unpublished content
Click this link to publish new pages or changes to existing pages

Figure 14-3: Changes or unpublished pages will cause this publishing link to show.

Publishing the site with Google Page Creator is much easier than with some other Web-design programs. All you need to do is choose the page you want to publish, and then click the button. There's nothing else for you to do. Google Page Creator handles it all. And because you can access the Publish button or command in a variety of ways, you can work in the way that's most comfortable for you.

There's even another way to preview your pages. If you're not in the page editor when you publish your Web page and you want to see it after it's been uploaded to the Web, click the URL next to the Page Manager heading. This takes you to a preview of your Web site that's accurate and live. Your page is published, and you can begin sending visitors to the site.

Unpublishing Your Site

Just as you wanted to put a site on the Web, there may be times when you want to remove a page from that site. Again, it's a simple process that can be accomplished in a couple of different ways.

One way to unpublish your site is right from the Page Manager screen. All you need to do is place a check mark in the small box beside the thumbnail for the page that you want to unpublish. Then click the More Actions drop-down menu shown in Figure 14-4.

From the menu, select Unpublish. The Page Manager loads briefly, and then the colored block around the page you chose to unpublish turns yellow, indicating that the page has not been published.

Another option for unpublishing a page is available on the Edit Page screen. Just open the Web page that you want to unpublish and then click the Unpublish link at the bottom of the page, as shown in Figure 14-5.

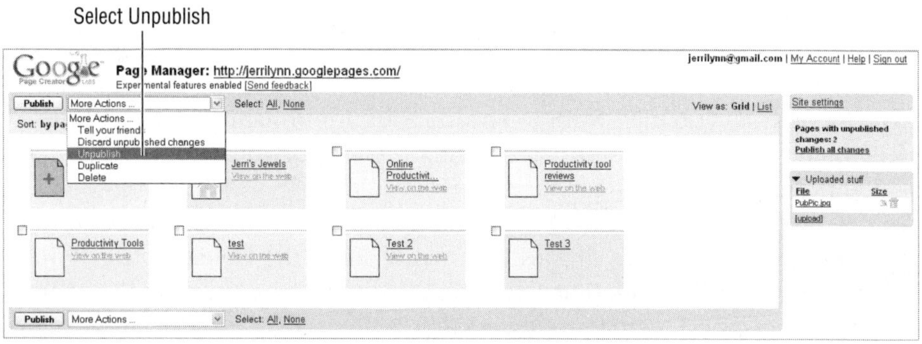

Figure 14-4: The More Actions menu contains additional controls for your Web page.

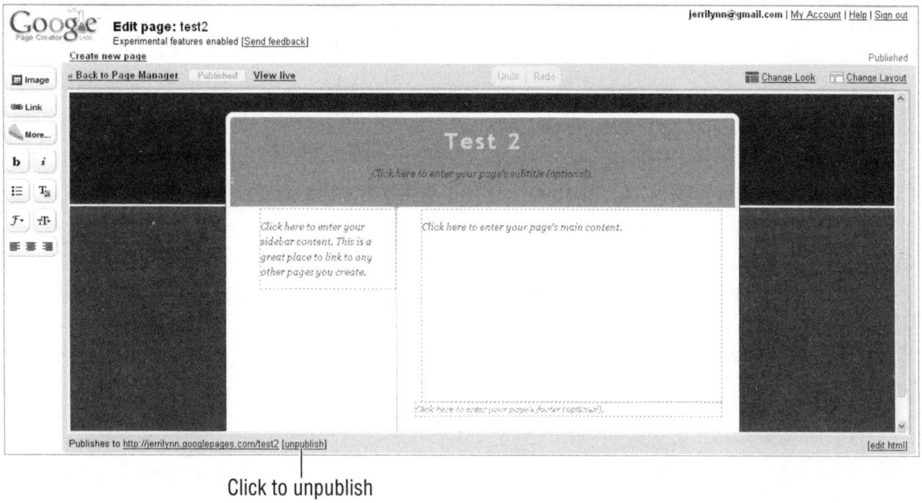

Figure 14-5: You can unpublish a page from inside the Edit Page screen, too.

When you click the Unpublish link, you are prompted to confirm that you want to unpublish the page. Click Yes, and the page loads briefly; then a message like the one shown in Figure 14-6 appears letting you know the page has been unpublished.

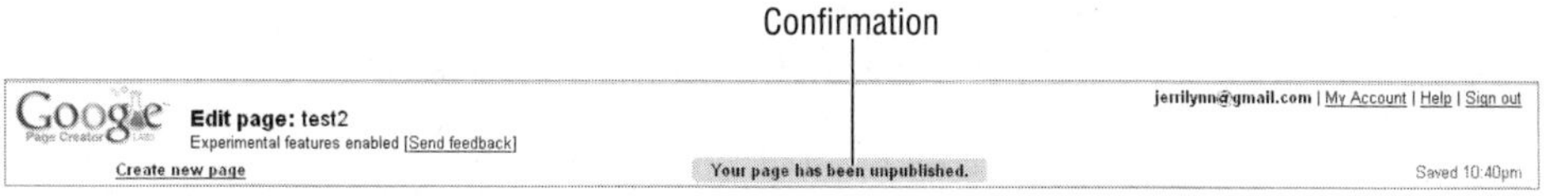

Figure 14-6: You'll see confirmation that your Web page has been unpublished.

When you return to the Page Manager screen, the colored block around the page thumbnail will have changed to indicate the page has been unpublished, too.

One more thing you may want to know about unpublishing pages is how to delete them after you've unpublished them. After all, you won't want those pages cluttering up your Page Manager forever, right?

To delete a page, place a check mark in the small box next to the page, and then from the More Actions drop-down menu, select the Delete option. You'll be prompted to confirm deletion. Click Yes to confirm, and then the Page Manager loads briefly and the pages disappear.

CAUTION **Be cautious when deleting Web pages. Once they're deleted, you can't get them back. This means that if you decide later that you want the pages back, you'll have to recreate them completely.**

Unpublishing and deleting Web pages are common activities when you're designing or updating your Web site. With Google Page Creator, you don't need to change everything just to unpublish or delete a page. Instead, it's a simple point-and-click process that will have your unwanted pages removed within minutes.

Moving On

Google Page Creator is a simple-to-use Web-page creator. Everything you need to put together a professional Web page in the shortest time possible is available in this program. You'll find that it's not nearly as feature-rich as some other Web-design programs, but it's also not as expensive or as complicated.

With Google Page Creator you can do everything that you need to do to put together a nice Web page. From a consistent design and layout to easy editing and unpublishing capabilities, you'll find the program user-friendly and capable enough if you're not a graphic designer or don't want to take the time to learn everything there is to know about Web design.

Even if you're a more advanced Web designer, you'll probably be able to get some use out of the program because some HTML editing features are truly useful if you're familiar with HTML. Either way, Google Page Creator is a good basic Web-page creation program. And it does have its advantages.

PART

V

Google Calendar

Life is busy. There's work, and all the appointments related to work. Then there's your personal life, which you also have to keep track of. You know, doctor's appointments, church functions, social events. Everyone wants a piece of your time. And if you happen to have a spouse or children (or both), then you have their schedules to keep up with, too.

How's a person supposed to handle all that stuff? You could use a paper calendar. And you'd have to carry it with you everywhere you go. Another option is to use an electronic calendar, like the one available in Microsoft Outlook. But then your calendar is locked on your computer and you have no way to take it with you.

Here's an idea. How about using Google Calendar? This is a Web-based calendar that you can access from anywhere. It will integrate (to a point) with your Outlook calendar, and if you really need to print it, you can. On top of that, you can have multiple calendars — one for your personal life, one for work, one for the ball team, and even one for your spouse — but you can access them all from one point, with a single view, so you'll always know what's going on.

Keep reading. This section shows you how to find and use Google calendar to get your life organized and keep it that way.

CHAPTER

15

Hello, Google Calendar

Keeping track of everyday life is far more difficult today than in the past. And that's before you add work and all of its associated requirements to your schedule. I have a friend whose day starts at 5 A.M. He's a single father, so he's up getting kids ready to meet the school bus at 6 A.M. and 7:45 A.M. Then he's off to work.

During the course of a day at work, he might have dozens of different appointments to keep up with. Then there are orthodontist appointments, doctor's appointments, appointments with teachers, and organized sports and other activities. He has trouble keeping track of it all.

He's tried using Outlook, but he can't access his home computer from work, so he doesn't have the family schedule while at work or his work schedule at home. Other Web-based calendars don't have all of the features he needs (such as keeping separate calendars with a single view), and they have no option for sharing the calendar with family and friends.

That's where Google Calendar comes in. Google Calendar is a Web-based scheduling application that allows you to keep track of multiple calendars from a single location, share calendars with others, and add dates from other calendars with a few clicks of a button. It's the busy person's answer to a calendar that meets all your needs.

Why Use Google Calendar?

So what's so great about Google Calendar? For starters, it's Web-based. But there are plenty of other Web-based calendar applications, right? Of course there are, but they aren't Google, and they don't all give you the features that you're going to find in the Google Calendar application.

Being Web-based is an excellent advantage for most programs. Web access gives you the ability to view the program from anywhere at any time as long as you have an Internet connection. It means your calendar is no longer in one place while you're in another. But it's also not all there is to Google Calendar.

Another benefit of Google Calendar is that you have a main calendar but you can also keep multiple other calendars — as many of them as you like.

So you can keep a calendar for your appointments, another for your spouse's, a third to keep up with your children's events and school schedules, and yet another for your parents, friends, or other people. Or, if you own a business, your main calendar may be for your business in general, with subcalendars being for each of your salespeople, a training schedule, or even an employee schedule.

The multiple calendar structure also allows you to view your calendar alone or with all your other calendars (and even subscribed calendars) enabled, so you have a global view of what your schedule looks like. And you can assign each calendar a different color to make it easy to tell quickly which appointment belongs to whom.

Google Calendar also gives you options for embedding a calendar into your own Web site so you can keep site visitors clued into what you're doing. And you have the option of creating RSS feeds for your calendars so that you, or anyone you allow to have access to your calendars, will receive a notice when a new appointment is scheduled.

On that note, a very nice feature of Google Calendar is the ability to have your appointment reminders e-mailed to you via the Gmail service or you can add your calendar to your personalized Google start page. In fact, if you have Gmail, you can quickly add events, right from your Inbox. And if that's not enough connectivity for you, you even have searching capabilities (using Google's search technology).

Are those enough reasons for you? If not, there's one more you might consider. Google Calendar is free. As in you-pay-nothing-no-matter-how-much-you-use-it free. Some calendar applications, even Web-based calendars, can have pretty steep licensing fees. Outlook (which includes Microsoft's answer to calendaring) will cost you about $110 for an upgrade, and if you're purchasing the full version of Outlook, you can expect to pay $200 or more for the software. And Outlook doesn't include the ability to access calendars using the Internet.

GOOGLE DESKTOP

Google Calendar is one of those nifty little programs that integrate with several other Google programs, including Google Desktop. Not familiar with Google Desktop? It's a program that requires a quick download and install, but once it's installed, you can access your Gmail, calendar, photos, weather, a scratchpad, and even news — right from your desktop.

You can download Google Desktop as part of the Google Pack (`http://pack.google.com`) which is a collection of different Google programs that you might find useful. Or you can download it directly from the Google Desktop page at `http://desktop.google.com`.

Once you've downloaded and installed Google Desktop, you can use it to index and search your computer, and you can add various gadgets to it to access different Google programs such as a Google Analytics viewer or even an Amazon.com best-seller list. Customize the desktop to meet your needs and desires. Then everything you use from Google can be right at your fingertips.

So there are plenty of reasons you might want to use Google Calendar. And not all of them have been addressed yet. As I cover the functionality of Google Calendar in this section, you may find even more reasons to use the program.

Navigating Google Calendar

Google Calendar is a very easy-to-navigate program. To get started with Google Calendar, go to `www.google.com/calendar`. Then, if you have a Google account, sign in with your e-mail address and password. If you don't have a Google account, you can learn how to sign up for one in Chapter 2.

The first time you sign into Google Calendar, you are prompted to enter your first and last names and your time zone. After you enter this information, you are taken to the default view of your calendar, as shown in Figure 15-1.

Getting around once you get into Google Calendar is fairly intuitive. You can navigate through a calendar by clicking a date in the small calendar on the left side of the screen, or by clicking a date in the full view of the calendar that takes up the main part of your screen.

In addition to those controls, you'll find small left and right arrows directly above the calendar on the left side. These arrows will cycle you through your calendar in increments according to your current view. So, if you're viewing your calendar by four-day increments, then clicking the right arrow takes you forward four days and clicking the left arrow takes you back four days.

There is also a Today button next to these two arrow buttons. This button allows you to return quickly to the current date on the calendar.

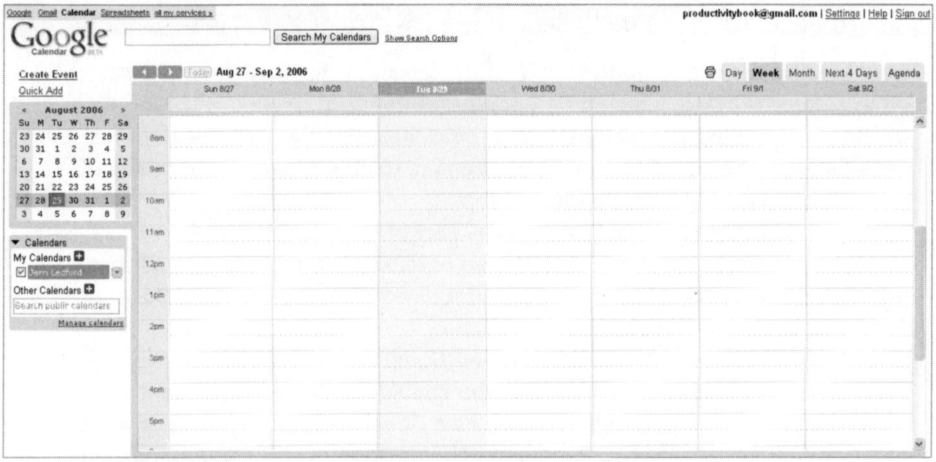

Figure 15-1: The standard is a week's view of your main calendar.

Setting Your Settings

The default view of your calendar is probably set to one week. To change this default view, use the tabs on the right. You have options to view your calendar by the day, week, month, next four days, or by the agenda.

The view for the next four days is customizable. If you prefer to have a different view for the next four days tab — which is actually the custom tab — then you can change that by clicking the Settings link in the top-right corner of the page. When you click that link you're taken to the Calendar Settings page, shown in Figure 15-2.

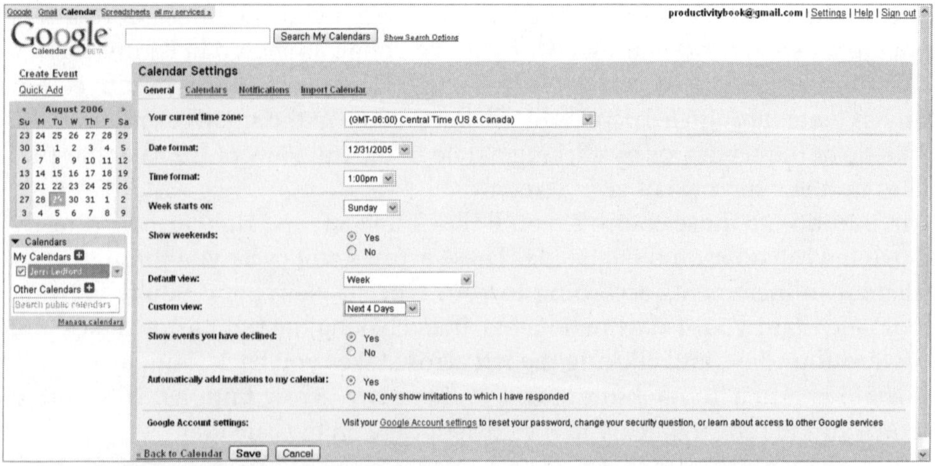

Figure 15-2: Use the Calendar Settings page to set the options for your calendar.

On this page, you can change:

- Time zone
- Date format
- Time format
- The day the week starts on
- Whether or not to show weekends
- Default view
- Custom view
- Whether to show declined events
- Whether to automatically add invitations to the calendar
- Your Google account settings

To change the custom view, select the drop-down menu in the custom-view line, and then select the view that you would like to have available. You can choose from two to seven days or two to four weeks, whichever view suits you.

When you finish adjusting your calendar settings, click Save and you are returned to the view of the calendar you were using before you clicked the Settings link.

There are other navigational controls in Google Calendar, but all of them integrate with the functions of the calendar, so you learn more about them in the pages that follow.

Moving On

Google Calendar offers an accessible, and affordable, solution to your calendaring needs. You can choose your views, keep multiple calendars, even color-code the calendars if you need to. And it's accessible from the Web, so you can use your calendar from anywhere you have an Internet connection.

Google Calendar is easy to use when it comes to functionality such as adding appointments, adding additional calendars, and even sharing your calendars. But all those functions are covered in the upcoming chapters, so keep reading.

CHAPTER

16

Using Google Calendar

Google Calendar, like all the Google applications, is easy to use. A few clicks put your appointments all in one place. But there's more. You can also add whole calendars, set up e-mail reminders, and invite others to join you at appointments.

You can get reminders from other people's calendars if an event is scheduled on a calendar you subscribe to. You can sort your appointments by calendar so that you can view them all or only certain types of appointments. And you can even do some far-out things such as pulling up a calendar with the national holidays of friends abroad or a calendar that records a shared interest, such as the birthdays of famous musicians.

Ultimately, Google Calendar is the tool you need to get control of your life. And because you can do it all online, you can stay in control, no matter where you happen to be. All you need is an Internet connection.

Creating New Calendars

One calendar is enough to keep up with everything you do, right? Well, maybe not. Sometimes it's useful to have separate calendars for your work and home life, or for your social obligations. Some of us even need several calendars to help us schedule everything.

Fortunately, Google Calendar enables you to set up as many calendars as you need, and then you can see a consolidated view of all those calendars or view them one at a time, depending on your needs.

When you signed up for Google Calendar . . . If you haven't done that, pop back to Chapter 15 and do it quick. It's easy. Really. Now where was I?

Oh, yeah. When you signed up for Google Calendar, your main — or default — calendar was automatically created for you. Now you can add as many different calendars as you like.

To add a calendar from scratch, click the plus sign next to My Calendars as shown in Figure 16-1.

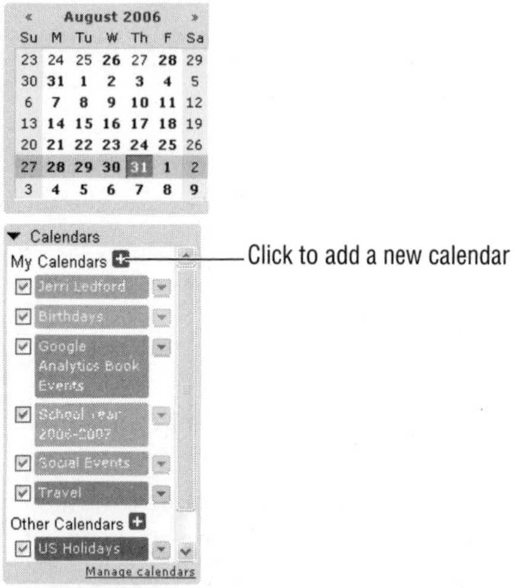

Figure 16-1: Click the plus sign next to My Calendars to add a new calendar.

You are taken to the Create New Calendar page, where you need to enter a name for your calendar, a description of it, a location for calendar events, and a time zone.

TIP **Google Calendar also has a neat feature that comes in very handy. When you share your calendar with someone else, or they share a calendar with you, appointment times are automatically adjusted to your time zone. So, if your friend shares a calendar with you, but he's in the Eastern time zone and you're in the Central time zone, you'll see all of the appointments on that calendar in Central time. No more mistakes when converting times!**

You can also choose your sharing options from the following:

- **Do not share with anyone.** This keeps your appointment information private.

- **Share all information on this calendar with everyone.** This makes your entire calendar public. This is useful for an organizational calendar, but for personal calendars you should be cautious when using this option.
- **Share only my free/busy information (hide details).** This is a better option for making personal calendars public. This option allows others to see when you are free and when you are busy, but they cannot view any of the details of your appointments.

Finally, you'll find options on the Create New Calendar page to share with individuals (instead of public/private sharing). To share your calendar, enter in the text box provided the e-mail address of the person with whom you'd like to share (as shown in Figure 16-2), and then click the drop-down list next to the e-mail address field to set permissions for that person.

CAUTION **Always remember that true privacy in cyberspace is rare. Even if you're careful about whom you share with, that person can always pass information along to someone with whom you have chosen not to share. Choose your friends wisely, and share sparingly.**

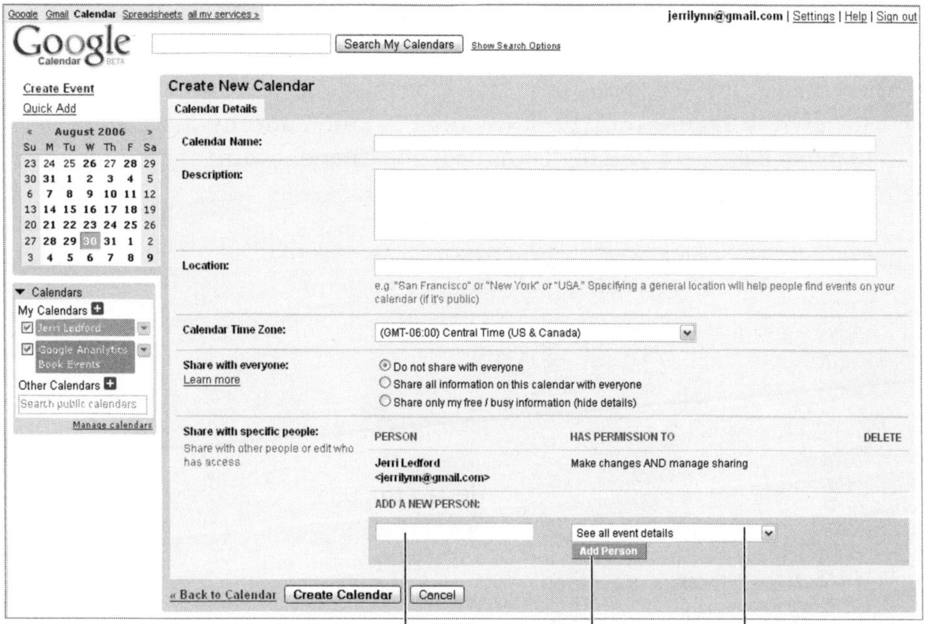

Figure 16-2: Invite others to view or add to your calendar.

After you enter the e-mail address and set the permissions, click the Add Person button to add that person to your calendar. Alternatively, if you select the e-mail address from the list of available e-mail addresses that appears as you're typing, then the person will be added and another line will appear for additional people.

When you've entered all your calendar-sharing information, click the Create Calendar button to create your new calendar. If you're inviting others to share the calendar with you, Google Calendar will check to see if those people have Google Calendar accounts. If they do not, you'll see a warning message like the one shown in Figure 16-3.

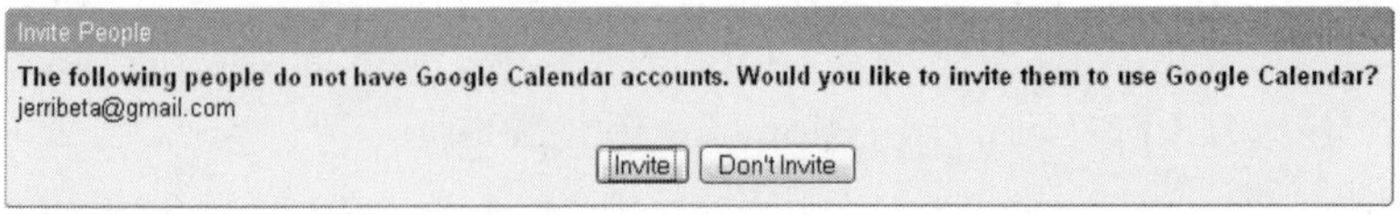

Figure 16-3: Choose if you want to send a Calendar account invitation.

Select Yes if you want to send an invitation to the person you'd like to include. The invitation will automatically be sent to that person. You won't see it before it's sent, but you will receive an e-mail notification that the invitation was sent. If you select Don't Invite, the person is not notified of the calendar, but it will still be created. If you want this person to have access to your calendar, you'll have to send the invitation, and they will need to accept it.

When this is finished, your new calendar is added to your My Calendars list, as shown in Figure 16-4. Each calendar is automatically assigned a new color to make it easy for you to distinguish one calendar from another on your main calendar view.

Figure 16-4: New calendars are added and color-coded for quick recognition.

Adding Other Calendars

In addition to the personal calendars that you can create, there are what Google Calendar terms "other calendars." These include public calendars, friends' calendars, and holiday calendars.

To add one of these other calendars, click the small plus sign next to Other Calendars, below the list of your personal calendars. You are taken to a page like the one shown in Figure 16-5, where you can select the type of calendar that you want to add.

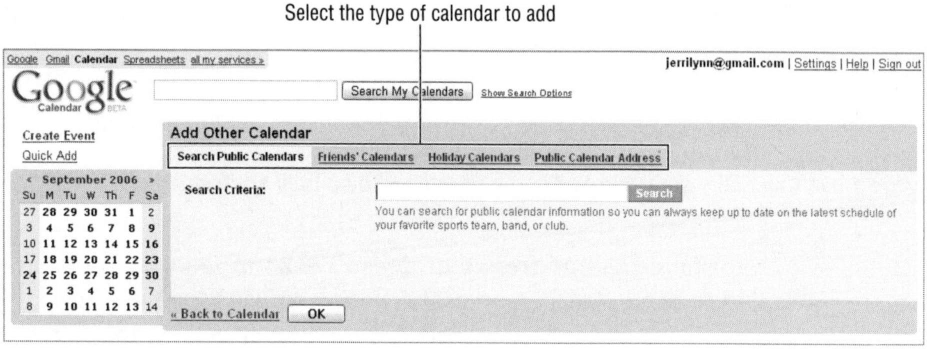

Figure 16-5: Other calendars include public, holiday, and friends' calendars.

Public Calendars

Public calendars are those that others have created and made public. If you're interested in blues music, one of the searches that you might perform would be for a calendar that lists birthdates for blues musicians. Search Google Calendar for Blues Birthdays, and you come up with a list of all the calendars created by both Google and other users listing birthdays for blues musicians.

You can preview each of the calendars by clicking the Preview button below each description, and when you find a calendar that you'd like to add to your collection, click the Add Calendar button to the right of the description. The calendar is then added to your list and you won't be prompted to confirm the addition.

Friends' Calendars

Friends' Calendars are those that have been added to Google Calendar by people you know. When you click the Friends' Calendars link, you are taken to a page, like the one shown in Figure 16-6, where you can search for your friends' calendars using their e-mail addresses.

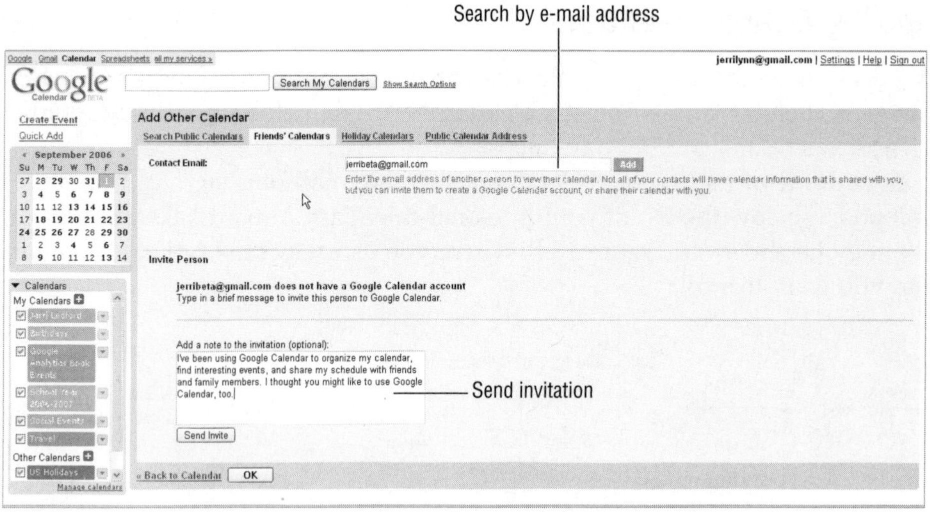

Figure 16-6: Calendars are listed and can be searched by e-mail address.

If you search for an e-mail address that doesn't exist in Google Calendar, you are prompted to send that person an invitation to use Google Calendar. Only calendars that your friends have made public will appear in this list, so don't be surprised if you can't find a calendar that you know should exist. It probably does; you just don't have access to it.

Holiday Calendars

Here's a really neat feature of Google Calendar. By clicking the Holiday Calendars link at the top of the Add Other Calendar screen, you can add a holiday calendar to your listing for about 40 different countries and religions.

When you click the Holiday Calendars link, you are taken to a list of the calendars available. Scroll through the list until you find the one (or more) that you want to add and then click the Add Calendar button to the right of the description. That calendar will be added to your calendars.

This feature can be used to keep up with your own holidays as well as holidays in other countries or religions. In other words, you can look really thoughtful if you have friends in other countries or who practice other religions and you remember to help them celebrate their holidays. (But alas, if you want to add a local event that means something special to the friend, like Little Burnt Bay Day in Newfoundland, Google won't let you add to the holiday calendar. Instead you have to add it to your own personal calendar.) The Holiday Calendars feature is also a good way to keep up with days that business associates may not be working.

Public Calendar Address

One last option for adding other calendars to yours is the Public Calendar Address link. This link takes you to a page where you can enter the public address of another calendar that you want to add to your own.

How do you get those addresses? Usually other people who have created a Google Calendar share them with you. But you can also get them through someone else who has access to that address. (Remember the earlier privacy warning?)

To add a calendar to your list by address, copy and paste (or type) the address into the text box provided and then click the Add button. The calendar is added to your list.

Viewing Some or All Calendars

With these different calendars, you may want an overview of all the appointments included in each one. Or you may not. But if you do want to see all of your appointments at once, you can.

Beside the name of each calendar is a check box. Each calendar with a check in that box will be shown on your calendar view. If you remove the check from the box (by clicking it), the appointments from that calendar are removed from your view. So, you have the option to view all, some, or even none of your calendars in the main view.

Adding Appointments

Once you've set up your calendars, you can begin adding appointments to them. Adding an appointment is easy, and you've got several options, so you can add them in a way that works for you.

The most intuitive way to add items to your calendar is to click directly in the time slot in which you want the appointment to appear. An event balloon appears, as shown in Figure 16-7.

In the balloon, enter the title for the appointment that you're creating and select the calendar on which you want the appointment created. If you're satisfied with the default time allotted for the appointment (1 hour), click Create Event and the appointment is created on your calendar.

You're not limited to just the settings included in the balloon. If you prefer a different time frame, or if you want to set up a reminder for the appointment that's different from your default reminder, click the edit event details link at the bottom of the balloon.

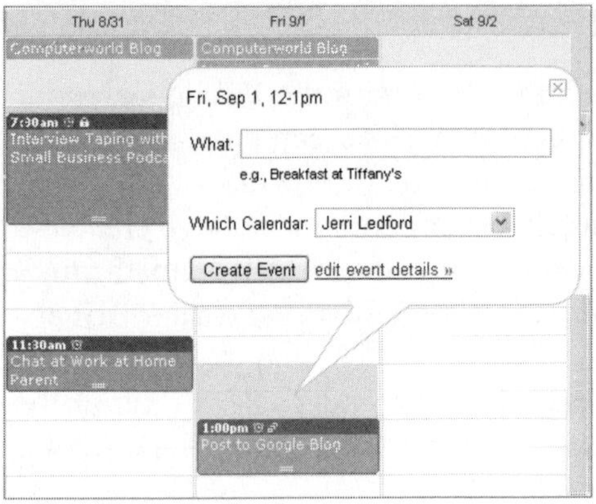

Figure 16-7: Click a time slot on the calendar to create an appointment.

You are taken to an expanded view of the Event Details, as shown in Figure 16-8. Use this view to enter more precise details about your appointment.

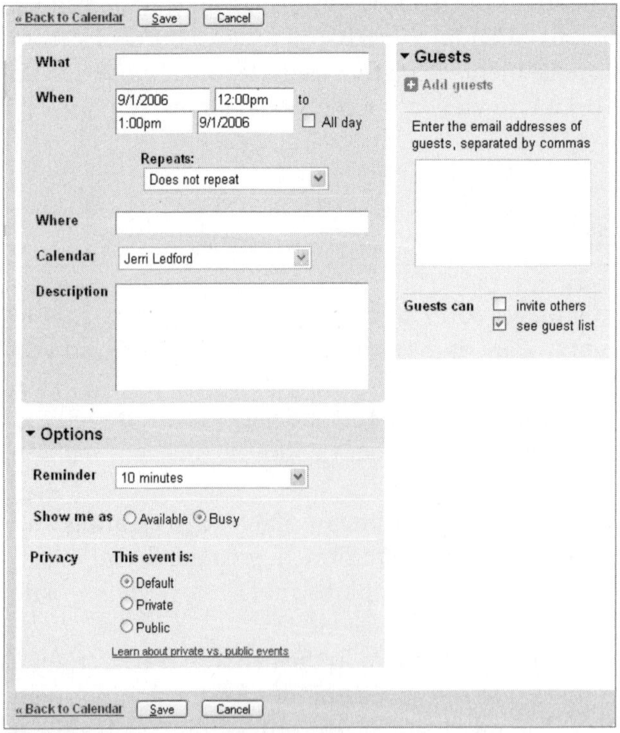

Figure 16-8: The Edit event details option lets you be more precise in setting appointments.

Inviting Others to an Appointment

In this view, the option to invite others to your appointment (Google refers to it as "Add guests") is also available. If you're putting together a meeting, party, or other event that others might want to attend, you can create an invitation to a single person or group of people.

Finish entering the appointment information. If the guest tab to the right is collapsed, expand it by clicking Add guests. Enter e-mail addresses of those you wish to invite, and select whether guests have the option of inviting others or viewing the guest list. Then click Save. When you do, you are prompted to send invitations to the people listed (if you have guests listed). Click Send and the invitations are sent and the appointment created in your calendar.

The e-mail that's sent to those you're inviting will look like the one shown in Figure 16-9. Those invited can choose to accept, reject, or remain uncommitted to the invitation by clicking Yes, No, or Maybe.

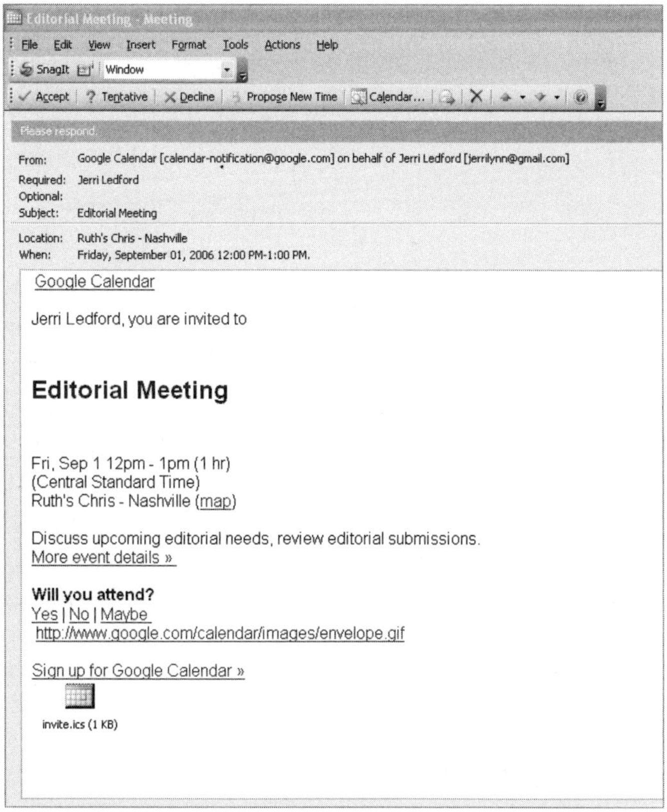

Figure 16-9: Those invited are sent an e-mail requesting their attendance.

No matter which response those invited choose, they are taken to a Web page where they have the option to change and submit their response or view details and the names of others invited. (You get this last option only if you checked the See guest list box on the event-details page.) In addition, there's an area, shown in Figure 16-10, that allows guests to leave comments about the meeting. This area can be used for discussions between you and those who plan to attend, before the appointment time.

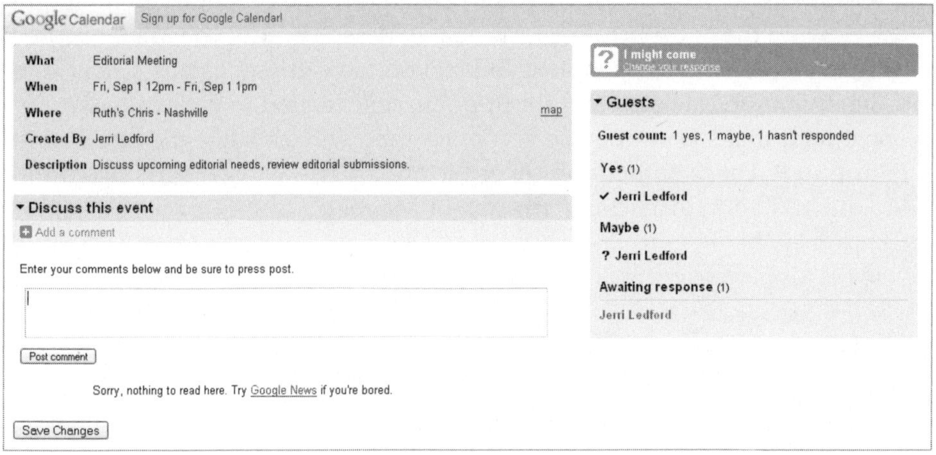

Figure 16-10: Those invited can send their responses and comments from this page.

You won't be notified when someone accepts or rejects your invitation, but to check the status, all you need to do is click the appointment on your calendar. You are taken to a view that shows you nearly the same information, including any comments, that is shown in Figure 16-10.

Create Event Option

Another way to add an appointment to your calendar is to click the Create Event link near the top-left corner of the main view of your calendar page. This link takes you to the more detailed view used for setting new appointments. Fill in the information requested, and click Save. The new appointment is added to your calendar, just as it was before.

Using Quick Add

Another option for creating appointments is the Quick Add link just beneath the Create Event link. Quick Add works a little differently from the other ways discussed previously.

To add an appointment using this option, click Quick Add and then type into the text box that appears a phrase that indicates the kind of appointment that you want to add (as shown in Figure 16-11). For example, you could type: *Editorial meeting with Jerri Ledford tomorrow at 2 P.M.*

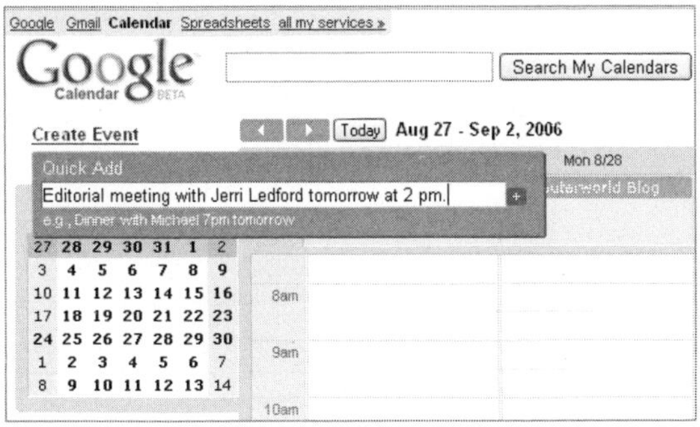

Figure 16-11: Type a phrase for the appointment you want to add.

Quick Add uses an interpretation technology to interpret words you type into the text box to create an appointment. So, after you type your phrase, click the small plus sign to the right of the text box and the appointment will be created, in the correct time slot, on your calendar. You can check to make sure your instructions were interpreted correctly.

Adding Appointments from Gmail

One last option for adding an appointment is to do it from Gmail, if you're a Gmail user. (If you're not, you learn how to sign up for a Gmail account in Chapter 25.)

If you receive a message in Gmail that contains meeting information, or a meeting request from another calendaring application, open the message and then, from the open message view, click the More actions drop-down menu and select Create Event, as shown in Figure 16-12. You are taken to the event creation page on Google Calendar. Fill in the appointment information and then click Save Changes. The appointment is created and you are returned to Gmail.

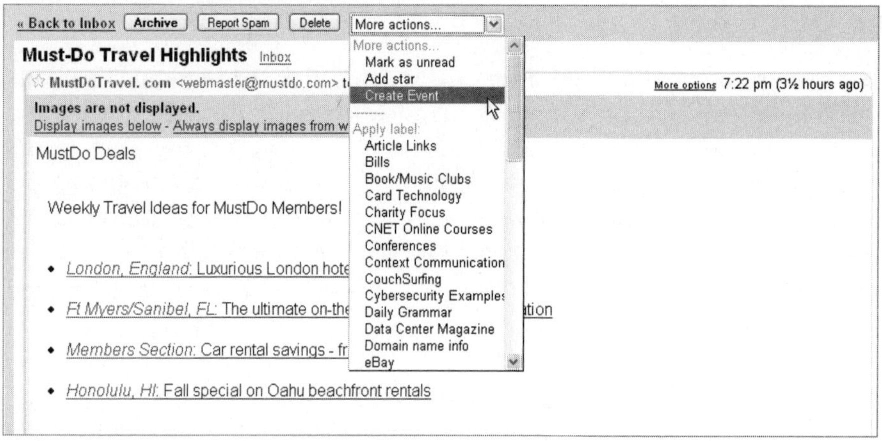

Figure 16-12: Create appointments for Google Calendar from Gmail.

Personalizing Calendars

Once you've added calendars and appointments to your Google Calendar account, you can personalize each calendar with different colors and settings.

Each time you create a new calendar, it's automatically assigned a color, which helps to differentiate the appointments on one calendar from those on another. However, for personal reasons, you may prefer to change the colors of those calendars. No problem.

Beside the name of each of your calendars is a downward arrow that indicates a drop-down menu. Click that arrow and then select the color that you'd prefer for that calendar, as shown in Figure 16-13. The color will not only change on the calendar name, but it will also automatically change for any appointments that have been entered into that calendar.

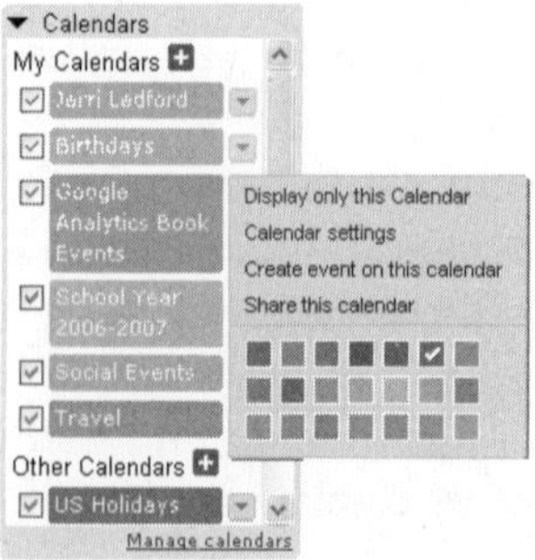

Figure 16-13: Use the drop-down menu to change the color for calendar entries.

You can also reset or change the calendar settings that you created when you first set up the calendar by clicking the drop-down menu beside the name and then selecting Calendar Settings. This will take you to a page that looks like the information page you filled out when you created the calendar.

Make any changes that you want to make and then click Save. This allows you to reset the calendar name, description, time zone, and sharing settings. You read more about the sharing settings in the next chapter (Chapter 17) but for now you should know this is where those settings are located.

Additional settings for your calendars can be found when you click the Manage Calendars link at the bottom of your list of calendars. This link takes you to the Calendar Settings page you saw earlier in this chapter. On this page, you can change general information about your calendars; specific information about them, as you saw above with the Calendar Settings menu; and the way your notifications are handled.

Setting Notifications

The Notifications link is especially helpful, because this takes you to the page shown in Figure 16-14, which allows you to set how you'll be notified about upcoming appointments. Using this page, you can set default reminder times and methods. There's even an option that enables you to have reminders sent to your cell phone. And Google Calendar supports nearly 20 different cellular service providers, so chances are this feature is available to you.

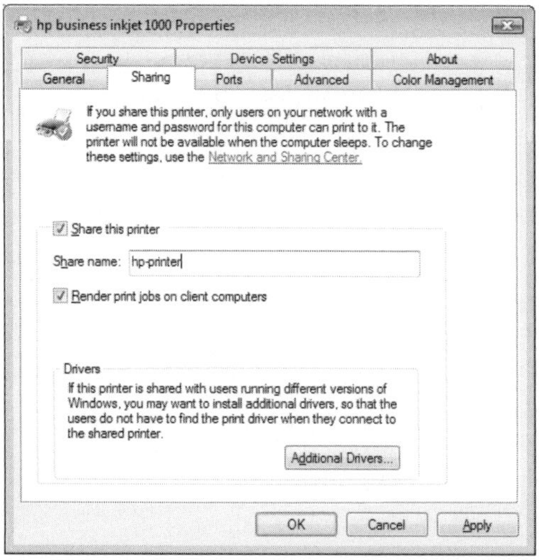

Figure 16-14: Set the ways in which you're notified about calendar appointments.

Setting up cell-phone notifications requires that you enter your cell-phone number into the space provided and then click the Send Verification Code button. After a few minutes, a text message is sent to your phone.

Enter that code into the space provided and click Finish Setup. If the setup is successful, the status changes to Phone Number Successfully Validated. If you enter the code wrong, you receive an error message, and you'll need to reenter the validation code.

Once you're signed up for notification by phone, then each time you have an appointment with a reminder set, you receive a text message to notify you that the appointment time is coming up. If at any time you want to stop receiving cell-phone notifications, go to Manage Calendars → Notifications and clear the box (or boxes) in the SMS column. After you've made your selections, click Save and you'll no longer receive SMS notifications. When you're ready to turn them back on, just place the check mark back in the box (or boxes).

Moving On

Google Calendar is a useful, Web-based calendaring application. With the options to add multiple calendars, link to others' calendars, personalize your calendars, and create appointments on your calendar in various ways, you might think there's just nothing more to add.

You'd be wrong. Google has excellent sharing and search capabilities, and you can even print your calendar in case you need (or just want) to have a print copy. All of these options are covered in the next chapter, so keep reading.

CHAPTER

17

Even More Calendar Tools

On the surface, Google Calendar looks like a simple program with only the most basic capabilities. But as you've seen in Chapters 15 and 16, there's more to Google Calendar than meets the eye. And I'm not finished yet.

There are still RSS capabilities, searching capabilities, and printing capabilities to explore. You can invite other people to view and edit your calendars. You can even import calendars from other calendaring applications. And you're going to learn how to do these things in this chapter, so keep reading.

Using an RSS Reader

If you subscribe to multiple calendars, especially if those calendars belong to someone else, you know how frustrating it can be to try to keep up with new appointments. If you don't remember to check the calendar regularly, you might miss something. Shared calendars also create a problem. If you're sharing a calendar with other people who have permission to add events and appointments to the calendar, then you could miss something if you don't check it regularly.

Instead of banging your head against the computer screen because you missed a really great concert featuring your favorite local group (because you forgot to check the calendar), why not just set the calendar up with a feed reader so you're notified whenever there are changes to it? You can, you know.

You can also share your feed URL with others who might be watching your calendar.

Let's step back just a touch. What's a feed reader, you may be wondering. This is a tool that collects the posts in news feeds and delivers them to you, usually as an e-mail. You may have heard feed readers referred to as RSS (Really Simple Syndication) feeds. If you subscribe to blogs or news feeds and have new posts delivered to your e-mail box, then you're probably using a feed reader.

Now, how does adding a shared calendar to a feed reader work? It's pretty simple, actually. Using your feed reader (if you don't have one, a ton of them are out there that can be found with a quick Google search), you enter a URL into the program. It then watches the calendar and you receive a notice when something about the calendar changes or is updated.

To add a calendar to your feed reader, you need a URL to paste into the feed reader, and not just any URL will do. You need a very specific URL that's coded to tell the feed reader where to look and what to watch for in your calendar. You can find that URL by clicking the small arrow next to any calendar. Then select Calendar Settings from the menu that appears.

This will take you to the Calendar Details page. On this page, near the bottom, you'll find a section labeled Private Address, as shown in Figure 17-1.

In the Private Address section are three buttons: XML, iCAL, and HTML. The iCal button generates a URL that you can use with iCalendar-enabled products. iCalendar is another calendaring application that you can learn more about on the Web.

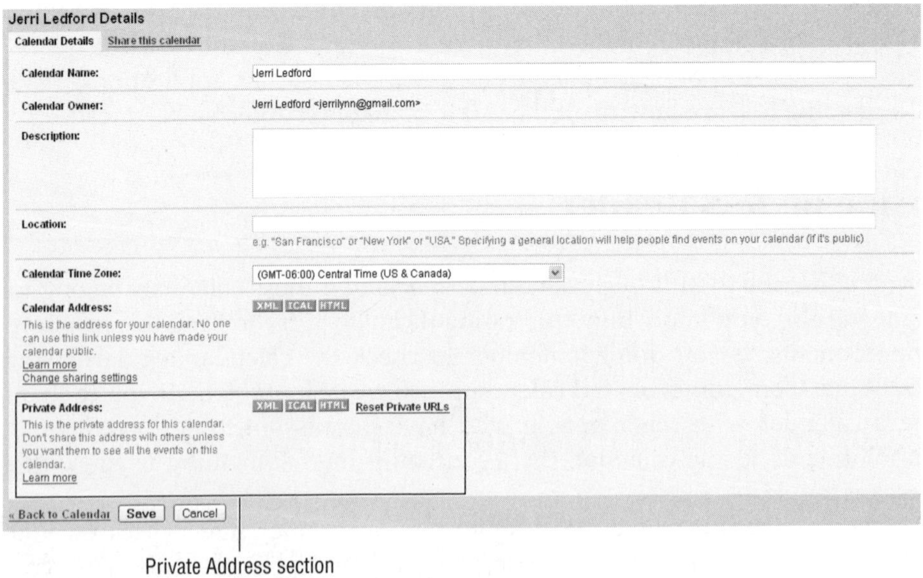

Figure 17-1: You'll find the feed URL in the Private Address section.

The HTML button generates a URL that you can copy and paste directly into a Web browser to view your calendar. The link takes you to a copy of your calendar with limited capabilities. One of the things you won't be able to do from that link is to create new appointments on your calendar. However, you can edit an existing appointment.

Use the XML button to generate a link that you can paste into your feed reader. Click the XML button and a pop-up window, like the one shown in Figure 17-2, appears showing the URL you need for the feed reader. Copy and paste the URL into the feed reader, according to the directions that are specific to that application.

Figure 17-2: Copy the URL provided and paste it into your feed reader for updates.

Once you've set up the calendar in your feed reader, you are notified of changes that are made to the calendar each time they're made. (Unless your feed reader is set to send you digests, in which case you'll get updates on a daily or weekly basis.) No more trying to remember to look at the calendar. And you'll never miss another appointment because you didn't know the calendar had been added to or changed.

Resetting URLs

One more link in the Private Address section that you might want to be aware of is Reset Private URLs. Clicking this link resets all of your URLs. This means that any existing feeds you have for your calendar will be invalidated so your feeds won't work properly.

You'll use this link when you've been sharing your calendars with others via a direct link and you want to change this. It's something that may never happen if you've been careful about handing out your link. But it's nice to know the option is there should you need it.

Embedding Your Calendar in Your Web Site or Blog

Many Web sites, especially those built around events, have calendars embedded in them to make it easy for visitors to learn when events are taking place. Google Calendar offers a feature that allows you to embed a scaled-down version of Google Calendar into your Web site or blog.

This function does require that you understand HTML and have access to the HTML code that makes up your Web site or blog, but it's not a difficult function to use.

To embed a calendar in your Web site or blog, the first thing you need to do is make your calendar public. To do this, click the small arrow next to the calendar that you want to add. Then, from the menu that appears, click the Calendar Settings option. This takes you to the Calendar Details page.

On the Calendar Details page, click the Share this Calendar link, near the top of the page (under the title). On the page that appears, click the radio button next to the option for Share all information on this calendar with everyone.

TIP **If you want to save a step, you can click the arrow next to your chosen calendar title, and then click the Share this Calendar option. You'll be taken to the same page as above.**

When you click this button, you are asked to confirm your selection. Click Yes to confirm and return to the sharing information page.

Next, click Save to save your choices and return to the calendar view.

CAUTION **Be aware that when you choose to share your calendar with everyone, anyone searching through Google Calendars can find and access your calendar. If you plan to embed a calendar on your Web site or blog, consider making a calendar especially for that purpose and adding only the information that you're certain you want to share with others.**

Once you've set your sharing options, you can generate the HTML code that you need to paste into your Web site or blog code. Navigate back to the Calendar Details page (click the arrow next to the calendar you want to embed and select Calendar Settings from the menu that appears). Then, click either of the HTML buttons near the bottom of the page. A Calendar Address pop-up window appears with the HTML address for your calendar and a short message that includes a link for the Configuration tool. Click this link to be taken to a page where you can configure HTML code for your Web page or blog, as shown in Figure 17-3.

Now, in this Configuration tool, there's already a URL that's been generated from the information in your Calendar Settings. However, you can change that URL to meet your specific tastes by entering a new or different title, specifying what controls to show, if any, and defining the height and appearance of the calendar.

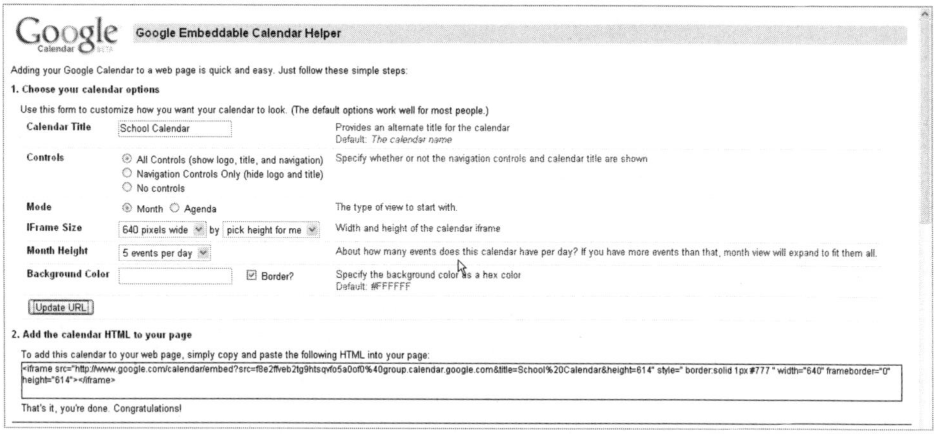

Figure 17-3: Use the Configuration tool to create the code for your Web site or blog.

If you make any of these changes, you can click the Update URL button and the HTML code is updated. (It may be updated automatically, but it's always best to click the Update URL button to ensure that changes are configured.)

Near the bottom of the URL configuration page, you'll see a preview of how your calendar will look on your Web site. Any changes you make to the properties of the link will be reflected in the preview. This is how the calendar should look when you embed it in your Web site or blog.

Once you have the code for your calendar, you can put the calendar on your Web site or blog by copying the code that the Configuration tool generated and pasting it into the HTML on your site or blog. How this is accomplished will vary according to the way in which you have designed your site or blog and how much control you have over that site or blog.

When you paste the code into the HTML, you may want to try it in a few different places until you get the placement you want. You can move the code around your page as it suits you.

Once you've embedded the code in your Web site or blog, any changes you make to your calendar are reflected in the calendar on your site automatically. There is no need to update the calendar in both places.

Embedding calendars on your Web site or blog makes a lot of sense if you have events that you want the public to be aware of. For example, if you are conducting a marketing tour or embarking on a speaking circuit, then having a calendar on your site that lists the dates of your engagements is one way to draw people to attend. Just remember that calendars shown on your Web site or blog must be made public so don't put anything on them that you don't want other people to see.

Importing Calendars

Another feature mentioned in passing in the last two chapters is the ability to import calendars from another calendaring program. Microsoft Outlook is one of the most commonly used calendars, and it's also one that can be imported into Google Calendars.

To import a calendar into Google Calendars, you must first export it from the program that you're currently using to your hard drive in a file format that can be imported into Google Calendar. How you do this will vary according to the type of calendar, but for Microsoft Outlook, you would export your calendar as a CSV file. Make note of where you're exporting the file to, as you'll need to locate it when it comes time to upload the file.

Currently, Google Calendar supports only two file formats, CSV and iCal. When you've exported your calendar from your current calendaring application to your hard drive, you should log in to Google Calendar and go to Manage Calendars.

On the Calendar Settings page that appears, click the Import Calendar link near the top of the page (beneath the title). You are taken to a page like the one shown in Figure 17-4.

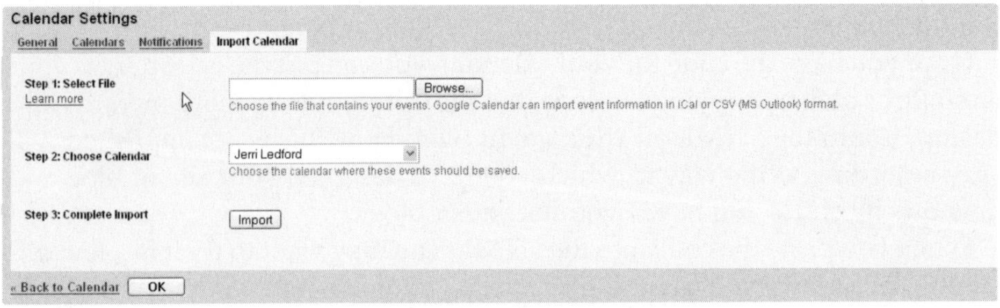

Figure 17-4: Upload CSV or iCal calendar files to Google Calendar.

In Step 1, navigate to the file that you exported from your current calendar application. To do this, click the Browse button and locate the file on your hard drive. When you find it, click the file and then click Open.

In Step 2, choose the calendar on which you want the events from the imported calendar to appear. This can be any of the calendars that you've already created, but you cannot create a new one. So, if you decide that you want to create a calendar specifically for the file that you're importing, do that before you begin importing the calendar file.

In Step 3, complete the import process by clicking Import. This will import the file into your Google Calendar application and you'll be shown how many files were processed, and how many were processed successfully, as shown in Figure 17-5.

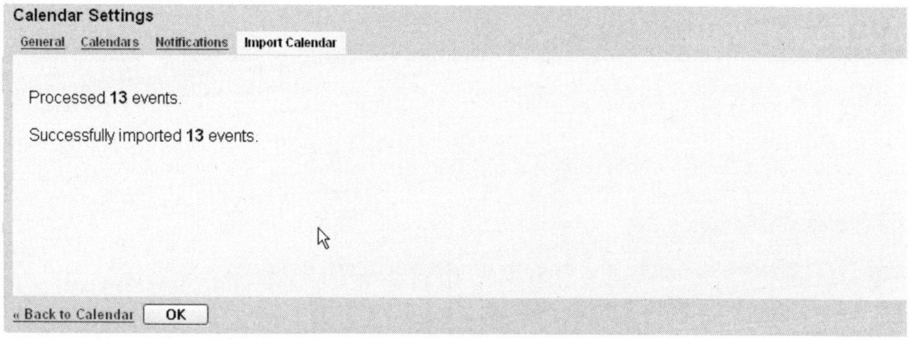

Figure 17-5: You'll see how many files were processed and imported successfully.

When you've reviewed the information that appears on the screen, click OK to return to your calendar view. Once you import a calendar, there's no way to un-import it. If appointments appear on your Google Calendar as the result of an import and you don't want them there, your only choice is to delete those appointments one at a time.

Deleting Appointments

Perhaps you've imported calendars with appointments you don't want or an appointment has been canceled. Whatever the reason, occasionally you need to remove an appointment. To do that, click the appointment in your calendar. As shown in Figure 17-6, the appointment balloon appears.

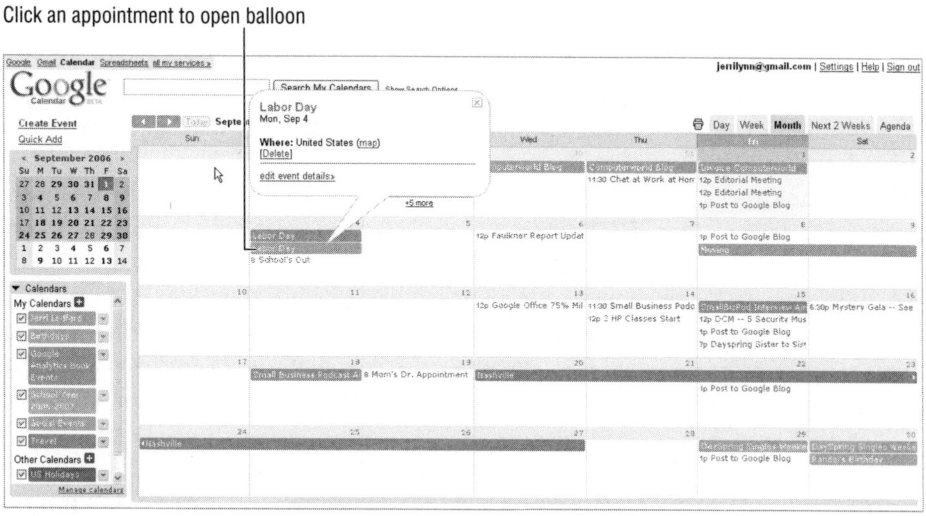

Figure 17-6: Click an appointment to open options.

In the balloon, click Delete. If the appointment is one of a series of appointments that recur at regular intervals, you'll be prompted to choose to delete Only this instance, All events in series, or All following, as shown in Figure 17-7.

Figure 17-7: Choose to delete just one occurrence or all occurrences.

The option Only this instance deletes only the appointment that you've chosen. The option All events in the series removes all of the appointments in the series, including past ones. And the option All following deletes all occurrences of the event from the selected day forward.

These options appear only if the appointment you're deleting is a recurring one. If it's a single occurrence, when you select Delete, that appointment is deleted, and the balloon closes.

Unsharing Calendars

A time may come after you've shared a calendar with someone when just deleting appointments won't be enough. Instead, you may want to remove someone's access to your calendar. This is a useful feature if you're sharing a calendar with employees and one of them leaves the company. It's also useful if *you* leave the company. Or maybe you've been sharing your calendar with friends or family and your circumstances change, so that you no longer need (or want) to share a calendar with them.

To remove someone's ability to share your calendar, click the small arrow next to the calendar name and then select the Share this calendar option. You'll be taken to the calendar details page, where you should see all of the people with whom you've chosen to share your calendar.

If you want to remove someone, click the trash can to the right of their name, as shown in Figure 17-8. That person's access to your calendar is removed.

CAUTION **Use caution when deleting user access to your calendars, especially for calendars that someone else has invited you to use. Deleting access to the calendar could also affect the person who invited you.**

From this screen, you can also change the permissions that each person you've added to the calendar has. Beside each name (except your own) is a drop-down menu. Click this menu and you can select the permissions that you want other users to have.

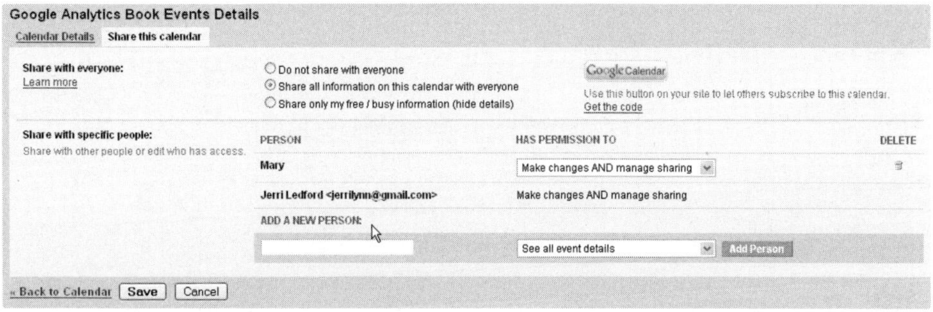

Figure 17-8: Sharing options can also be used to "unshare" calendars.

Unsharing is almost as easy as sharing in Google Calendars. Click a few buttons, and you can remove or alter access for anyone whom you've invited to share your calendar. Just remember that once you've removed someone's permissions to view and edit your calendar, you have to re-invite them in order to add them back.

Searching Calendars

Some people schedule activities and appointments months in advance. The only problem is that when you schedule an appointment that's far off in the future, you may not remember whether you added it or not. And finding an appointment should be easier than flipping through month after month of appointments.

It's not difficult with Google Calendar because there's a search function that uses the power of Google Search capabilities to search your calendar for a specific appointment or activity.

Above your calendar, you should see a Google search box. To find an appointment or activity on the calendar, click inside the text box beside the search options and type the term, name, or title that you'd like to search for. Then click Search My Calendars.

Google searches through all the appointments on your calendar. Then, as shown in Figure 17-9, you are taken to an Agenda view of your calendar that lists only the appointments relevant to your search.

If the search doesn't return the results you're looking for, you can also use the Advanced search options by clicking Show Search Options next to the Search my calendars button. When you click this link, you are taken to an expanded view of search options, as shown in Figure 17-10.

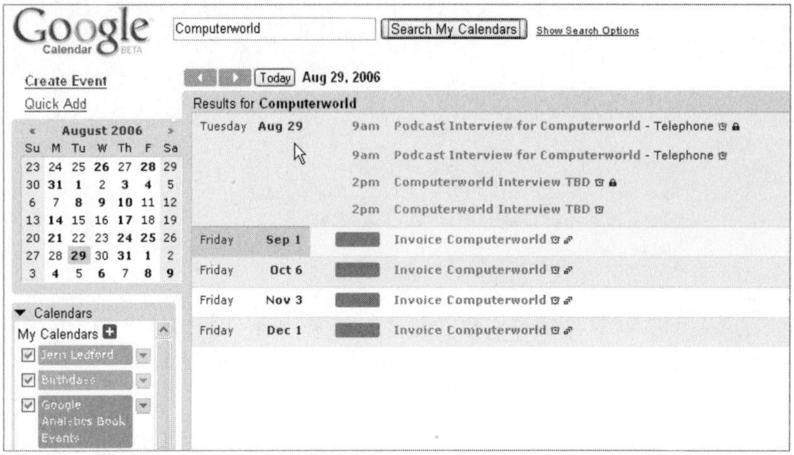

Figure 17-9: Search results are returned in the Agenda view for ease of use.

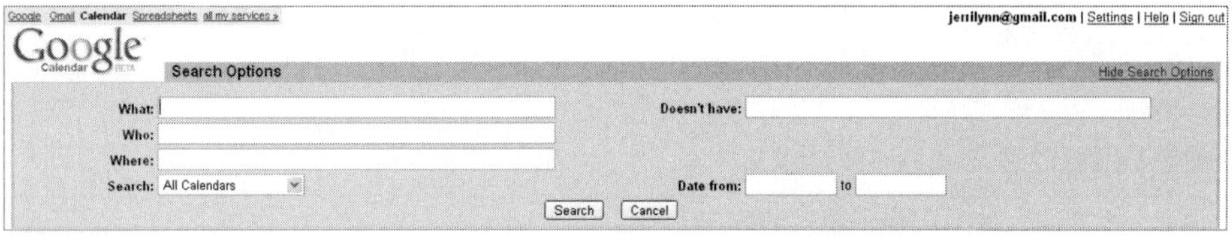

Figure 17-10: Advanced search options give you more searching power.

Fill in the fields for additional search information, and then click Search. Google Calendar then performs the more advanced search.

You don't have to fill in all the information in the Advanced Search options. You can use only the fields that you find most relevant, or you can use them all. But the ones you use will be determined by what you're looking for and how you've labeled it.

The power of Google Search in your calendar makes it easy for you to find the appointment you're looking for very quickly. Just a few clicks of a button, and it will be right there.

Printing Calendars

One last option is the ability to print your calendars. I'm one of those people who love electronic stuff, including gadgets and software, but there are still some things that I'm old-fashioned about. My calendar is one of those.

I have no problem entering appointments in digital format, but I travel so much that I also like to have a paper copy of my calendar available when I can't get an Internet connection on my computer. Printing a calendar one page at a time works best for me.

With Google Calendar, you can print one or all of your calendars with the click of a button. Just open the calendar that you want to print and then click the small printer icon at the top of the calendar (to the left of the Search Results tab). Then follow the onscreen directions, and you'll have a printed calendar to carry with you no matter where you go.

Moving On

Google Calendar has so many options that it's hard to believe it's a free program that you can access from the Web. Importing calendars and deleting them, even using Google search capabilities and embedding calendars into your Web site or blog — these are just some of the things you can do with Google Calendar. And features are still being added to it.

Already you have more power and usability than you get with most other calendaring applications. These features make it easy for you to get organized and stay that way.

Once you set up your calendars, you won't have to worry about missing an appointment or forgetting it. You can enable reminder settings and RSS feed readers to keep you updated on what's happening with your shared calendars.

Ultimately, Google Calendar is much more usable (and useful) than it appears to be on the surface. So don't stay on the surface. Flip back through the last three chapters and learn all you need to know about Google Calendar.

When you're done, you can read the next part of this book, which addresses a useful tool called Google Notebook.

PART VI

Google Notebook

Are you a note-taker? Do you wish you had a way to collect the bits and pieces of interesting articles, product descriptions, or research papers that you find on the Web — aside from printing and highlighting them all, that is?

Google Notebook is the answer you're looking for. Using Google Notebook, you can capture items of information from the Web, along with the Web addresses they came from, and keep all this stored in one place.

You can also use this program to collect information and then publish your notebook to share with others. Are you in a study group that's putting together a presentation about the great financial wizards of the fourteenth century? No problem. You can do all your Internet research, collect your findings in a notebook, and then share it among other members of your group with just a few clicks of the mouse.

Keep reading. There's plenty more information in the next part on Google Notebook and the ways in which you can put it to use.

CHAPTER

18

Hello, Google Notebook

The one thing missing from the Internet is a place to take notes. In fact, that's a drawback to computers in general, but the Internet exacerbates the problem. Often, people find they need to print page after page of a Web site, just to have a printed copy of something they need to keep up with.

The alternative to printing pages from the Internet is to take notes. That's a pain, too. Because there is so much information on the Web, you could spend days taking notes about a particular subject or topic. There just has to be an easier way.

Of course there is. One of the productivity tools that Google makes available is called Google Notebook. It's a program that you can use to take notes as you surf around the Internet. When you've collected all the notes that you want to take, you can print them so you'll have a hard copy.

It's a useful program for anyone doing research online. And it's easy to access, although to be most useful it does require that you download a small plug-in for the browser that you're using.

Google Notebook currently is compatible with both the Firefox browser and with Microsoft Internet Explorer 6.0.

NOTE **You can use Google Notebook without the downloaded plug-in. However, the notebook is not nearly as useful if you have to copy something and then surf to the Google Notebook Web site each time you want to collect a bit of information. Even if you're working with two browser windows or tabs open, you'll find the process cumbersome. Downloading the browser extension makes using Google Notebook much easier and more effective.**

Why Use Google Notebook?

Google Notebook sounds like a neat application, but why would you want to use it? Simply put, because it's useful for gathering information in a single spot that you can refer back to often.

Maybe you're researching a new product line that you'd like to include on your company Web site, and you want to search around the Internet to find out what other companies are carrying that product, in what range they have it priced, and how they feature it on their site. You can surf to each site you find in a Web search and print out all of those pages or take notes by hand about what you find, but wouldn't it be much easier to simply copy the information you need into your Google Notebook and then print it all at one time?

Not only does that take far less time and effort than your other alternatives, but it also puts all of that information into one place where you can keep up with it until you're finished with it completely. When you're done, all you have to do is delete it.

Google Notebook also has a publishing feature that allows you to publish your notebook to the Web so others can view it. If you're part of a group or team, this feature makes it easy to share notes and research without having to print and distribute multiple copies of your notes. Your teammates or group members can also add their own notes if you choose to allow them editing capabilities. The collaboration can speed the time it takes to find the right research and to gather other people's input to the research that you've gathered.

You learn about many other features of Google Notebook in additional chapters in this part, but I'll mention one more here: source attribution. Whenever you add a note to your notebook, even if it's as short as a couple of words, the source of the words is also added to your notebook. So Google Notebook pulls double duty by collecting all of your sources and providing a list of links for you to refer to if necessary.

Navigating Google Notebook

In order to access Google Notebook, you need to log on to the Google Notebook site. You can go to `www.google.com/notebook` to access the program. You'll be required to enter your Google account name and password to gain access. Then you'll be prompted to download the browser extension that you need to use Google Notebook as part of your browser.

If you do download the extension, you have to restart your browser after it's installed. When you do, instead of being taken to your home page the first time you open your browser after installation, you are taken to an overview page about Google Notebook. This page includes general information on how to use Google Notebook.

When you've finished looking through that information, click the Google Notebook Overview link at the bottom of the page to be taken to additional information about Google Notebook. From there, you can click the Google Notebook Home link to go to your Notebook home page.

Default and Custom Notebooks

The first time you log in to Google Notebook, you'll see a few links, and the heading My Notebook, as shown in Figure 18-1. This is the default notebook that Google creates when you open your account. You can immediately begin adding notes to this notebook by copying and pasting them here.

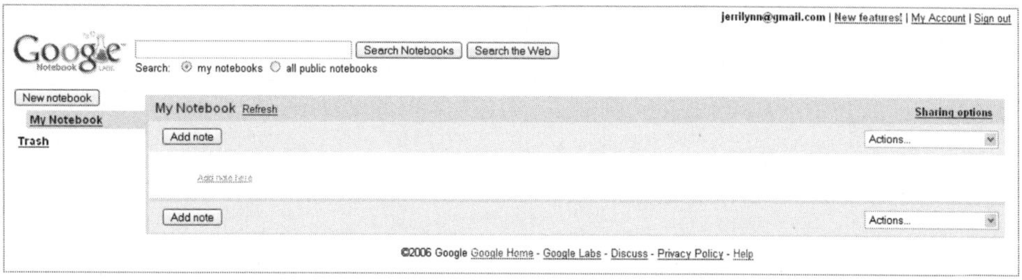

Figure 18-1: My Notebook is created when you open your account the first time.

If you want to add additional notebooks to your collection — possibly for different topics — you can do that by clicking the Add Notebook link on the left side of the page. When you do, you are taken to a page that looks like the one shown in Figure 18-2. Enter the name for your new notebook in the text box provided and click OK.

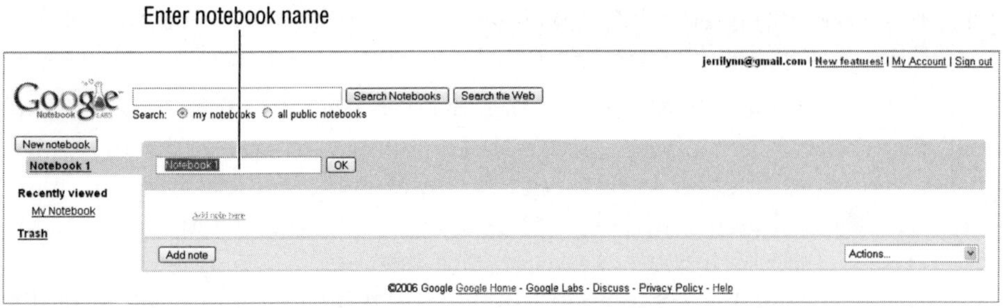

Figure 18-2: Add new notebooks after using the Add Notebook button.

After you click OK, the name of the notebook is changed in your notebook list on the left and you are taken to the body of the notebook.

Add Notes

To add notes to the notebook you've just created, click the Add note button and a text editor appears on the page where you can type text, as shown in Figure 18-3. When you're adding notes using this method, even if you copy and paste those notes from the Internet, you will not see any attribution for them. The attribution is available only if you're using the browser plug-in.

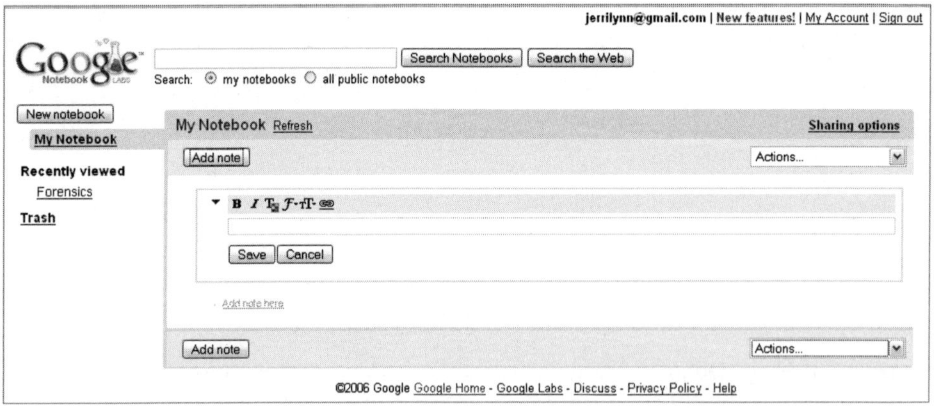

Figure 18-3: Use the text editor to type or paste notes into your notebook.

Using the Browser Plug-In

The Google Notebook browser plug-in is an optional element of the notebook plan. My recommendation is that you use the plug-in. Without it, the Google Notebook program isn't as powerful as it could be.

After you've downloaded and installed the plug-in, you'll see a notebook icon at the bottom of your Internet browser screen. This icon, shown in Figure 18-4, is how you'll control your Google Notebook when you're surfing the Web.

Figure 18-4: The Google Notebook icon, in the bottom-right corner of your browser

To use it, find a section of text on a Web site that you would like to include in the notebook. Highlight the text, and then click the notebook icon. As Figure 18-5 shows, the browser controls for Google Notebook expand.

Now, to add the text you've highlighted to your notebook, all you have to do is click Add note. Just the title and the URL of the note that you're adding will be displayed in this mini-notebook. When you're ready to look at all of your notes, click the Actions drop-down menu in the upper-right corner of the mini-notebook and select Go to full page view. That takes you to the Google Notebook Web page where you can edit, add to, delete, and share your notebook.

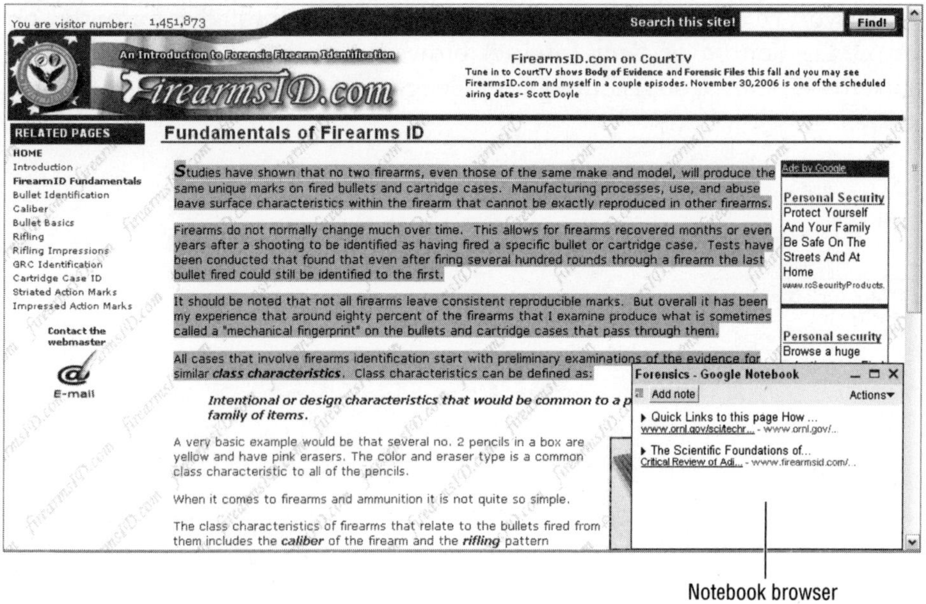

Figure 18-5: The Google Notebook browser controls — for adding notes and more

Navigating Notebooks

Once you're back on the Google Notebook Web site, you can navigate through your various notebooks by clicking the title of the notebook on the left. This will take you to the full view of the notebook so that you can scroll through, print, and even share your notebook with other people.

One very handy feature is the ability to type your own words directly into the notes that you have clipped from the Web. To do this, double-click within the text you've copied and the screen will change. The background goes white and your cursor appears. Now you can add your own notes.

TIP **If you're adding your own notes within the text of notes that you've clipped from the Web, finding those notes might be a little difficult later on. To make it easy to locate your own comments, change the color of the text that you're entering using the toolbar near the top of the page. And if you're collaborating with other people, each person can choose a different color text so their words are easy to identify.**

Another useful feature, especially if you've collected a variety of notes from around the Web, is the ability to expand and collapse your notes. As shown in Figure 18-6, there's a small arrow at the top and to the left of each note you've collected. The direction of the arrow indicates whether the note is expanded or collapsed. A downward arrow indicates the note is expanded; an arrow that points to the right indicates the note is collapsed.

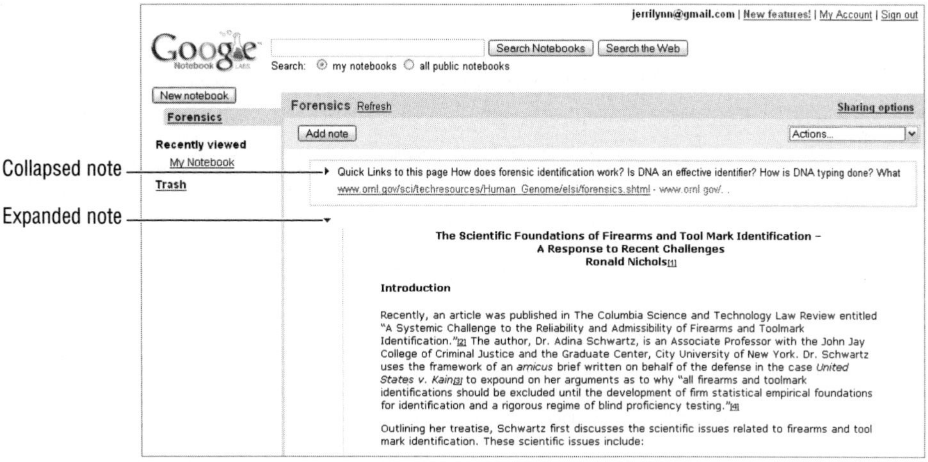

Figure 18-6: Use the arrows to change how notes are displayed.

More Notebook Actions

Once you're back on the Google Notebook Web site, you'll find a drop-down menu, shown in Figure 18-7, that gives you more options for the tasks that you can accomplish with those notebooks.

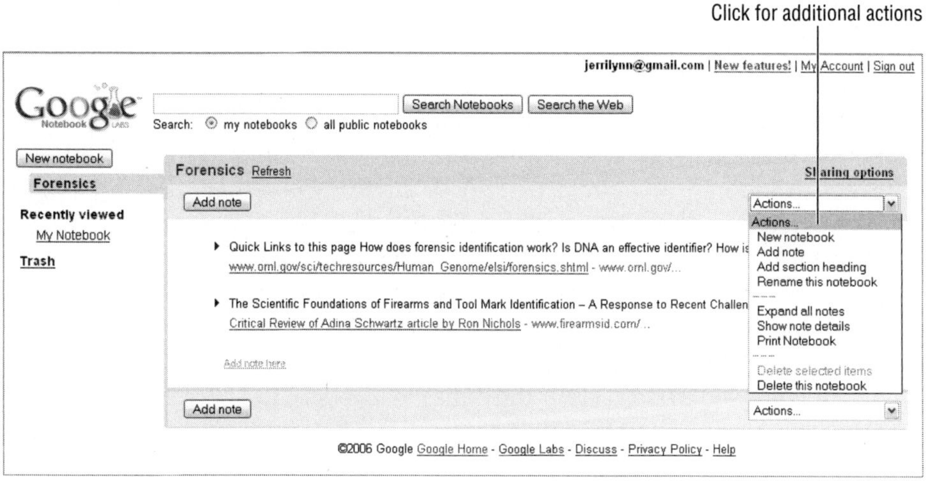

Figure 18-7: Use the Actions menu to accomplish more tasks.

The options included in that menu are as follows:

- **New Notebook:** Begins a new notebook. You are prompted to enter a notebook name, just as you were the first time you created a notebook.
- **Add Notebook:** Adds a new notebook to your collection. This works in much the same way the New Notebook option works.
- **Add Section Heading:** Allows you to add section headings for organizational purposes. You can separate your notes by heading for easy locating.
- **Rename This Notebook:** Gives you the ability to change the name of the notebook that you're currently working in.
- **Expand All Notes:** Expands all of the notes within your notebook. This results in scrolling pages of text if there are more than a few lines in your notebook.
- **Show Note Details:** This adds lines to each of your notes for the time and date the note was collected and for the URL from which the note was pulled.
- **Print Notebook:** Allows you to select printing options and print your notebook.
- **Delete Selected Items:** Deletes the selected note from the notebook.
- **Delete This Notebook:** Deletes the entire notebook.

Using these controls, you can manage and organize your notebooks very quickly. This means less time searching for the right source attribution, the paper note that you know you stuck right here, or the comments that you've written on the one note that contains all the information that you need.

Sharing Your Notebook

One last feature is the ability to share your notebook with other people. As mentioned previously in this chapter, sharing has a lot of benefits. You and others can collaborate on a project, a trip, or anything else that you might want to do cooperatively. And you can do it all from the Web, so you can trade notes back and forth without the risk of losing something.

To share your Google Notebook, select the notebook you want to share from your Notebook list. Then, click the Sharing link in the top-right corner. You are taken to a page like the one shown in Figure 18-8.

Now all you need to do is enter the e-mail address of the person with whom you want to share the notebook and click Save Settings. You can also enter multiple addresses, separated by a comma, to invite more than one person at a time.

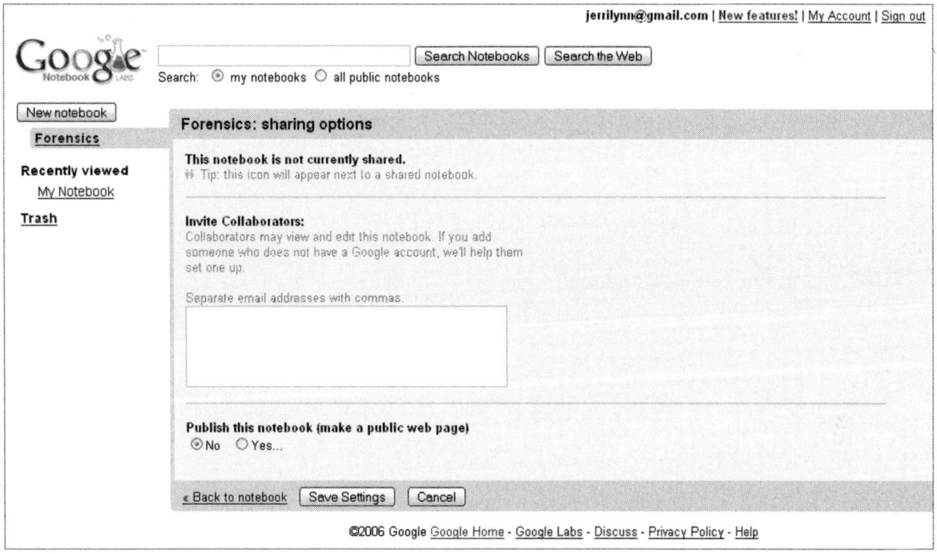

Figure 18-8: Use this page to share your notebook with other people.

You'll also notice an option on the sharing page that gives you the ability to make your notebook public. If you select Yes and then click Save Settings, your notebook is saved as a Web page and will be locatable with a search engine within a few hours. Use this option only if you truly intend to share your notebook with anyone who happens to stumble upon it.

Moving On

Google Notebook is a very valuable tool if you do much research on the Internet. It doesn't really matter what the purposes of the research are; what's more important is that you'll be able to catalog and return to information that has value to you. You can even share this information with other people if you want to.

As you move forward in the remaining chapters in this part, you'll learn more about the power of Google Notebook. Topics that were skimmed over here will be addressed in more detail in coming chapters. And you'll find that Google Notebook is the tool that you've been waiting for.

So keep reading. There's much more to come.

CHAPTER

19

Google Notebook Mini

Many people carry some kind of small notebook with them for recording thoughts and information. It's usually a pretty simple notebook, sometimes with strange little jottings that don't mean a lot to anyone but the owner. Google Notebook offers a feature very similar to this notebook, only it's electronically based. And you may find it's easier to understand than the notes that you hastily jot into your paper notebook.

The Google Notebook Mini is a smaller version of the Google Notebook Web page, and in order to use it, you have to download the Google Notebook extension for the browser that you're using. This extension can be found at `www.google.com/notebook`.

Before you can use the Google Notebook Mini, you'll have to download and install it, but it's a fairly small program that shouldn't take you more than about five minutes to put in operation (assuming you're using a broadband Internet connection).

Locating the Mini

After you've downloaded and installed the browser extension for Google Notebook, you need to close and reopen your Web browser. When you reopen your browser, the icon for Google Notebook appears at the bottom of your browser screen. You saw the picture of this icon in Chapter 18.

The only way to access the Notebook Mini is through this link, and without the browser plug-in, you won't be able to access the Notebook Mini at all. There are no other links to the program in other areas of Google Notebook. And there's no way to have access to the Mini if you don't download and install the plug-in.

Once you've done that, all you need to do to access your Notebook Mini is to click Open Notebook. This will open your last-used notebook in a small pop-up window at the bottom of your browser screen, as shown in Figure 19-1. If you don't happen to be logged in to your Google account when you click the link, you'll be prompted to log in before you notebook is displayed.

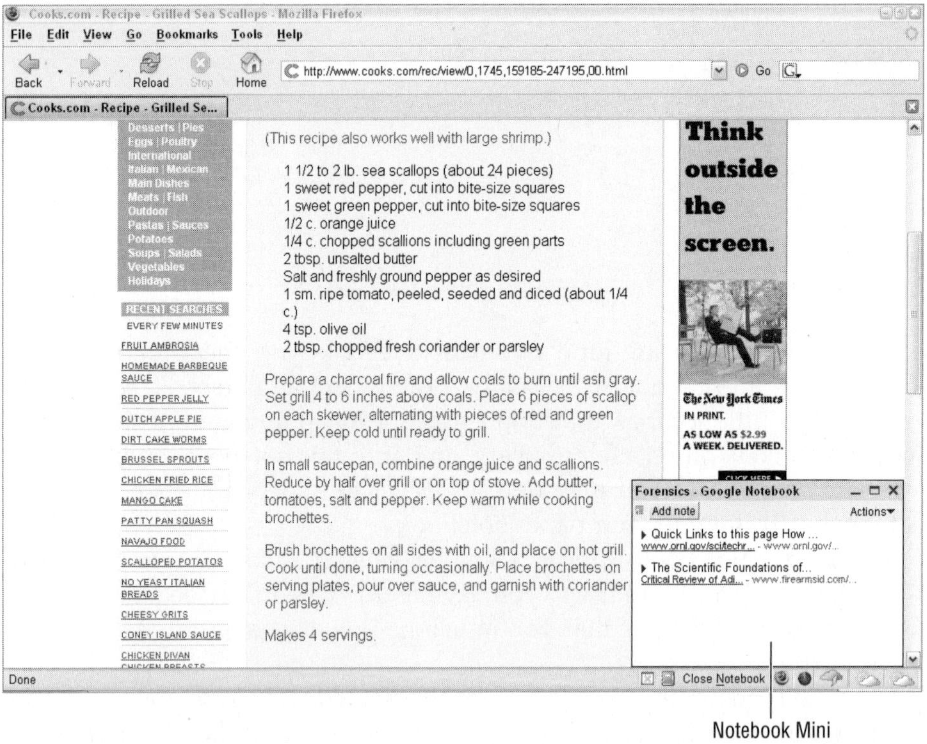

Figure 19-1: The Google Notebook Mini is a small, unobtrusive way to access notes.

Adding to the Mini

From the Notebook Mini, you can perform a few functions. The first is to add notes to the notebook. As you learned in Chapter 18, all you need to do is highlight what you'd like to paste into the notebook and then click Add Note. The note is added, in abbreviated form, to your notebook.

If, while you're performing your research, you want to access the full text of the notes that you are adding (or have added), then you can click the small arrow next to the note. If the arrow is pointing to the right, then the text of the note is hidden. If the arrow is pointing down, the text of the note is displayed. This works much the same in the Mini as it does in the full-page notebook.

Another option with the Mini is to change the notebook to which you're adding notes. The Notebook Mini is always opened to the last notebook that you were using. But that doesn't mean you have to go to the full-page notebook to change the notebook you're adding notes to. All you need to do is click the notebook-list icon, shown in Figure 19-2.

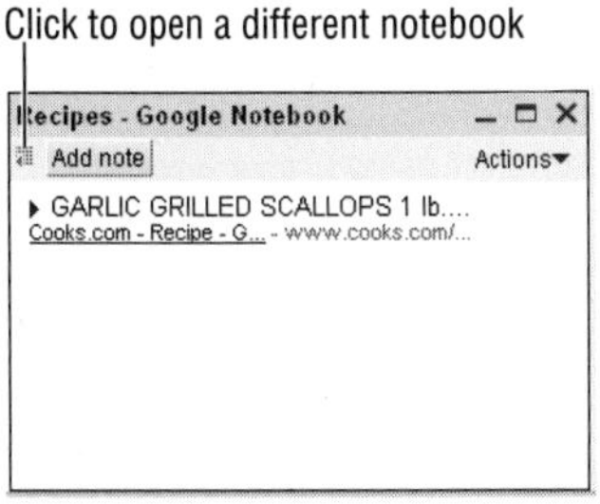

Figure 19-2: Use the notebook-list icon to add notes to another notebook.

When you click the icon, the pop-up window will expand to show you a list of the different notebooks you have already created and to which you can add notes, as illustrated in Figure 19-3.

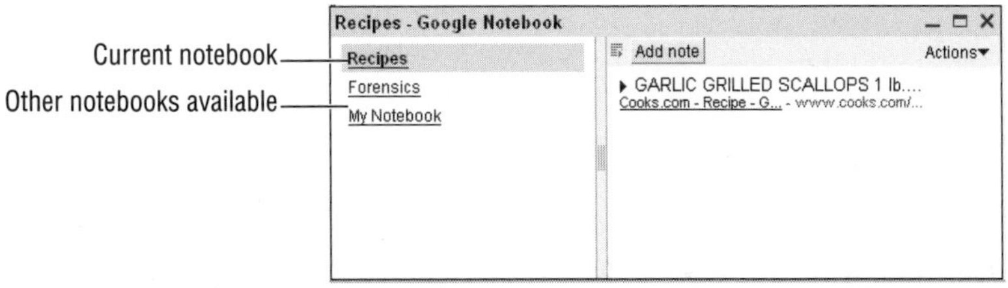

Figure 19-3: The window expands to allow you to choose a different notebook.

In the list of available notebooks, the one that you're currently using should be highlighted. The titles of the other notebooks should appear as blue links. To open a notebook, click the title of the notebook to which you want to add something.

You can switch between these notebooks as often as you like, but remember that if you end your session and come back later, your notebook will open to the last notebook used.

Editing Notes

Once you've added notes to your Notebook Mini, you may want to edit them without going to the full-page view. You can.

When you add a note to your Notebook Mini or when you click on any note title in your Notebook Mini, you should see a small Edit link appear on the note, as shown in Figure 19-4.

Figure 19-4: The Edit link disappears when you're working with other notes.

To edit that specific note, click the Edit link, and the editing view of the Notebook Mini appears, as shown in Figure 19-5. In this view, you can add or delete text, and add text effects such bold or italics.

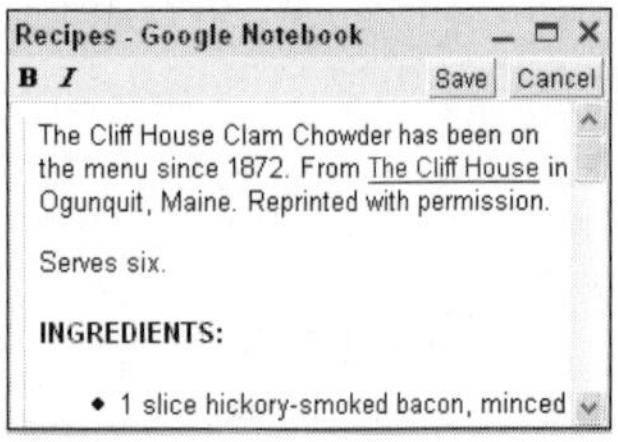

Figure 19-5: Use the Edit view of the Notebook Mini to add to or change notes.

When you're finished editing your notes, click Save. The changes you've made will be saved and you'll be returned to the note view of your notebook.

Organizing Your Notebook Mini

When you're adding notes on a specific topic to your Notebook Mini, you may decide that you'd like to assign those notes to several subtopics. Google Notebook gives you an option that allows you to add headings directly to the Notebook Mini.

To add a heading to a notebook, click on the note below which you would like the heading to appear. (A small frame will appear around the selected note.) Then click the Actions drop-down menu, as shown in Figure 19-6.

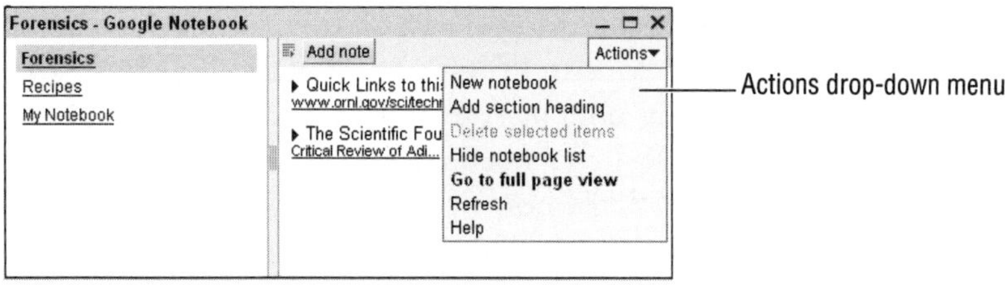

Figure 19-6: Use the Actions drop-down menu to add headings to the Mini.

Then select the Add section heading option. As Figure 19-7 shows, each new section heading appears with a text box in which you can enter the title of that section. You can create as many section headings as you want. For this illustration, I created two: Techniques and Section 1.

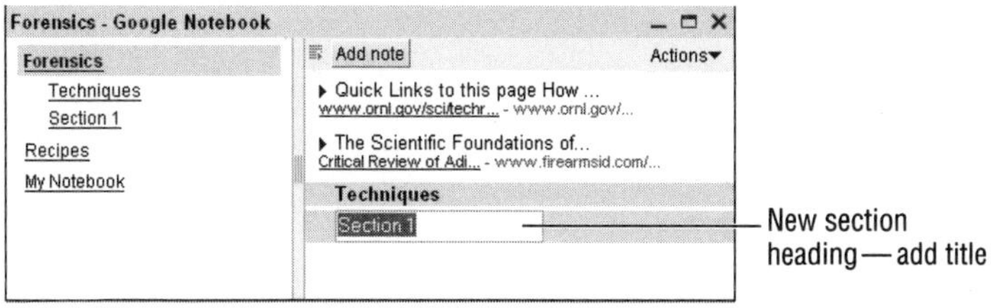

Figure 19-7: Type a section title in the text box provided.

After you've typed the desired section title in the text box, either press the Enter key on your keyboard or click away from the section heading you've just entered. The section title will appear in the Mini.

Now when you want to enter a note into a specific section of your notebook, just click the section title and add your note as you ordinarily would. The note will be inserted into the notebook under that heading.

The one drawback to this capability in the Notebook Mini is that once you place a section heading in your notebook, you can't rearrange it, nor can you rearrange the notes that are under the heading. You do have those options in the full-page view of your notebook, but I cover all of that in Chapter 20.

Editing and Removing Notes and Headings

I'm very good at assuming that every piece of information I come across during research is of value. Then later, I look at all the information I've gathered and realize that much of it is worthless. If you're at all like that, then having the ability to delete notes and headings or even just to edit them is a big plus.

Google Notebook makes editing easy. As you saw in the last section, clicking on a note causes an Edit link to appear. When you click the Edit link, you can change, delete, or add text to any note in your notebook.

But if you have a note or heading that just needs to go away completely, how do you delete it? First you need to click the note or heading. This tells the Notebook program that you want to work with that specific note and not the last one that you entered.

Next, click the Actions drop-down menu again. And then select the Delete selected items option. This enables you to delete the note or heading you clicked on at the beginning of the process. After the note has been deleted, you'll see a confirmation message, like the one shown in Figure 19-8.

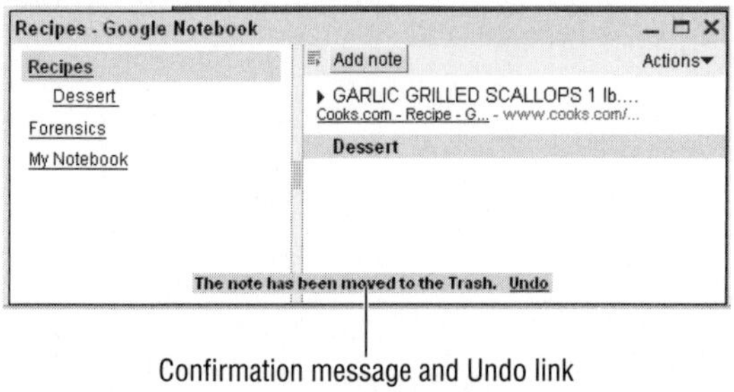

Figure 19-8: A confirmation message appears briefly after you delete a selection.

The confirmation message stays only until you perform another action with the Notebook Mini so if you're not watching for it, you may miss it.

There's also an Undo link in that message so if you accidentally delete an item you didn't intend to delete, you can retrieve it by clicking that link. Just be cautious when deleting headings because all of the notes under the heading will also be deleted.

Moving On

Google's Notebook Mini is nearly as powerful as the full-screen notebook, as you'll see in the next chapter. You can add notes, create headings, and even edit and delete items from the Mini.

Of course, there are a few things that you just can't do, including rearranging your notes in a way that makes the most sense to you and sharing your notebooks. However, you do have those capabilities, and you learn all about them in Chapter 20.

CHAPTER

20

Using Notebook: Full-Page

As useful as the Notebook Mini is, sometimes what you really need is a full-screen working area. One such time might be when you're adding your own notes to the notes you've collected from the Web. It's hard to write anything of any substance when you have only a small window available to write in.

You'll also find that a few functions are just plain missing from the Notebook Mini. These functions, such as sharing capabilities, the ability to rearrange your notes and headings, and the ability to print your notes, are important capabilities that you don't need all the time but will need occasionally.

So although it may seem a little redundant, there actually is good reason to have both the full-page notebook and the Notebook Mini. Ultimately, the combination of the two equals a very powerful, easy-to-access note-taking program. If you begin using it regularly, you may find that you just can't live without it.

Viewing the Full-Page Notebook

The first time you saw the full-page Google Notebook was probably when you signed into Google Notebook for the first time. And now you may be wondering how in the world to get back to that point. You can actually get there in a couple of ways.

One way to reach the full-page notebook is to log directly in to it on the Web (go to www.google.com/notebook/). This is a useful option if you're not already using the Notebook Mini to gather notes from the Web.

If you're using the Notebook Mini, you can access the full-page version in a way that's probably a little easier. From the Mini, simply select the Actions drop-down menu and then choose the Go to full page view option.

If you're using a Firefox Web browser, another tab will probably open (but depending on your setup, it could be a whole new window) with the full-page notebook displayed. If you're using Internet Explorer, then the page you're currently viewing will likely be replaced with the full-page notebook.

I've used the terms "probably" and "likely" here because your browser settings could affect the way the full-page notebook is displayed — whether it's opening in another tab, another window, or the same window. Regardless, you should ultimately end up at the full-page notebook view.

Editing and Changing Your Notebook

Once you get into your full-page notebook view, you have several of the same options that you had when you were using the Notebook Mini. You can add, change, edit, and delete notes, but you can't add notes simply by copying them and clicking the Add note here link. As you may remember from Chapter 18, you can use that link only to copy and paste information or to type it yourself, and no source notation will be included with those notes.

You'll also find the Actions drop-down menu available in the full-page view, as shown in Figure 20-1. This menu, however, includes more and different links. Those links and their functions are also covered in Chapter 18.

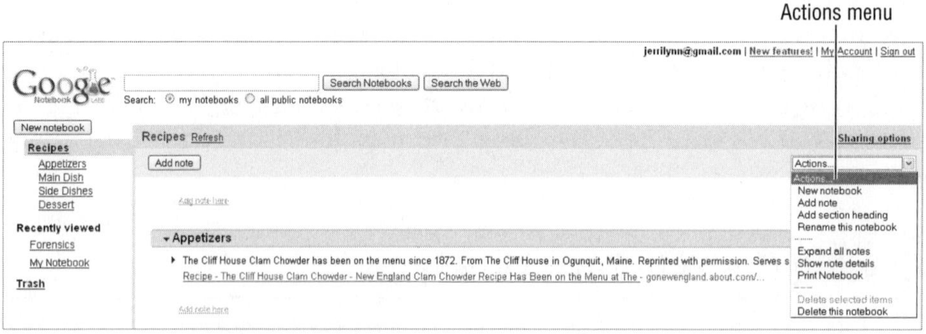

Figure 20-1: The Actions menu in full-page view contains several extra commands.

Rearranging Your Notes

So let's get to the new stuff. For some people, editing notes is nearly as important as gathering them. That's because the notes are of little value until they mean something to you, and until you put them in an order that makes sense, that just won't happen.

Fortunately, rearranging your notes and headings is easy. All you have to do is click and hold the note or heading that you want to move and then drag it to the spot where you want to put it. Using these steps, you can arrange and rearrange your notes as often as you like.

Searching for Notes

When you're working on a particularly involved topic, you might find that you've taken so many notes that you don't know what you have and what you don't or even where the information might be located. Google being Google, there is a search capability included in the full-page notebook view (see Figure 20-2).

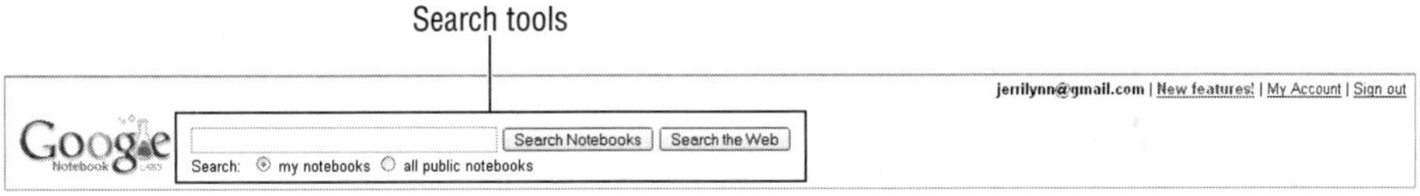

Figure 20-2: Use the search capabilities to find your notes or those of others.

You can use this search capability to find notes in any of the notebooks that you've created or to find notes that others have created and made public. I searched for "seafood recipes" and pulled about 27 results from others who have made notes public that contain seafood recipes. When I clicked on one set of notes, I was taken to the public view of that notebook, shown in Figure 20-3.

If you have information you think others might be interested in, you may be wondering how you can have your notebooks included in those search results. You will find that information in the next chapter on sharing your notebooks.

Printing Your Notebook

It's important to learn how to print your notebooks. You may think you've left printing behind, but if you use notebooks very long, the time will come when you'll want to see that paper printout.

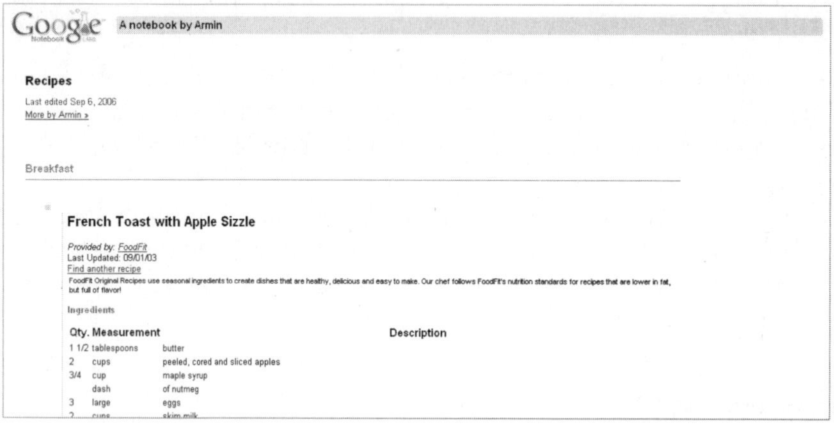

Figure 20-3: Public notes appear as a basic Web page when someone views them.

You can create notebooks that include your favorite recipes from the Internet and then print them for family or friends. You can create a notebook that has information about every destination you plan to visit on your European vacation, and then print the notebook to take with you. Or you can create a notebook that contains reviews of a new product that you want to carry in your store; then you can print the notebook to pass around with your sales pitch. You're limited only by the number of ways you can imagine how to use the vast amount of data available on the Internet.

To print any notebook that you have in your notebook list, just open that notebook, and then from the Actions menu select the Print notebook option. As shown in Figure 20-4, the Print dialog box appears. Select the printer you want to use and then click OK and your notebook should print. Because the notebook Web page is effectively set just as a printable Web page should be set, your notebook should print without any difficulties at all.

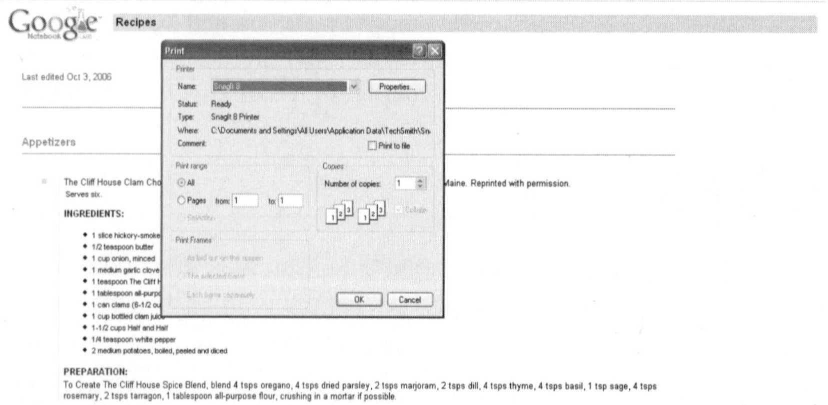

Figure 20-4: Select your print options and then click OK to print your notebook.

Moving On

You can use Google Notebook in a great number of different ways. And the full-page view of Google Notebook gives you a few additional controls that you don't have with the smaller Notebook Mini.

For those of you who are driven to organize everything, the full-page notebook view gives you all the organization controls you need. And if you like to add lots of your own notes, there's the larger-sized text editor. You can even search and print from the full-page notebook, which isn't possible with the Mini.

About the only thing that leaves is sharing your notebook. You learned as a kid that sharing is a good thing. And everything you need to know about sharing (at least about sharing your Google Notebook) is included in the next chapter, so keep reading.

CHAPTER

21

Sharing Your Notebooks

The Google Notebooks program has so many uses that you could probably keep experimenting forever, but eventually you may want to share your notebooks with others. You may want to share because you're working with a group. Or you may just think others would be interested in the information you've collected.

No matter what your reasons, the capability to share a notebook is useful — as long as it doesn't take some complicated process to make it happen. Fortunately, Google Notebooks makes sharing easy, a quality that's appealing in most of the Google productivity tools.

Which Notebooks to Share?

Before sharing a notebook, think it over carefully. When you share, the people you're sharing with have access to all of the information you've included in the notebook. There's no way to share only portions of a notebook.

Making your notebooks public, which is slightly different from sharing them, also makes your information available to others — in this case, "others" means anyone who searches for and finds the notebook.

When you're considering sharing a notebook, remember that you probably don't want to share one that has personal information or information that's sensitive even though it's not personal. For example, you may choose not to share a notebook that you've used to collect notes for your new novel, if you don't want others to have access to the idea, plot, or character traits that you've included in the notebook.

Once you've addressed the security concerns of sharing your notebooks, however, you can publish or share any notebook that you've created. Both processes are simple and shouldn't take more than a few minutes to complete.

FINDING YOUR WAY WITH GOOGLE MAPS

You might choose to share your notebook because you're planning a trip with one or more other people. Lots of families use Google Notebook to plan vacations, and business associates use it to plan business-related travel. And of course, travel means using a map to find your way.

Did you know that Google has a mapping application? It does. And it's a very good one. Using Google Maps, you can get directions from one place to another or you can find businesses or attractions in a specific location. And there's nothing to download in order to use Google Maps.

All you have to do is go to `http://maps.google.com`. **Once there, you can use Google's natural language search capabilities to search for addresses, places, attractions, or any other map-related topic you can think of.**

Sharing Your Notebooks

Before I cover the steps for sharing your notebook with someone, let me quickly clarify the difference between sharing and publishing notebooks. To share your notebook is to invite *specific* people to view and even edit the notebook. Sharing requires that you know the e-mail addresses of the people you would like to share or collaborate with.

Publishing your notebook is making it public for anyone who chooses to search for it. You may not even know these people exist. But they'll be able to find your notebook through the search function. To do that, they need to enter a search term, so you can improve the number of times your notebook is found by including only information relevant to the topic you're collecting information about.

When you're ready to share your notebooks — and this can be done anytime between notebook creation and deletion — you first need to open the notebook that you want to share. If you're already working on the notebook, you probably don't need to take any action at all. If you're not using the notebook that you want to share, however, all you need to do is select the right notebook from the notebook list on the left side of the full-page notebook view.

TIP **When you're ready to share or publish your notebook, be sure that you switch from the Notebook Mini to the full-page notebook view. The options for sharing and publishing are not available in the Mini view of your notebook.**

With your notebook open, click the Sharing options link in the upper-right corner of the page. You'll be taken to a sharing options page, similar to the one shown in Figure 21-1.

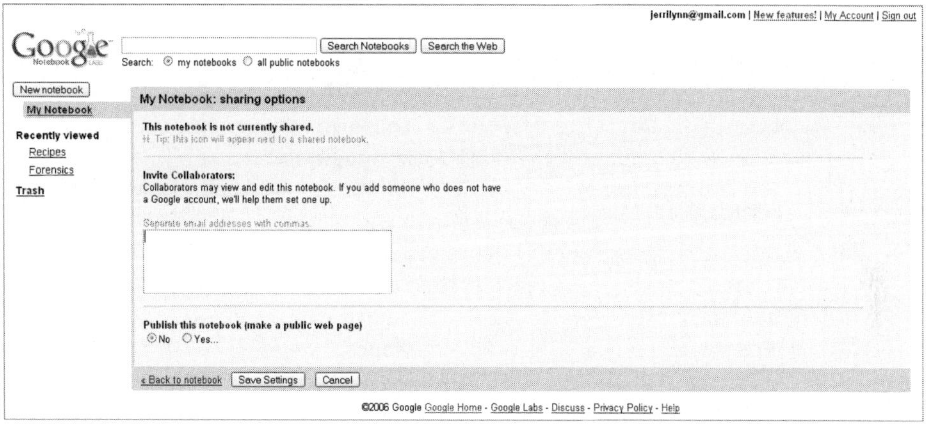

Figure 21-1: The sharing options page allows you to share or publish notebooks.

To share your notebook with other people, enter collaborators' e-mail addresses into the text box provided in the Invite Collaborators section of the page. You can enter as many e-mail addresses as you like; just remember to separate the addresses with commas.

When you've entered all of the e-mail addresses for people with whom you wish to share the notebook, click Save Settings. An e-mail window, like the one shown in Figure 21-2, appears.

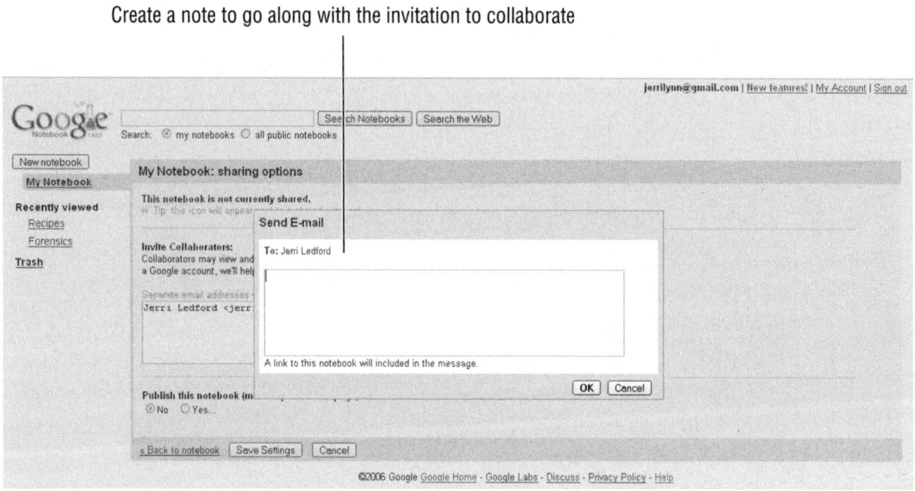

Figure 21-2: Use the e-mail window to write a note to invite others to collaborate.

In the text box provided, write a note to the people you're inviting to share your notebook. When you've completed your message, click OK. Your notebook page will reload, and then you should see one indicator (resembling two tiny figures) next to the title of the notebook, and another indicator in the top-right corner of the notebook that confirms you're sharing this notebook with other people, as shown in Figure 21-3. The indicator in the upper-right corner also shows how many people you're collaborating with.

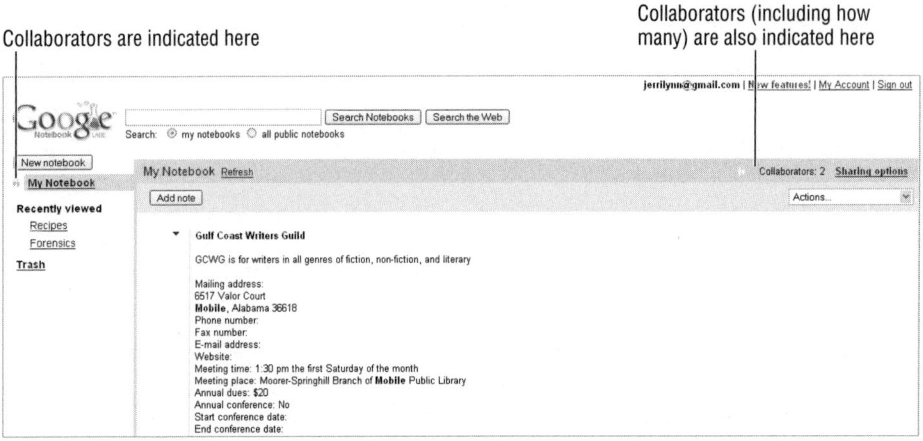

Figure 21-3: Collaborators are indicated in two places on your notebook page.

Once you allow someone else to collaborate on a notebook with you, that person has the ability to add, remove, or change the listings in the notebook, just as you do. One thing the collaborator can't do, however, is delete the notebook from your program. Instead, if you're sharing with someone who no longer wants access to your notebook, that person can select Sharing options from the top-right corner in the full-page view of that notebook. Then, a dialog box like the one shown in Figure 21-4 appears.

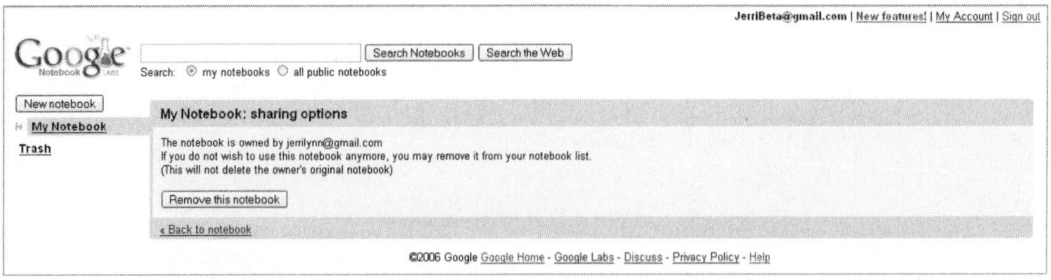

Figure 21-4: Collaborators see this message when they select Sharing options.

The message explains to users that the notebook belongs to you, and they can quit sharing it, but that this will not delete the notebook for you. If that's what the user would like to do, then he or she can click the Remove this notebook button below the note to remove the notebook from view. This also removes that user's ability to edit the notebook. In order to gain access to it again, the user would have to click the link provided in the invitation e-mail originally sent.

Managing Collaborators

On your side of the collaboration, you may find times when you just don't need a collaborator any more. For example, if you're collaborating with someone in your company and that person leaves the company, you may want to remove collaboration status to protect your data.

From the full-page view of the notebook that you're sharing, click the Sharing options link in the upper-right corner. This takes you back to the sharing options page, but now you should see a list of the people who are collaborating on your notebook with you, as shown in Figure 21-5.

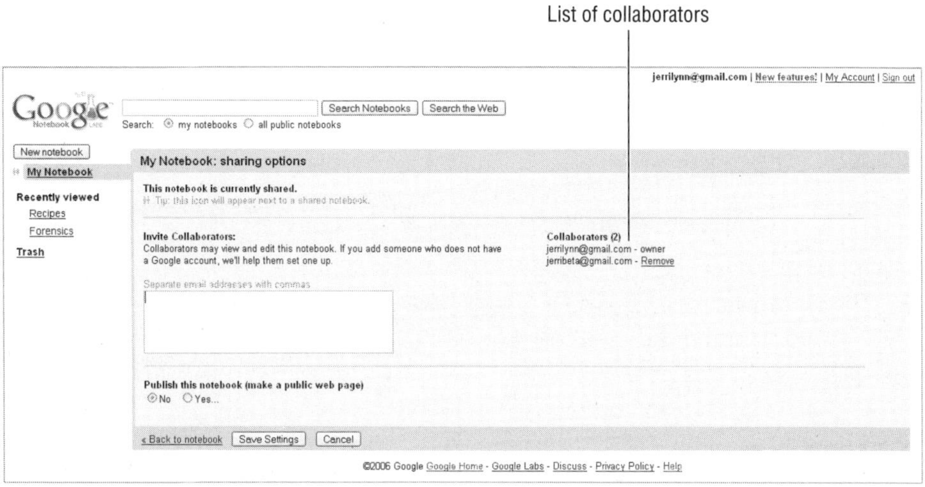

Figure 21-5: Collaborators are listed so you can see with whom you're sharing.

Next to the name of each person on the list (except you, the owner) is a Remove link. To remove someone from sharing your notebook, click this link and then click Save Settings. Be cautious about using the Remove link, however, because you won't be prompted to confirm your command. The user will simply be removed from the list. And don't forget to click the Save Settings link. If you don't click it, the user will not be removed from accessing the notebook.

If you decide in the future that you need to share the notebook with that person again, you can send another invitation, using the same steps you used previously to invite the person for the first time.

Publishing Your Notebook

Just as you can share your notebook with selected users, you can also publish it for the rest of the world to see. Publishing is a little different from sharing, simply because of the audience that sees your notebook. However, the steps to publish aren't any more difficult than those you took to share your notebooks.

Begin by opening the notebook that you want to publish and then click the Sharing options link. When you're taken to the sharing options page, you'll see a section below the collaboration section that's titled Publish this notebook (make a public web page).

Beneath the title are two radio buttons. To publish your site, click the Yes button. The settings page will expand, as shown in Figure 21-6, to include the ability for you to invite others to view the published notebook, the URL of the notebook once it's been published, and a space for the name you would like to have appear on the notebook.

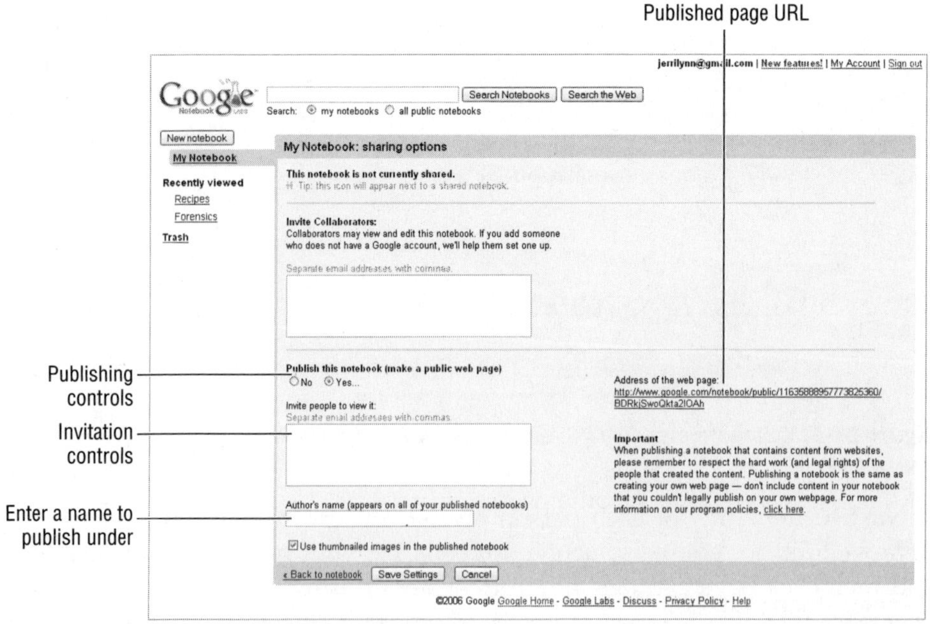

Figure 21-6: Your Settings page will change to give you additional publishing capabilities.

The information requested is not required. But it will make your published notebook more attractive and will help get the word out about it, so enter as much information as you can. When you're finished, click the Save Settings button at the bottom of the page.

If you've chosen to send an e-mail announcement to people to let them know about your published notebook, then the e-mail form you saw back in the sharing section will appear. Type any note that you want to include with the invitation and then click OK.

Your notebook page reloads, and again you'll see the icons that you saw when you shared your notebook. These icons will be located next to the title of the notebook and in the upper-right corner. The difference, however, is that this time the icons are indications that your page has been published, rather than shared. Also, as shown in Figure 21-7, you'll have a link in the upper-right corner to view your published notebook as it appears to other people.

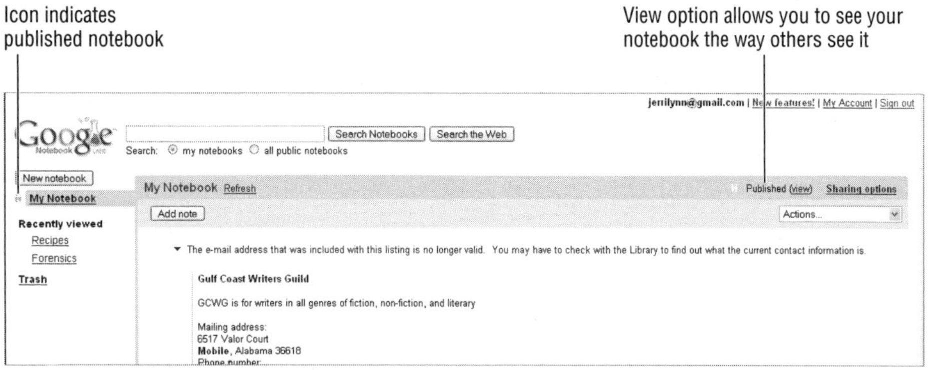

Figure 21-7: When your notebook is published, you'll be able to tell this at a glance.

Unpublishing Your Notebook

Just as you may want to publish your notebook so other people can see it, a time may come when you want to unpublish it. This is especially true if you publish a notebook containing very timely information that will be useless within a few days or weeks.

Google Notebook also contains an unpublishing option for your notebook, and it's easy to use. From the full-page notebook view, open the published notebook that you want to unpublish and then click the Sharing options link in the upper-right corner.

When you're taken to your sharing options page, simply click the No radio button under the publishing option, and then click the Save Settings button.

You'll be returned to the full-page notebook view for that notebook, and within a few days Google will stop publishing your notebook.

NOTE **When you unpublish your notebook, you may expect it to stop publishing immediately. However, with Google Notebook, it could take a few days for the unpublishing of your notebook to take effect and for the notebook to be removed from Google's search databases. Nothing to worry about — just remember that it takes a few days for the notebook to disappear from public view.**

Moving On

If you do a lot of Internet research, you'll find that Google Notebook becomes indispensable very quickly. It's easy to use, and between the full-page notebook view and the Notebook Mini, you have as much power as you'll ever need for taking notes on the Web.

Adding notes, printing, sharing, and even publishing your notebooks are straightforward activities, and all require few steps to accomplish. So what are you waiting for? Give Google Notebook a shot. It's a useful tool that can improve your effectiveness in just a few short minutes.

PART

VII

Google Talk

Communication is the lifeblood of any organization. On a given day, you could spend a third or more of your time on the phone or using a chat service to discuss business. And then there are personal communications. After you leave work, whether work is at an office downtown or the dining room table, you'll probably spend another hour or more talking on the phone, and e-mailing or chatting with friends and family.

Communications also happen to be one of your biggest expenses at work and at home. You can figure the average home telephone line costs around $80 a month, and that's before you call your brother who lives in Seattle and your best friend who's in Tuscany on sabbatical. And if you work in an office or own a business, the corporate phone costs are going to be even higher.

There's an answer to those painful bills, however. It's Google Talk — a free communications program that lets you have phone conversations or chat with your colleagues, friends, customers, or family.

This section of the book explains the benefits of Google Talk and how to use it.

CHAPTER

22

Welcome to Google Talk

Communication is everything. Think about it. How many people do you know who don't have cell phones? And most people have both a cell phone and a home phone, and in many cases those same people also have e-mail and use instant messaging regularly.

Today's world requires that you be available every possible moment. Work needs you, even when you aren't there. Or your family needs to know where you are, when you'll be home, and what you're bringing for supper. You need a cell phone so you'll never be out of touch.

If you're working on the computer, and have an Internet connection, then an instant-messaging program allows you to stay connected to people anywhere in the world without your having to worry about the expense of picking up the phone.

Our world requires that you have the most immediate means to communicate all the time. Google knows that, so they've created the Google Talk program.

As of this writing, Google Talk is still in beta testing, but that doesn't make it any less exciting. You can use Google Talk to talk with or send instant messages to your friends and acquaintances. It not only helps you stay in touch, but also reduces the cost of doing so.

Why Use Google Talk?

If you already have a home phone and an instant-messaging program you like, you may be wondering why in the world you'd want a program like Google Talk. There's one easy answer. This program, like the others we've covered in this book, is free.

Free isn't everything, however, and there's more to Google Talk than just the fact that the program itself is the ultimate bargain. Probably the most compelling reason to use it is that it also reduces the amount of money you spend on long-distance telephone calls.

In an office setting, especially one that involves offices in other areas or countries, Google Talk can greatly reduce the cost of communication between locations. For example, if your company has offices in Houston and Miami, you can install Google Talk on all of the employees' computers to enable employees to make calls between the offices for free.

The same holds true for calls to other countries, or even telephone service in your home. Google Talk works like many other VoIP (Voice over Internet Protocol) programs, such as Skype and Vonage's soft phone. Software provides the tools with which to have a telephone conversation. And the Internet provides the method by which the call is transported.

The result is that you can make telephone calls that travel from one place to another via the Internet, and it doesn't cost you a dime. It doesn't matter if those calls are going to the opposite side of the world or to the next office.

There is a rub, however. Google Talk is currently available only between Google Talk subscribers. Anyone you call using Google Talk must have a Google Talk account — you can't call people who have other VoIP accounts or who use traditional telephone service.

You might also want to use Google Talk because there's no limit on that use, as there is on some other VoIP services. Skype does have a free version of its VoIP service, but as with Google you can call only other Skype users.

Downloading and Installing Google Talk

The one aspect of Google Talk you might find slightly unappealing is the program's download procedure. Because Google Talk allows you to talk to or instant message with other people, you need some type of indicator on your computer that authorizes and helps to complete calls and instant messages. That capability is included in the download you'll need to perform if you want to use Google Talk.

To get started using Google Talk, go to `www.google.com/talk`. When you log on to the Google Talk Web site for the first time, you'll see information about the program and a link to download the Google Talk software. Click the Download Google Talk button.

The download should begin automatically. Select a location on your hard drive to save the file, and when the download is complete, close out of all of your windows, navigate to the file, and then double-click it to begin the installation.

Installation is short, and when it's finished, you need to sign into the Google Talk window that launches, using your Google account information or your Gmail account information.

How Google Talk behaves after you sign in is determined by whether or not you have a Gmail account. If you do have a Gmail account, when you sign into Google Talk for the first time the program will be populated with the contact information that you've stored in Gmail, as shown in Figure 22-1.

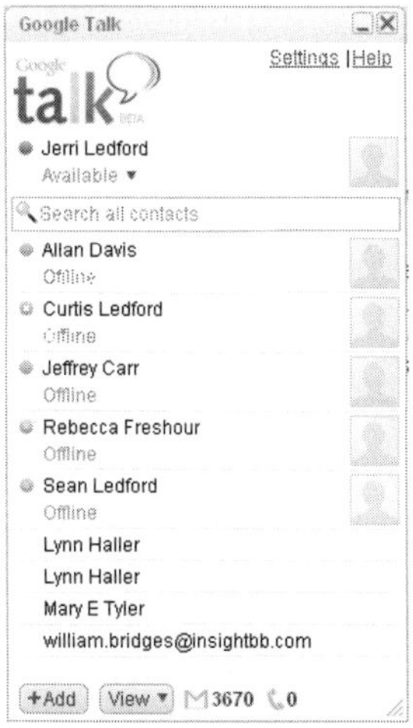

Figure 22-1: Google Talk is automatically populated with your Gmail contacts.

If you don't use Gmail, then Google Talk will open but your contact list won't automatically populate. You'll have to manually add the people with whom you would like to communicate. You learn more about how to add contacts to Google Talk in Chapter 23.

For now, let's look at how you get around in Google Talk. In Figure 22-2, you can see each of the commands and navigational aids for Google Talk labeled.

- **Settings and Help:** These links take you to your settings page, where you can change program settings, or to the Help page where you can learn more about specific tasks in Google Talk.
- **Your Availability:** You have the option to set yourself as available or busy, and you can also set some music options in this menu.

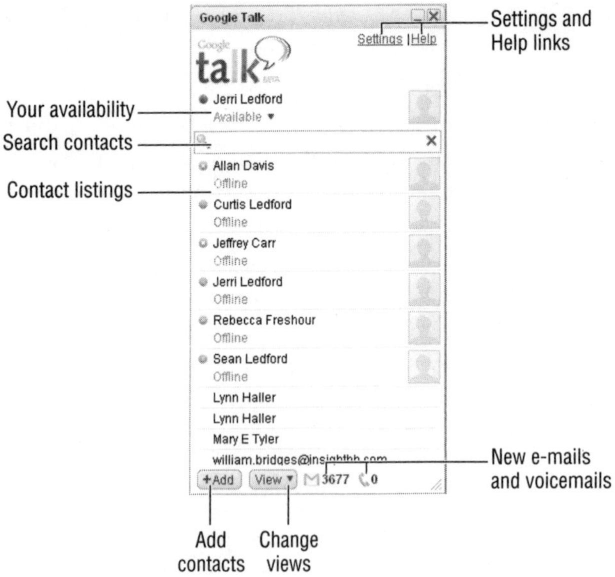

Figure 22-2: Getting around in Google Talk is a matter of selecting the right option.

- **Search Contacts:** Quickly find your contacts using the search capabilities included.
- **Contact Listings:** This is a listing for each of your contacts. By default, Gmail contacts are listed first in alphabetical order and then all other contacts are listed in alphabetical order. You can click a contact's name for options on how to communicate with him or her.
- **New E-Mail and Voice Mail:** These two icons show you how many new e-mails and voice mails you have available. If you click either icon, you are taken to your Gmail account e-mail or voice-mail view.
- **Change Views:** You can change how you view your contacts from this option.
- **Add Contacts:** Use this button to add contacts to your contact list.

Most of these options have submenus that allow you to perform more tasks and organize your communications in a manner that's convenient for you. You learn about most of the submenus in coming chapters.

One that should be covered here, however, is the Settings menu. When you click the Settings link in the top-right corner of the Google Talk window, a settings dialog box appears, like the one shown in Figure 22-3.

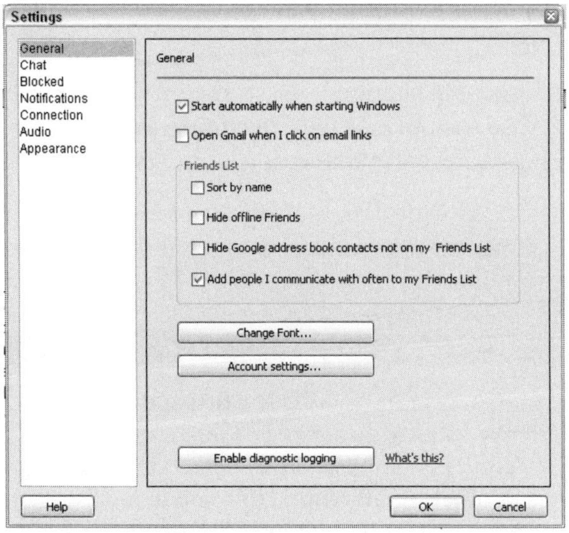

Figure 22-3: Use the Settings menu to change how Google Talk behaves.

By default, the Settings dialog box appears on the General page, but on the left side of the window that opens is a list of seven other pages that also contain settings options:

- **General:** The General page allows you to change how Google Talk opens and behaves. From this screen, you can also set options for your friends list, change your account settings, and troubleshoot the program.
- **Chat:** The Chat page lets you decide whether you want to keep logs of your chats or not. Logs are a great way to keep a record of instant message conversations. But keep in mind that they contain the entire conversation, so if you say something you don't want getting around, you might want to remove the chat log or turn off the logging option.
- **Blocked:** This is a list of the names that you have blocked from instant messaging or calls using Google Talk. From this screen you can unblock other users.
- **Notifications:** On this screen, you set how you're notified about incoming instant messages and call indicators that show your friends are online. There are also controls here for e-mail notifications.
- **Connection:** Change the way you connect to Google Talk.
- **Audio:** Set your audio preferences on this screen. You can change how your audio behaves when you're on a call and when you have an

incoming call. There's also an option to share your Music History with Google's Music Trends service.

- **Appearance:** On this screen, you can change how your contacts appear in the Google Talk window. Use the options here to choose a style that contains or does not contain pictures, and that meets your style.

The Settings option is about making Google Talk more convenient (and more fun) for you to use. Use these settings to personalize Google Talk, and then you're ready to begin using the program.

GOOGLE MUSIC TRENDS

Google Music Trends (`www.google.com/trends/music`**) is a listing that Google compiles of the most frequently listened-to songs by Google users. If you agree to have your music preferences monitored by Google, that data will be used (along with thousands of others' preferences) to compile the list shown on the Web site above. It's like a "Top 20 Hottest Hits" list, except that Google users are the only ones who get to vote.**

Moving On

Google Talk is a neat little program that has some potential to save you time and money when communicating with other people. It does require that you download a small piece of software and install it on your hard drive, but that small download could save you a lot in the long run.

And if you're already a Gmail user, then the power of Google Talk becomes even more concentrated. Using the two programs together will let you communicate in ways that you never thought would be possible.

In the next chapter, you learn about one of those ways: instant messaging. The power of Google's instant-messaging program will probably be enough to make you want to use it, so keep reading. There's still a lot to learn.

CHAPTER

23

Instant Messaging

Google Talk is actually an integrated communications program. What this means is that you can use the program for both instant messaging and for voice conversations. However, because it integrates with Google's Gmail, you also can use it to access your Gmail account (if you have one).

Instant messaging is probably the most widely used feature of this program. Most people today use, or have used, instant messaging for one reason or another. You've actually used instant messaging if you've ever dealt with a Web-based customer service program that enables you to chat live with a customer service or tech support representative.

It's more likely, however, that you've used it to chat with your friends online or your coworkers, without having to pick up the phone. And that's the beauty of instant messaging. It's a communications method that allows you to "talk" and continue what you're doing online, whether you're wading through e-mail or checking out the latest deals on eBay. You can multitask, and if you don't want to be bothered, it's easy to make yourself unavailable.

Google Talk gives you all these capabilities and a few more.

Using Google Talk for Chat

You can use Google Talk for two things: chatting and talking. Talking is covered in the next chapter, so let's consider chatting. Google Talk is set up to make it easy to chat with your friends, as long as they are Google Talk or Gmail users — with a few exceptions.

In addition to letting you chat with Google Talk and Gmail users, Google Talk will also let you chat with people who use other instant messaging platforms, as long as those programs are based on open-source technology. Here's a quick list of the other instant-message clients that Google Talk can chat with:

- Adium
- GAIM
- Chat
- Miranda
- Psi
- TrillianPro (This program is not free.)

These chat programs aren't as widely used as AIM, or Yahoo! Messenger, but they are cross-functional with Google Talk, in case you know people who happen to use them.

Set Up a Contact List

When you're ready to begin chatting with other people, the first thing you need to do is set up a contact list. If you're using Gmail, your contact list should set up automatically, as you learned back in Chapter 21, and you can add new contacts easily. Even if you're not a Gmail user, setting up a list isn't difficult. Begin by opening the Google Talk window, and then click the +Add button in the bottom-left corner of the window. As Figure 23-1 shows, an invitation window opens. Enter the e-mail address into the text box of the person whom you'd like to invite to chat, and then click Next. Alternatively, Gmail users can choose contacts from their contact lists.

Figure 23-1: Use the invitation window to invite others to use Google Talk.

The next screen that appears will contain a prewritten invitation to the person you're inviting. You can leave this invitation as it is, or you can change it by typing your own words in the space provided. When you've finished with your message, click Next.

The final screen is a confirmation that you've completed the invitation. The invitation has not yet been sent, however, so you have to click the Finished button to send it. After you do, the window closes and you are returned to your Google Talk window. As shown in Figure 23-2, your friend's address now appears in your Google Talk window with an invited notation next to the person's name. If your friend accepts your invitation, the invited notation disappears. If the person rejects the invitation, he or she will be removed from your contact list.

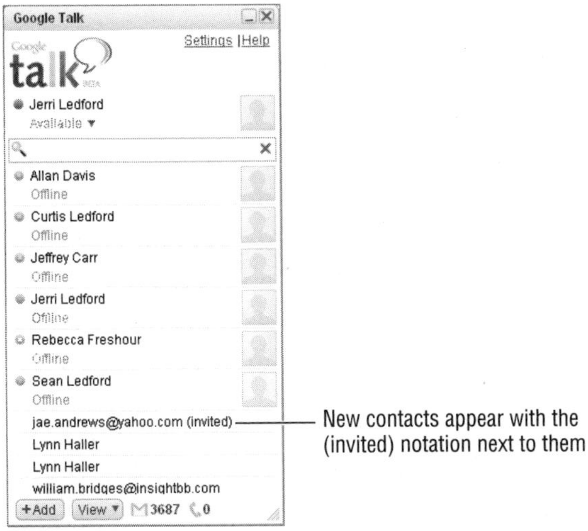

Figure 23-2: Friends show up as "invited" until they accept or decline your invitation.

Chatting with Others

Once you have populated your contact list and are ready to chat with someone, it's easy to do. First, pull up the Google Talk window. Any of your contacts who are online will be displayed at the top of your list with green dots next to their names, as shown in Figure 23-3. Contacts who are offline will not have the green dot next to their names.

To chat with someone, place your pointer over that person's name. (Remember that you can contact only those with green dots next to their names because those without dots are offline.) If you place your pointer over a name that has a green dot, a pop-out window appears, as shown in Figure 23-4.

Figure 23-3: Contacts who are online will have a green dot next to their names.

Figure 23-4: Place your cursor over a name to see communications controls.

In the pop-out window, click the Chat option. The chat window will open. Type your message into the text box provided and then press the Enter key. Your message will be sent to the person you chose to chat with.

When you're finished chatting, simply close the chat window.

Chat Logs

You can log your chats, which is an especially useful feature when you're using Google Talk to chat with coworkers about projects or with family and friends about some activity that requires planning. A chat log is a record of your conversation.

By default, Google automatically logs your chats and stores those logs in your Gmail account, if you're using one. You can change your automatic log settings by clicking the Settings link at the top of the Google Talk window.

After clicking the Settings link, the Settings dialog box appears. Select Chat from the list on the left. On the chat settings screen, you can choose whether you want to log your chats or not.

If you choose to log your chats, you can access those logs anytime. From your chat window, click the small downward arrow on the right side of the screen. As shown in Figure 23-5, a pop-out menu appears. Select the View past chats option.

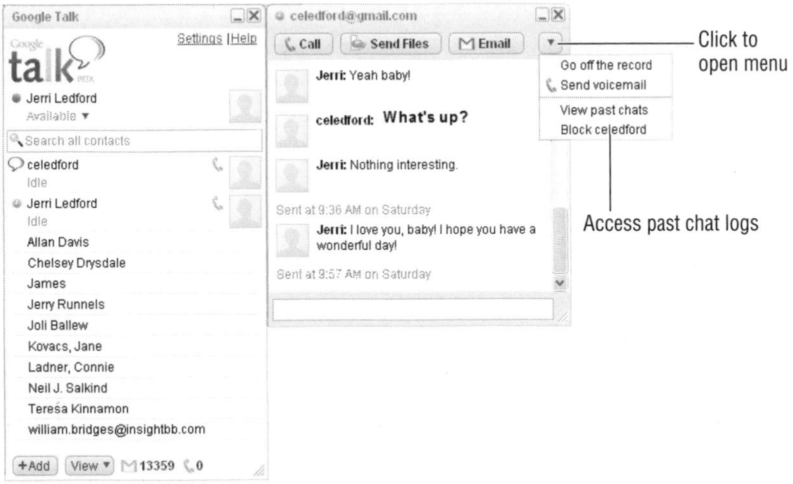

Figure 23-5: Access past chats with the person to whom you're currently chatting.

This option takes you to your Gmail account, where your chats are logged, as shown in Figure 23-6. From this option, however, you'll see only the chats that have taken place with that person. To view all of your chats, regardless of whom you were chatting with, click the Chats link on the left side of your Gmail account.

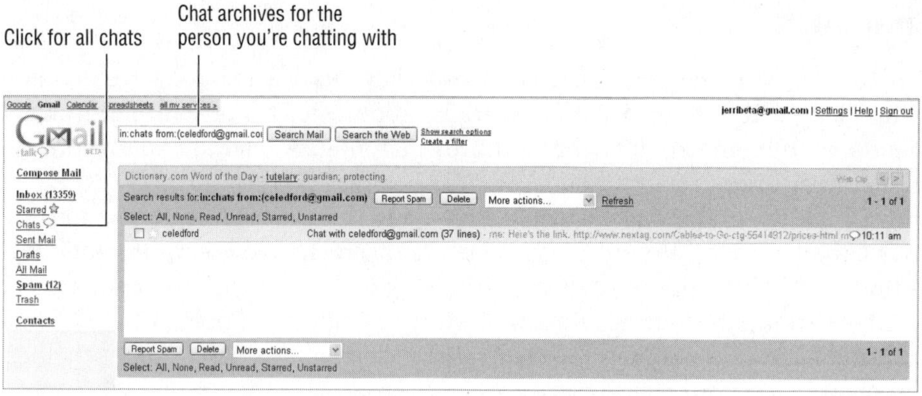

Figure 23-6: Chat logs are available from your Gmail account only.

There is a way to have an unlogged conversation with someone while still keeping regular logs of your chats. It's called "going off the record." To go off the record — and chat outside your log — click the small downward arrow that you used to access your chat logs. From the menu that appears, click Go off the record. As shown in Figure 23-7, a message appears in your chat window indicating you're off record. When you're ready to go back on the record, click the downward arrow again and select Stop chatting off the record.

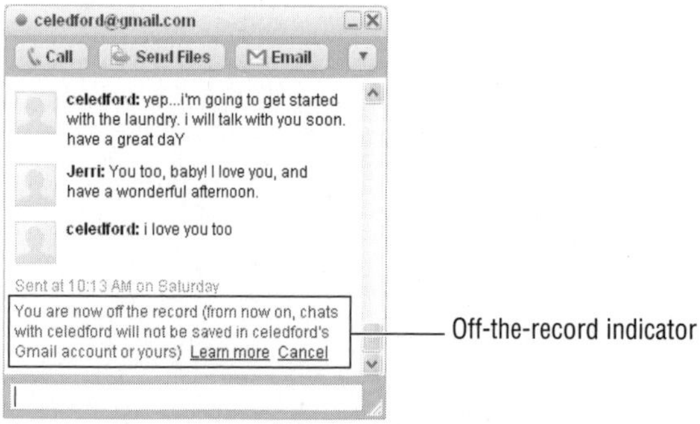

Figure 23-7: Chatting off the record temporarily stops the chat log.

Sending Files by Chat

One more interesting option is the ability to send files by chat. This is a really useful feature if you're collaborating with someone on a project or if you simply have photos or files you want to transfer to someone with whom you're chatting.

To send a file by chat, from the open chat window, click the Send Files button, as shown in Figure 23-8.

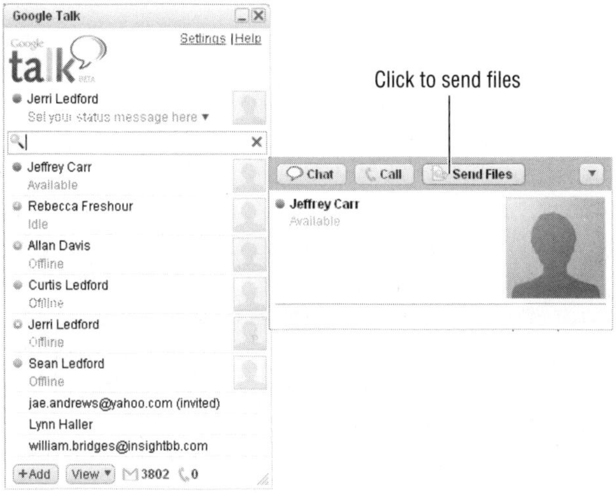

Figure 23-8: Click Send Files to send a file to the person you're chatting with.

A dialog box appears that you can use to navigate to the file you want to upload, as shown in Figure 23-9. When you find the file, select it and then select Open in the dialog box.

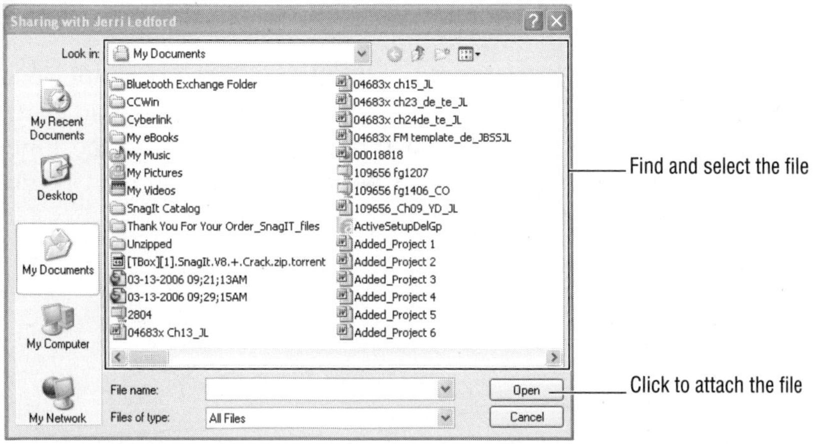

Figure 23-9: Use the dialog box to locate and attach the file you want to send.

The file will be inserted into the open chat window. The other person then needs to Accept or Decline the file. If they accept it, they'll be prompted to download the file and when the download is finished, they'll be able to access it.

Any file that you can send through e-mail you can send using Google Talk's Send File option. It speeds the way you communicate and makes it much easier to do so without interrupting the flow.

Chat to E-mail

Of course, sometimes when you're chatting with someone you may discover that you need to send him or her an e-mail. You can if you're using Gmail. All you need to do is click the Email button from the open chat window; your browser will be launched and you are taken to your Gmail account. What's more, a new message is started and addressed for you so that all you have to do is add a subject and the text of the message.

The neatest part of this feature is that you don't have to be having an active conversation with someone to send them an e-mail. From the main Google Talk window, you can place your pointer over any name on your contact list and then choose Email from the pop-out window that opens. Even if you're not chatting with someone, you are taken to your Gmail account and the new message opens, just as it does when you're talking to the person whom you choose to e-mail.

Moving On

Google Talk is a really useful program if you spend a lot of time online. You can chat with other people, and from within this chat you can also send files or e-mails, directly from the Google Talk program.

There's another option, too. It's the option actually to talk to someone, just as you would if you were to pick up the phone. In the next chapter, you learn everything you need to know about using this function. And by the time you're finished, you'll know everything you need to know to make Google Talk a convenient part of your daily workflow.

CHAPTER

24

Google Conversations

Nearly every home in the United States has a landline telephone, and it's estimated that more than a third of the world's population owns cell phones. And now telephone communication has a new capability. It's called VoIP — Voice over Internet Protocol. VoIP technology allows you to use your broadband Internet connection to make phone calls.

VoIP appeals because it's cheap and has many more features than plain old telephone service (called POTS). And Google Talk has a VoIP element, which allows you to talk to other Google Talk users.

Google Talk's VoIP element is called a softphone, meaning simply that it's a software phone — a piece of software acts as the telephone. If you're at all familiar with Skype, then you should have a pretty good idea of what the VoIP element of Google Talk is all about.

Equipment Needed

Some people are wary of using a service such as Google Talk because it requires that they have some equipment they don't ordinarily use when making telephone calls.

With traditional telephone service, you pick up the phone that you've always used and make a call. With VoIP, you use your computer to accomplish this, which means you also need speakers and a microphone. Most people prefer to use a headset that combines the microphone and speakers into a single device.

Not only do you need different equipment, but you also need to learn to connect differently. Instead of dialing a seven- or ten-digit phone number, Google Talk allows you simply to select a name. This may not seem like a huge difference, but making VoIP calls is just different enough to take some getting used to. Once you've learned VoIP, however, you may never go back to POTS.

Your first question may be where to get the needed equipment but, in fact, you may already have some of it. Many people can use the speakers and microphone that are installed on their computers (assuming they've installed a microphone — it's not standard equipment). Using these pieces of equipment will allow you to have a conversation without any trouble, although there *is* one possible worry.

When you're using your computer's speakers and a microphone to talk to other people with Google Talk, your conversations are broadcast through your speakers, just as any sound from your computer would be. That's why many people prefer to use a headset. And of course, Google can help you with that.

The Google Store (`www.googlestore.com`) carries a headset that you can use with Google Talk. You don't have to purchase it there, but it's convenient, and if you want complete freedom in using your Google Talk service, there's even a wireless headset available.

You also need a sound card in your computer. In most cases, it's already there and you don't have to worry about it. But if your computer is more than a year or two old, you should check to be sure your sound card will operate the headset you choose.

Having a Conversation

Once you have your computer set up — software downloaded, speakers and microphone or headset installed — you're ready to start having conversations. And of course, the conversation starts from the Google Talk window.

Sign in to your Google Talk program, and from the Google Talk window select the person you would like to call. Remember that to select a person you simply place your pointer over the person's name and wait for the pop-out window to appear.

To talk to others through Google Talk, they also have to be using the program, and they must also be online. If you try to call someone who isn't online, you'll receive a message telling you that.

From the pop-out menu that appears, click the Call button, shown in Figure 24-1. This initiates a call to your selected friend.

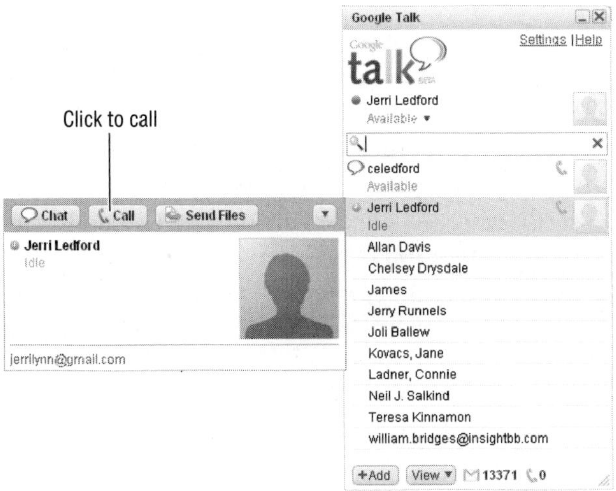

Figure 24-1: Select the Call button to initiate a call with another Google Talk user.

Inside the chat window, you'll see a message that says you're calling someone. This will change to show you're actually talking to the person or (if there's no answer) that you've left a voice mail, if you have.

When you've talked to the person and are ready to end the call, click the End Call button, as shown in Figure 24-2. (Hint: The End Call button replaces the Call button when the conversation is initiated.)

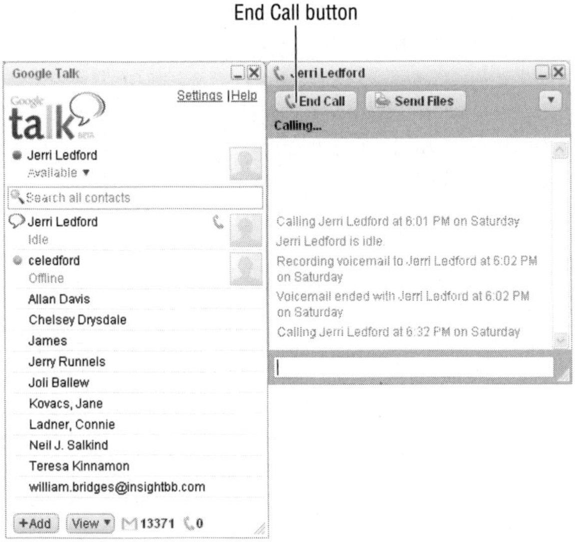

Figure 24-2: Click End Call to end your conversation.

Voice Mail

If your Google Talk friend doesn't answer your call, you can leave a voice mail, just as you would on a regular phone — with one condition. Your friend must also be a Gmail account user. When you're finished leaving your voice mail, click the End Call button and the voice mail will be delivered to the person you called. The next time that person signs on to Google Talk, a voice-mail indicator, like the one shown in Figure 24-3, appears.

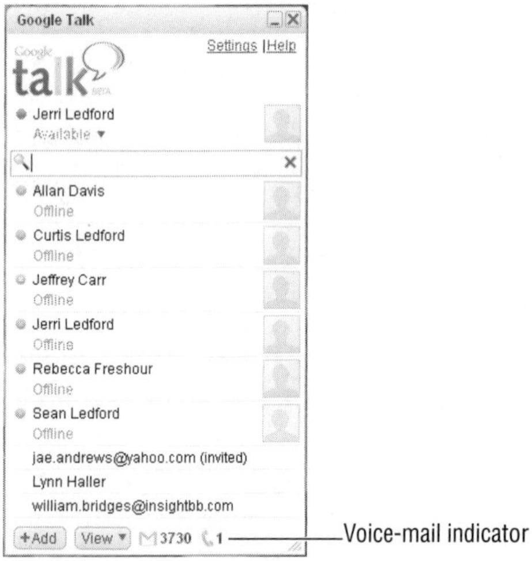

Figure 24-3: An indicator tells you how many voice mails you have waiting.

To listen to your voice mail, click the voice-mail indicator. A browser window opens and you are taken to your Gmail account. Then you can click on the messages that contain voice mails. The messages will open, as shown in Figure 24-4, to allow you to access playback controls. Click the right-pointing arrow to play a message, or download the message by clicking the Download as MP3 link.

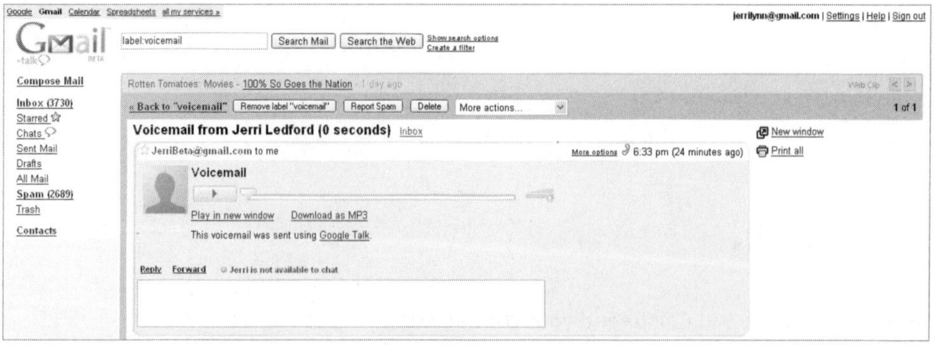

Figure 24-4: The voice-mail message has playback controls.

When you're finished listening to your message, you can leave it in your Gmail account or delete it. Either way, once you've opened the message, the voice-mail indicator will reset to zero.

Here's a neat capability. If you decide that you don't want to call the person back, you can reply via e-mail. Simply click the Reply button near the bottom of the message, and a reply e-mail is opened. Type your message and click Send.

Moving On

That's about all there is for Google Talk. It's a nifty little program that allows you to chat or talk to your friends, depending on which method of communication suits your needs. And if you happen to be a Gmail user (which you learn more about in Part VIII of this book), then Google Talk offers that much more functionality.

So what's next? Gmail, of course. Since we've covered nearly everything else, Gmail is the next logical step. So keep reading. There are still some things to learn.

PART VIII
Gmail

One of Google's first steps into hosted applications was also among the most-used applications on the Internet: e-mail. Except that Google calls its answer to e-mail Gmail. And this is one awe-inspiring e-mail program.

One of the most attractive draws of Gmail is the storage space that's provided — 2,500MB currently, and Google is increasing it all the time. For you, this means no more sorting through and deleting mail. Keep everything, and then when you need one of those e-mails, just search for it.

Gmail also has some interesting integration features with other programs we've covered in the past, and there's an out-of-this-world spam filter. Occasionally something will get through this filter, but not very often.

These features and more are covered in this section of the book. Gmail may be the next-to-last Google program explained in this book, but it's by no means the least exciting. On the contrary, Gmail is among the most useful Google programs.

CHAPTER

25

Welcome to Gmail

In the past decade, e-mail has become one of the most popular ways people stay in touch. Aside from the cell phone, it may be the most essential communication tool available. So essential, in fact, that every Internet service provider offers e-mail with its service.

Most free e-mail accounts, however, are nothing more than honey pots for spam. Sure, you can get legitimate e-mail in those accounts, but you sometimes have to wade through hundreds of spam messages a day to get to the two or three that you find useful.

Those accounts can also be less than secure, which means that you run the risk of having your personal information compromised if you're using a free e-mail account. But then Google's e-mail program hit the Internet and changed all the rules.

Gmail is Google's e-mail application, and it's everything that most other Web-mail applications are not. Gmail has functions you just won't find anywhere else. Read on and you'll see.

Why Use Gmail?

Web mail is Web mail. Right? If only it were that cut and dried.

All Web mail, no matter what developer creates it or what company provides it, has a few things in common. All Web-mail services are accessible through the

Web. Most of them offer some type of spam filtering (although the quality of that filtering varies widely). And most of them have other types of features that you may love or hate.

What makes Gmail different from every other Web-mail service on the planet is the way in which the program handles mail, and many of the other communication services that tie in with e-mail. For example, one recently added feature of Gmail is the integration with Google Talk that you learned about back in Chapters 22, 23, and 24.

No other e-mail application has this feature. And tens of thousands of users find the service not only user-friendly but also very useful.

Here's a quick list of what you can expect from Gmail:

- **Mega storage:** Most Web-mail programs top out at around 100 to 200MB of online storage. A few will push the envelope a little further, but Gmail operates on the premise that you shouldn't have to waste valuable time trying to decide what to save and what to toss. Its motto, "Search don't sort," describes the Google theory that e-mail should be useful, not frustrating.
- **Google search capabilities:** One of the most useful features of Gmail is the ability to use to Google's search capabilities to find any message you might need. The search feature uses natural language capabilities, so you don't have to learn any special way of creating search strings to find what you're looking for. And you can search in a variety of ways: by name, by e-mail address, by topic, or by keyword. Finding your messages in Gmail is easy.
- **Messages in context:** This is a feature unique to Gmail. All of the messages in a given thread are shown together. You'll never have to wonder what a message reply means or search for the original message to keep your responses in the context of a conversation. All of the messages are right there together, in abbreviated or expanded form (and you'll see how this feature works a little later in this chapter).
- **Hurray! No spam here:** The folks at Google take great pride in the spam filtering of Gmail. The company has designed (and continues to improve) a spam filter that catches most of the junk mail that comes to your account. Occasionally something will get past this monster filter, but if it does, you can label the offensive message as spam and the spam filter will catch any future instances of the message. It's intelligent, I tell you, intelligent!
- **Program integrations:** Many of the other Google programs (such as Google Docs & Spreadsheets, Calendar, Notebook, and Talk) integrate

with Gmail to create a powerful program that's really useful for more than just mail.

- **Customization options:** Gmail has filtering capabilities, labeling capabilities, and the ability to use an auto responder or forwarding service. These are just a few of the features you'll find in Gmail. All of these and more are covered in the coming chapters.

Gmail is also a free program, like most Web-mail services. With Gmail, you will find some advertising in your page and message layouts, but these ads are non-obtrusive, and they're usually targeted well. In fact, there may be times when you find the advertisements useful. It's hard to believe but true. And you'll seldom find the advertisements annoying.

TIP One fun feature of Gmail is its SPAM recipes. You'll find them linked from the top of your spam page. You'll be amazed what you can do with SPAM (the meat product, not the junk e-mail).

The usability of Gmail is off the charts. It integrates with most e-mail applications, such as Outlook, Mozilla Thunderbird, and Eudora, so you can download your messages to a program you're comfortable with. And if you want to use the program exclusively online, there are added benefits.

So, why should you use Gmail? The easy answer is because once you use it, you'll find that it's more usable and more useful than any e-mail program you've ever accessed.

Navigating Gmail

Getting around in Gmail is no more difficult than in any of the other Google applications. There are a few differences, and Gmail is a little more feature-filled than many other applications, but it's still not difficult. The WYSIWYG interface is back, and navigating it is a breeze.

Getting Started

At the time of this writing, Gmail is still in beta testing — albeit wide-spread beta testing. This means you can't get into Gmail without an invitation. If you don't already have an account, you have a few options. You can either find a friend or colleague who has a Gmail account and ask to be sent an invitation, or you can search online until you find a message board where Gmail account owners are bartering their available invitations.

One final option is to stop by the Google Productivity Book Web site and request an invitation (`www.googleproductivitybook.com`). As long as I have invitations available, I'll be happy to send them out on a first-come, first-served basis.

Once you have an invitation to the Gmail application, you need to get signed up. Click the link in the invitation e-mail that you receive, and you are taken to a Web page where you're prompted to create your Gmail account.

Enter your name, choose a user name and password, set your security and location settings, and then read through the Terms of Service and Privacy Policy documents. Finally, if you agree to the terms set forth in these documents, select "I accept. Create my account."

You'll be taken to a page that displays an overview of some of the most common features. When you're finished reading through that page, click "I'm ready — show me my account."

The next page that appears takes you through some of the chat options in Gmail. Make your selections and then click "Sweet! Go to my inbox." And you'll be taken to your Inbox.

As Figure 25-1 shows, your Inbox contains links to all of the navigation you'll need when using Gmail.

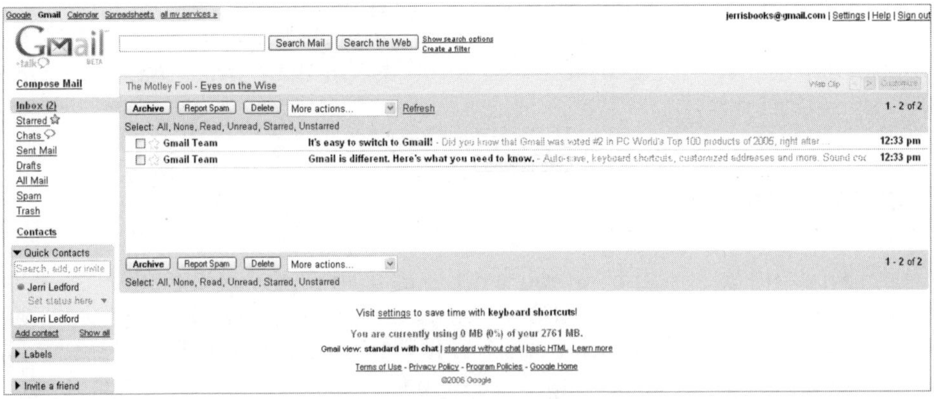

Figure 25-1: The Gmail Inbox contains all of your navigational links and your mail.

General Navigation

Getting around in Gmail is pretty self-explanatory. On the left side of the page is the main e-mail menu. Here you'll find links for the following:

- **Inbox:** This is where your mail will be displayed if you haven't filed or deleted it.

- **Starred:** Important messages can be starred to make them easy to find.
- **Chats:** If you elected to keep logs of all your chats when you created your account, this is where you'll find them.
- **Sent Mail:** A copy of all mail that's sent out is kept here.
- **Drafts:** If you're creating a message online and you get kicked off or sign off before the message is complete, the draft of the message is saved here so you can return to it later.
- **All Mail:** Every piece of mail that you have in your Inbox, folders, and other locations in Gmail will appear in this file. This is a useful file to have if you don't remember what category you assigned to a message.
- **Spam:** Well, it's spam. Google will keep it around for about 30 days, just in case something that's not spam ends up in this folder. After 30 days, the spam goes away (all on its own — you do nothing).
- **Trash:** Any mail that you've deleted will appear in the Trash folder for about 30 days. That's just in case you decide later that you didn't really want to delete it.

In addition to these links, there's also a link for your Contacts. When you click this link, a list of your contacts appears, as shown in Figure 25-2. Depending on how you set up your account, you can have e-mail addresses automatically added to your contacts when you reply to a message.

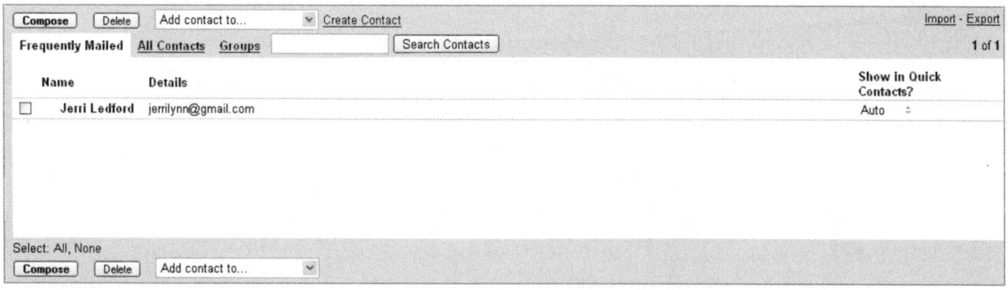

Figure 25-2: Your contacts list contains all your e-mail addresses.

Additionally, you can import an address book from another e-mail application such as Outlook by going to the Contacts page and then clicking the Import link on the right side. An upload dialog box appears. Click Browse to browse your computer and locate the contacts file you want to upload. When you find the file, click it and then click Open. You are taken back to the import page. Click Import contacts and the file is imported into your Gmail contacts list.

Finally, there are three smaller menus on the left side of the page, as shown in Figure 25-3. These menus allow you to manage your contacts, add labels to your messages, and invite friends to Gmail. I cover all of those functions in more detail in Chapters 26 and 27, so for now all you need to know is where they are located.

Figure 25-3: These menus help you perform common functions in Gmail.

Gmail Settings

In addition to the navigation bar on the left side of the page, you'll find your Gmail settings link at the top of the page, near the right corner. When you click the Settings link there, you'll be taken to the Settings page, as shown in Figure 25-4.

The Settings page contains a link system (like tabs) near the top of the page to make it easier for you to create settings that suit your needs. This link system includes the following pages:

- **General:** General settings are your language, keyboard shortcuts, vacation responders, signatures, and personal indicators. Each of these settings gives you control over how your incoming and outgoing messages appear and behave.
- **Accounts:** This page lets you set up how your outgoing messages will appear. Will they seem to come from your Gmail account or another account? You determine how it appears.
- **Labels:** You can set up the labels that you'll apply to your messages to help organize them. There are multiple places to do this, and you learn more about that in the next couple of chapters.
- **Filters:** Filters can be applied to incoming e-mail messages so that they are automatically deleted, filed, or left alone.

Figure 25-4: Use the Settings page to customize your Gmail application.

- **Forwarding and POP:** POP refers to the method by which some e-mail accounts can be downloaded using an e-mail program such as Microsoft Outlook, Mozilla Thunderbird, or Eudora. You'll find those settings as well as forwarding settings on this page.
- **Chat:** Set your chat preferences from this page — for example, whether you want to see all past chats or your full contacts list.
- **Web clips:** Web clips are headlines, tips, and blogs that might be of interest to you. Using this page, you can choose the Web clips that you'd like to receive as well as how you'd like to view them.

Each setting Google makes available in Gmail is designed to make the program easier for you to use. Once you're comfortable using the features, you'll find they're as powerful as other Web mail applications, if not more so.

Navigational links above and below your list of mail message allow you to Archive, Delete, and Report Spam with the click of a button. And you can use the drop-down menu located next to these buttons to perform more actions on your e-mail messages, including marking messages as read or unread, starring or unstarring messages, and applying labels to them.

Navigating messages in Gmail really is point-and-click easy, and Gmail gives you numerous options, in multiple places, so you can quickly choose the option that suits the way you work.

Searching Gmail

One last navigational element to be aware of is the search capability of Gmail. You'll find the Search function right near the top of the page, and you have two options: You can search just your e-mail or you can use Google to search the Web.

All you have to do to use this function is type the word, term, or phrase that you want to search for into the text box provided and then click either Search Mail or Search the Web. If you're searching your mail, the search results will appear on a page that looks very similar to your Gmail Inbox.

If you're searching the Web, your search results will be opened in a different page.

Moving On

Gmail is one of the hottest Google applications available to you. And it's also one of the easiest. It won't take you long to get up to speed on it.

Once you're comfortable using it, you'll find that you don't ever have to worry about your e-mail again. If you never want delete a message, that's okay with Google. Or if you're an ultra-organized person who wants to have all mail available, quickly and from anywhere, then you can use the tools provided to file everything neatly away.

Despite its ease of use, Gmail is a powerful e-mail application that will give you ways to communicate that you never thought possible. So read on and find some other treasures in this program.

CHAPTER

26

Using Gmail

E-mail as we know it didn't exist a couple of decades ago, yet today if we're without it for more than a few hours, we break out in hives. We need to be in touch, no matter where we go, and no matter what equipment we carry with us.

The great appeal of Gmail is that it doesn't matter what equipment you have with you when you travel. You can still check your e-mail; all you need is an Internet connection and some Internet-enabled device. And there aren't a lot of new things to learn with Gmail. The controls for creating and editing messages, sending and receiving messages, and even saving or deleting your message are easy to use. You'll find a few new capabilities with Gmail, but even those work much as you would expect them to.

Creating and Editing Messages

The two most-used functions of any e-mail account are creating e-mail messages and editing the ones you've created. With Gmail, the controls for these are right on the front page.

Begin by signing into Gmail. Go to `www.gmail.com`, enter your user name and password, and then click Sign In. By default, you should be taken to your Inbox. From here you can send messages or view your new messages.

To send a message, click the Compose Mail link, shown in Figure 26-1.

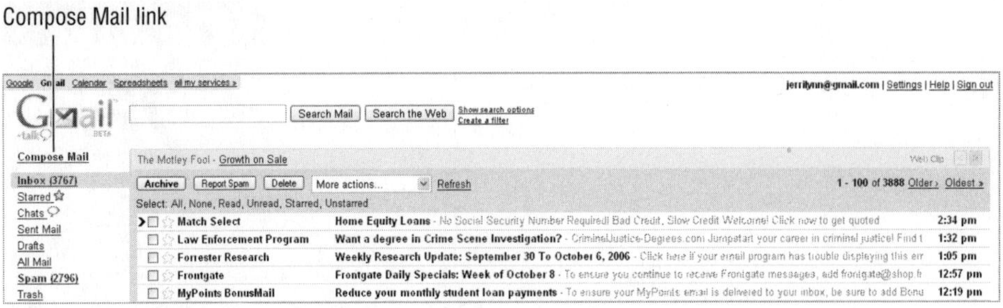
Compose Mail link

Figure 26-1: The Compose Mail link is at the top of the links on the left.

When you click the Compose Mail link, a new, blank e-mail message form appears. You simply add the address of the recipient, a subject line, and your message, and then click the Send button. However, you do have some additional capabilities if you need them.

One of these is to add event information to your message. To do this, click the Add event info link in the right corner of the message, as shown in Figure 26-2.

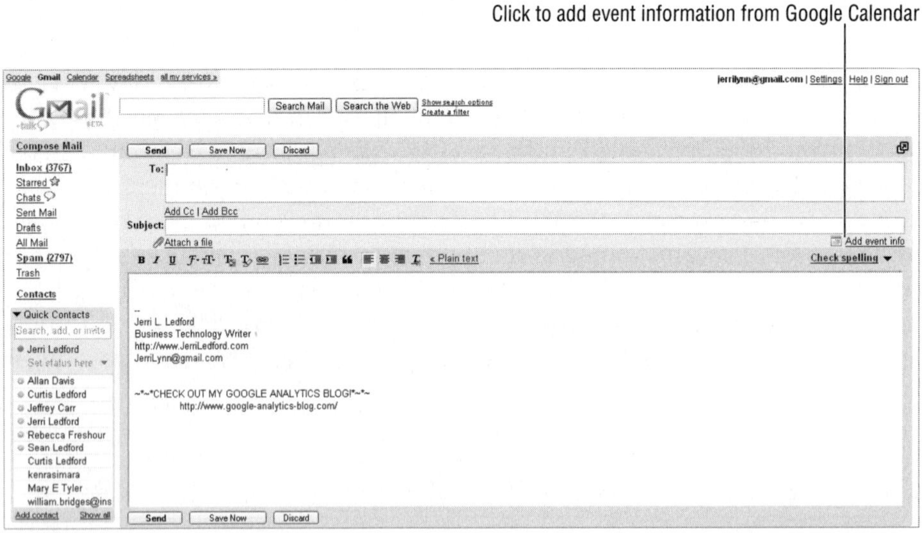
Click to add event information from Google Calendar

Figure 26-2: Click the link to add information about an event to your e-mail message.

When you click the link, additional lines are added to your message for the event title, the time and date, and the location. Figure 26-3 shows how the message will appear.

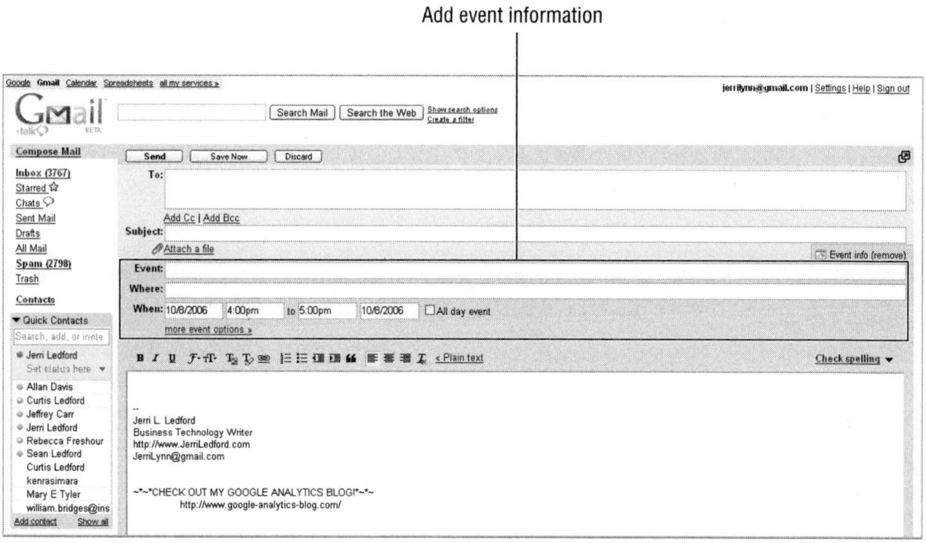

Figure 26-3: Add event information using the lines provided in your new message.

If you use Google Calendar, you can link your event information to your calendar. After you've entered your information, click the link (right below the event information) for more event information. A window opens with space for new event information for your Google Calendar, as shown in Figure 26-4. Enter your information and click Save changes, and the event is added to your calendar. You'll also be shown a confirmation page to ensure you know your event notice was created.

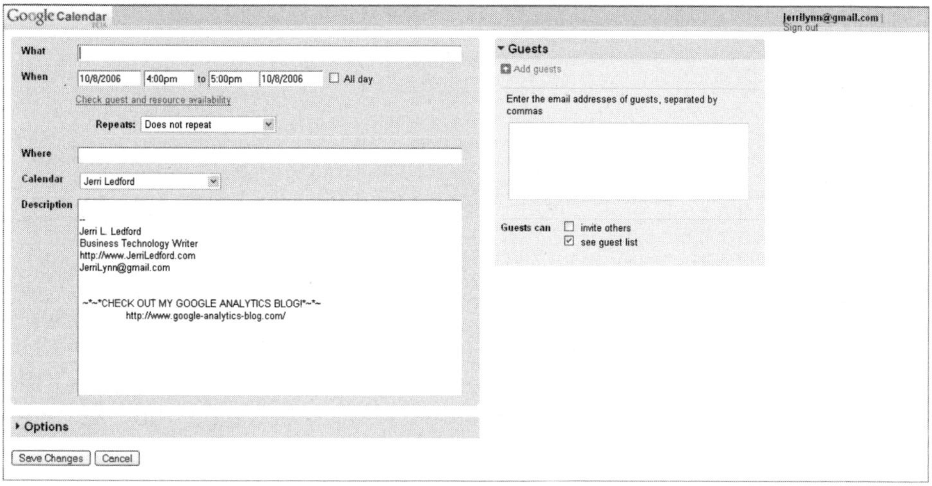

Figure 26-4: Add appointments from your Gmail account.

NOTE **For more information on Google Calendar, see Chapters 15–18.**

Back in your Gmail account, you may decide that you don't want to include event information in your message after all. You'll notice that the link you clicked to Add event information has changed and now reads Event Info (remove). Click that link to remove the information.

STAY CURRENT WITH GOOGLE ALERTS

There are all kinds of events and information floating around on the Web. You could spend days searching and not find everything there is to find. But Google can help you, and it won't take days. Google Alerts is an e-mail–based service that generates automatic e-mail notifications about events and search terms that you define.

Google Alerts is easy to use. All you have to do is go to `www.google.com/alerts` **and set up the alerts that you'd like to receive.**

You can choose from four categories of alerts: News, Web, News & Web, and Groups. And you have the option to receive them once a day, as it happens, or once a week.

Google Alerts can help you stay on top of any topic or event that interests you. All you have to do is create the alert and forget it.

Editing Your Message Text

Any time you're creating a text document, even an e-mail, you may find you need formatting, spell check, or other editing options. In a Gmail message, those options are below the subject line, as shown in Figure 26-5.

Editing toolbar

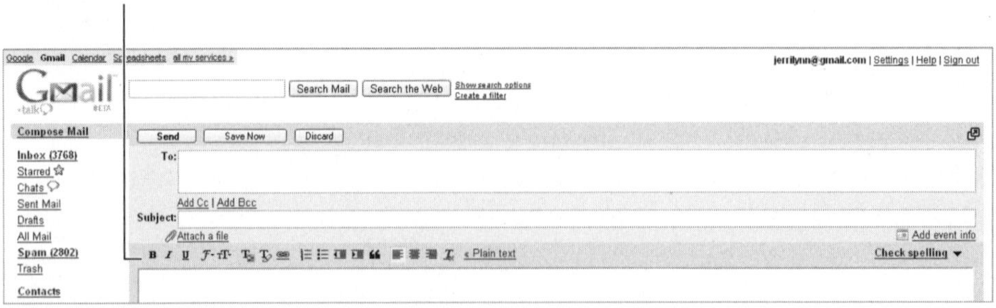

Figure 26-5: Use the editing toolbar to edit the text you've added to your message.

Included in the editing toolbar are options for:

- Bold
- Italics
- Underline
- Font (seven fonts available)
- Text Size (four sizes available)
- Text Color
- Highlighting
- Hyperlink
- Numbered List
- Bulleted List
- Indent Less
- Indent More
- Quote
- Left Justified
- Centered
- Right Justified
- Remove Formatting
- Plain Text (switches to Plain Text Editor)
- Check spelling (far right)

Adding Attachments

In addition to these options, you also can attach files to your message. Click the Attach a file link, just above the editing toolbar. A new text box opens in your message with a Browse button to the right of it, as shown in Figure 26-6. Click the browse button to locate the file that you want to attach.

If you want to attach another file to your message, click the Attach another file link. A new text box and Browse button will appear, as it did for the first file. Follow the same steps to attach a file as you did before.

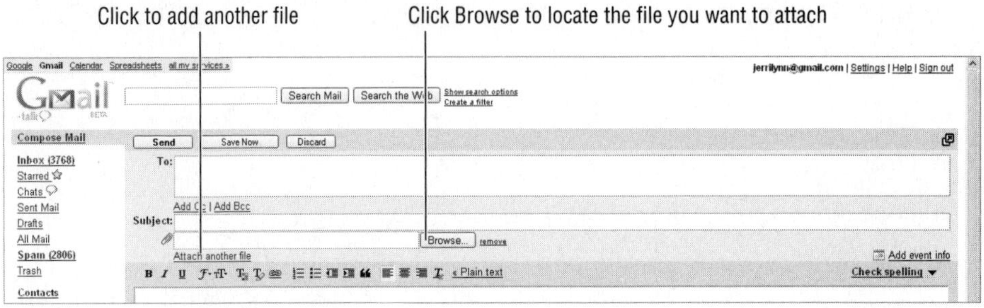

Figure 26-6: Attaching a file adds lines to your e-mail message, near the subject line.

Sending and Receiving Messages

Once you've created your message, sending it requires only the click of a button. When you finish creating your message, click the Send button directly above the text box where you entered the e-mail address of the person to whom you want to send the message.

To the right of the Send button are two additional buttons: Save Now and Discard. The Save Now button allows you to save your message as a draft. This is especially useful if you're interrupted and need to close out of Gmail before the message is finished. The message will be saved in the Draft file, which you can access by clicking the Draft link in the list to the left.

The Discard button discards your message. If you click the Discard button, you'll be asked to confirm your decision before the message is discarded.

Receiving Messages

If you're receiving your messages from Gmail's Web interface, you can see your new ones simply by logging into your Gmail account. If you keep your browser open to Gmail, the page refreshes automatically every few minutes and new messages appear in bold.

If the page doesn't refresh often enough to suit you, you can click the Inbox link on the left side of the page to refresh your Inbox.

Gmail's Web interface isn't the only way to receive your e-mail messages, however. Gmail can also be used with Outlook, Mozilla Thunderbird, Eudora, Netscape Mail, and a few other e-mail applications.

To send and receive messages using your preferred e-mail program, you first need to enable POP Download. To do this, click Settings in the upper-right corner of the Web page. This takes you to the Settings page that you saw in Chapter 25.

Next, click the Forwarding and POP tab near the top of the page, as shown in Figure 26-7.

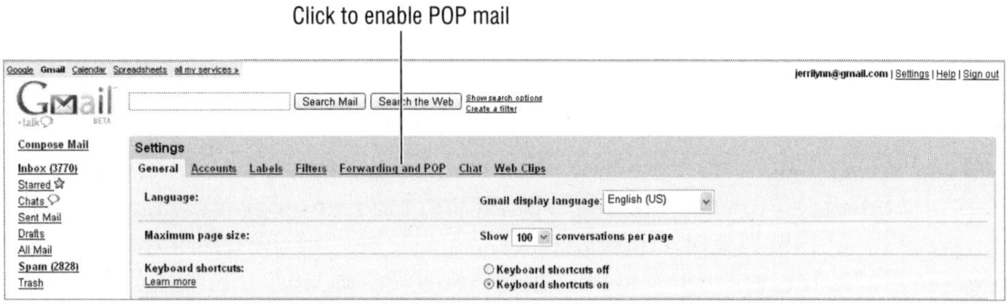

Figure 26-7: You can enable POP mail on the Forwarding and POP tab.

The Settings page will change to display your forwarding and POP mail preferences. In the POP Download section, click the preferred radio button under Step 1 Status. Then in Step 2, use the drop-down menu to set how you want e-mail to be handled after it has been downloaded. And finally, in Step 3, click the Configuration Instructions link to learn how to configure your e-mail application. These instructions will be opened in a different tab or window.

When you've finished setting your preferences for POP mail, click the Save Changes button at the bottom of the page. Your settings will be saved and you'll be returned to your Inbox. Now your POP mail is configured, and if you used the configuration instructions, your e-mail application should be configured so you can download messages to your favorite mail program.

Saving and Deleting Messages

Now you know how to send and receive messages, but what if you want to save a message that comes to you? Gmail's organizational structure is a bit different from that of most e-mail programs.

In Gmail, you don't have "folders" per se. Instead, Gmail uses a label system. This means that you label (or tag) your messages with a specific word or phrase; then all the messages with a given label are stored together.

When you want to store a message, you can either open the message or click the small square on the far left of the message line to select the message. Then, from the More actions drop-down menu, select New Label. As shown in Figure 26-8, a small dialog box opens with a text box in which you should enter the word or phrase you want to use for a label. After you've entered this label, click OK and the label is created.

Figure 26-8: Use the dialog box to create the label you want to use.

If you've selected a message and then created the label, that label will automatically be added to your message. But if you have another message to which you want to add that label, simply click the small box on the left of the message line, select the More actions menu (see Figure 26-9), and then click the label that you want to apply to the message.

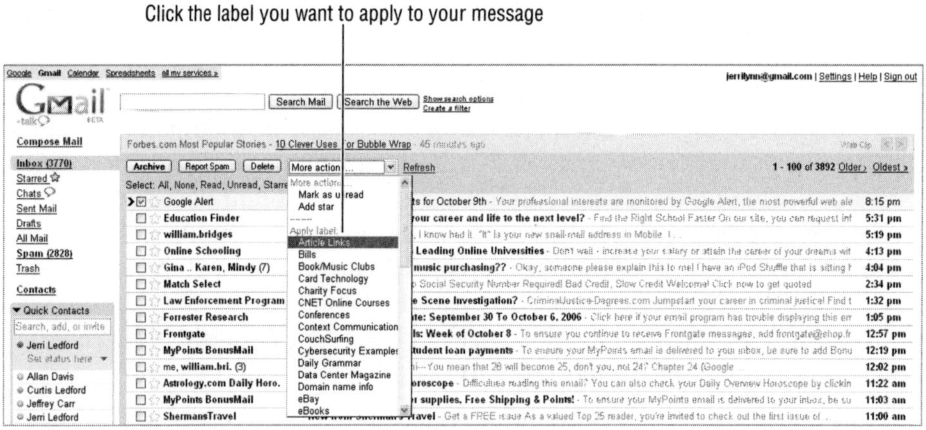

Click the label you want to apply to your message

Figure 26-9: It's easy to add a label to additional messages.

When you create a label for a message, a link for that label will appear in the list on the left side of your mailbox. This link is how you'll find all of the messages to which you've applied that label. To file your messages so they aren't in either your Inbox or the trash, click the small box to the left of each message that you've labeled and then click the Archive button near the top of the page.

This effectively files your messages away. If you never want to throw another e-mail away, you can file them. And if you really don't want to mess with adding labels, you don't have to. You can still select the messages and then click Archive. The messages are then filed into the All Messages file. You'll see a link to this file on the left side of the page.

Starring Messages

There's one more trick to filing your messages. Sometimes you need an easy way to keep up with a particularly important one. With Gmail, you can apply a star to a message, which provides a visual way to remind you that the message is important.

To add a star to any message, just click the small star in the message line, as shown in Figure 26-10. Then, even if you've filed the message away, you can find it easily by clicking the Starred link in the list on the left side of the page. This takes you to a view of only your starred messages.

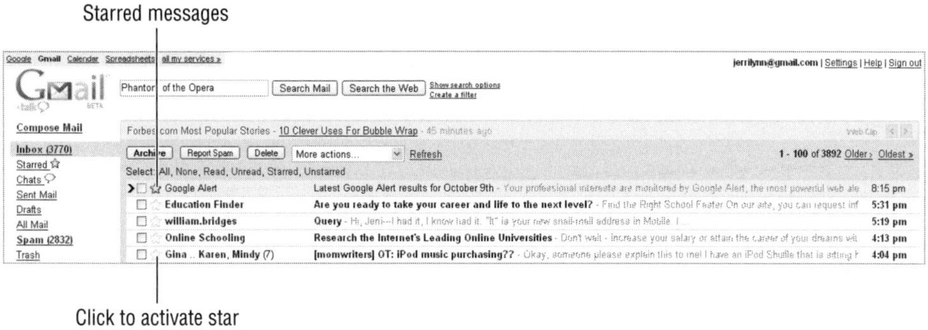

Figure 26-10: Click the star to flag your message as important.

When you no longer need your message starred, click the star again and it will be unselected, making it just an outline instead of a colored star. One drawback to Gmail's star system is that there are no additional colors available for your stars. They're all yellow, no matter the importance of the message that you're highlighting.

Moving On

Those are the basics of creating, editing, sending, and receiving e-mail. Let's not forget the organizing and deleting, too. These are the features that you'll use most often in Gmail. But they are by no means all the features available.

In the next chapter you'll see some of the more advanced features of the program, including how to filter your message, use auto-responders, forward messages, and, most exciting (for some people anyway), use Gmail with your mobile phone.

CHAPTER

27

Additional Gmail Features

Gmail is a full-service, Web-based e-mail program. Like the other programs that Google started in beta version, accessing Gmail in the beginning was a challenge. You had to score an invitation — and will still need one because technically the program is still in beta — before you could even sign up.

No one knows for sure when the beta testing of Gmail will end, but today Gmail is a little easier to gain access to — it's much easier to get an invitation, and far more of them are available than in the past. You can even send and receive invitations through the chat feature of Gmail. It has far more features than it had in the beginning, too. Features such as auto responders, mobile access, and filtering are the result of user feedback. And Google regularly adds features based on what users ask for.

This makes Gmail one of the most powerful Web-based e-mail programs on the Web. It's also one of the most popular. Yahoo! Mail and Hotmail give Gmail a run for its money, but neither program is as useful as the Gmail program. And that's due in large part to the additional features of Gmail.

Filtering E-mail

One of the features added to Gmail early in the process was the ability to filter your messages. Filters are basically guidelines that set up an "if/then" situation for mail. For example, you can set up a filter that would be the equivalent of: "If a message has the word 'invoice' in the subject line, then apply the invoice label to the message and archive it automatically."

With that filter in place, every e-mail that comes to your Inbox with the word "invoice" in the subject line will be tagged with the invoice label and automatically archived.

It's this functionality that many people find most useful; and in fact it's because so many people requested the filtering functionality that it was added to the program.

So how do you apply filters to your messages? It starts in the Settings screen. To get there, click the Settings link in the upper-right corner of your screen. This link should be in the same place no matter what folder (Inbox, Drafts, Starred, or Custom) you're in.

Clicking the Settings link will take you to the Settings page. Once you're there, click the Filters tab. You are taken to the Filters page, which should look something like Figure 27-1.

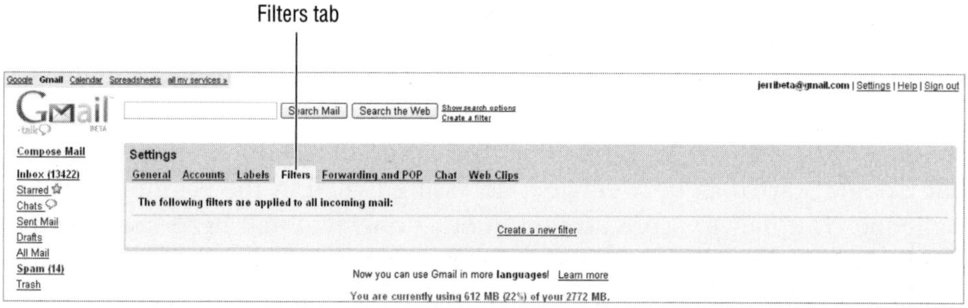

Figure 27-1: The Filters tab is where you'll create and monitor your filter settings.

If you have already set up filters for your Gmail account, those will be listed on this page. Let's assume you have not yet set up a filter. To set one up, click the Create a new filter link at the bottom of the page. The Create a Filter capabilities will appear at the top of the new page, as shown in Figure 27-2.

To create the filter, you have to design some parameters for it. Use the text boxes provided to set those parameters:

- **From:** In this space, enter the e-mail address from which filtered e-mails will arrive. This is a useful field only if you know what addresses your messages will come from. For example, if you know that you'll get e-mail from a specific company or person and you want to create a label for those e-mails only, then you can enter that e-mail address here.

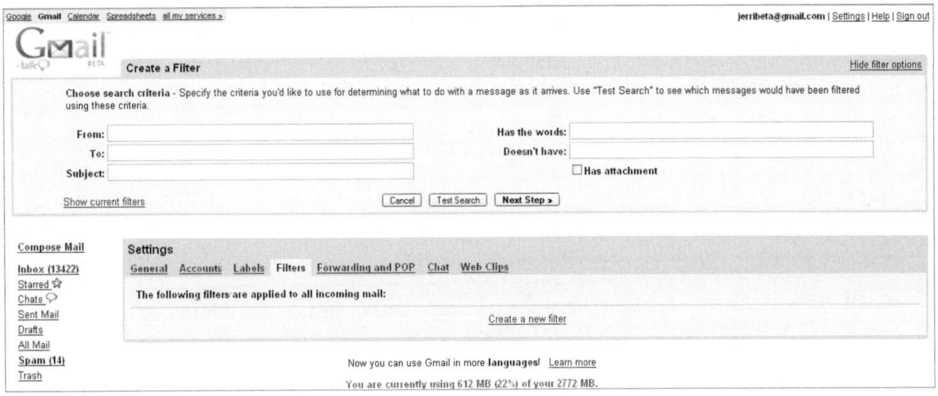

Figure 27-2: Use the filter-creation capabilities to create new filters for your e-mail.

- **To:** In this space enter the e-mail address to which the messages that you want to filter were sent. This may seem like a strange item to have on a filter, but it can be useful. If you're forwarding messages from your other e-mail accounts, their "To" addresses will be different from those of others sent to your Gmail. And you can set a Gmail filter to grab and file just those forwarded messages.
- **Subject:** If you know the specific subject of the messages you want to filter, enter that subject in this line. Some e-mails always have the same subject (i.e., marketing e-mails and e-mail newsletters).
- **Has the words:** Are there specific words that characterize e-mails you want to filter? Maybe you receive e-mails from a variety of people with a variety of subject lines, but all of the e-mails have the word "furniture" in them. You can create a filter, using this option, that specifically looks in the subject line and the body of the e-mail for the word "furniture." Messages containing the word will then be labeled and sent to a specific folder that you've set up for "furniture."
- **Doesn't have:** Are there specific words that are never used in your e-mail messages? This is really only useful if the word that you want to exclude is a common word that would ordinarily appear often. For example, if you want every message that doesn't say "Sale" in the subject or body of the message to be placed in a folder, then you can enter the word "sale" into this text box and those messages will be tagged accordingly.

Once you've set up the criteria for your filter, click the Test Search button to see what messages are in your Inbox that match the filter criteria. If you don't have any matches, you should consider adjusting your filter. Once it's set to your satisfaction, click the Next Step button.

The next step, shown in Figure 27-3, is to set up an action for your filter. Choose the action that you would like to be performed on the messages that meet your filtering criteria, and then click Create Filter.

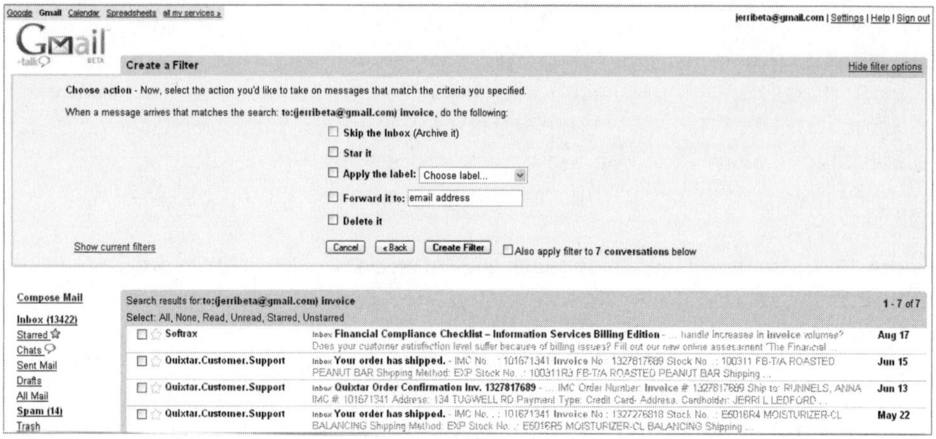

Figure 27-3: In the second step of filter creation, choose an action for the messages.

Next to the Create Filter button is an option to apply the filter to the messages that were found during the text run. If you would like your label to be applied immediately, or if there's an action you would like performed, place a check mark in the box to the left of this option.

After you click the Create Filter button, you are returned to the filter view of the Settings page, and your new filter will be displayed on the page, as shown in Figure 27-4.

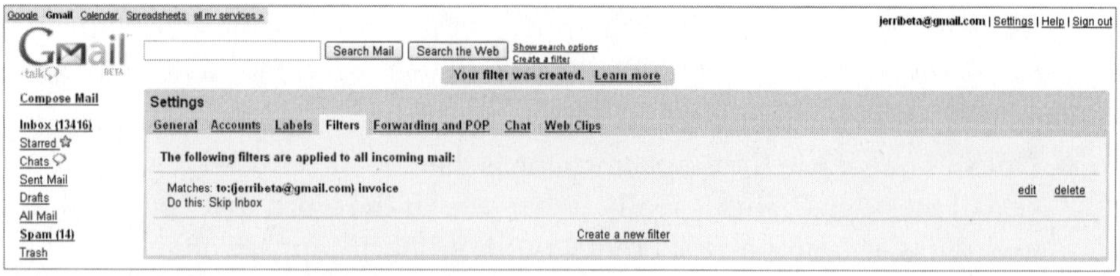

Figure 27-4: Filters are displayed on the Filters page.

If you decide later that your filter needs to be tweaked or deleted, you can use the Edit and Delete links at the far right of the filter view to perform these tasks.

Filters are easy to apply, and they have a variety of uses. It's up to you to decide just exactly how to use them to filter your messages in a way that makes sense to you.

Using Auto-Responders

In many Web-based e-mail programs, there's no auto-responder, even though this is an especially useful feature. An auto-responder is a little program, attached to your e-mail box, that can automatically send a reply to every message received in your Inbox. Most people use them to notify others when they are out of the office or on vacation.

Gmail didn't originally have an auto-responder, but this has since been added. Now if you're going to be away from your e-mail and you want to let others know you're away, you can set up an auto-responder message and have it sent for you.

To set up an auto-responder, first log into your Gmail account and then click the Settings link. You should automatically be taken to the General tab on the Settings page. If that doesn't happen, however, just click the General tab to be taken to that page.

Near the bottom of the page there's a section titled Vacation Responder (see Figure 27-5). This is what Google calls the Gmail auto-responder.

Figure 27-5: The Vacation Responder is the control for sending automatic messages.

To set the auto-responder to send a message to anyone who e-mails you while you're away, first activate the radio button next to Vacation responder. Then create a message to be sent in reply to anyone who e-mails you while you're gone. People usually choose to leave a message about when they are leaving and when they will return, but you can leave whatever message you want. Just type a subject and the body of the message in the text boxes provided.

Once that's done, all you need to do is decide who should get the auto-response message. If you select the check box below the body of the message, then your auto-response will be sent only to the people on your contacts list. If you don't select this option, the auto-response will go to everyone.

When you've finished using these settings, click Save Changes at the bottom of the page and your auto-responder is activated. You won't be asked to confirm your settings; you'll just be returned to your Inbox.

As Figure 27-6 shows, when you return to your Inbox, a banner message at the top of the window shows your Vacation Responder is turned on.

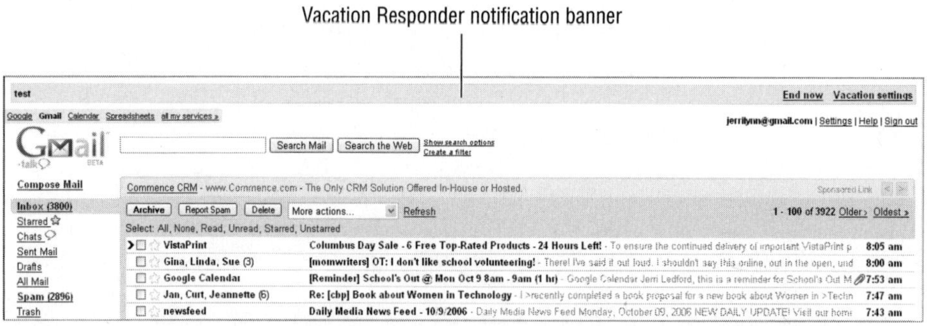

Figure 27-6: A banner message is displayed while your auto-responder is active.

On the far right side of this banner are two links. If you click the End now link, your auto-responder will be turned off. If you click the Vacation settings link, the General tab on the Settings page appears (where you originally set up the auto-responder). You can make changes to the auto-response message and settings or end the auto-response.

If you've never used an auto-responder, then you don't know what you're missing. But give it a go and you'll find it's one of the handiest tools you can have in your Inbox, especially if you travel frequently.

Forwarding Messages

I'm an e-mail junkie. I have multiple e-mail boxes on several services, and I have Outlook on both my laptop and desktop computers. I typically use Gmail for all my mail handling, but I like to have a copy of all the messages on all my

Gmail accounts in each of my e-mail boxes (I have five or six). It's a redundancy thing that ensures I always have what I'm looking for.

In order to do this I have to set up a complex system of forwarding messages from one account to another. Thank goodness for Gmail's forwarding capabilities.

Forwarding on Gmail basically involves just having your Gmail messages automatically sent to a different account. It doesn't have to be a Gmail account; it can be any e-mail account you like. And you might have several reasons for forwarding your messages. Maybe you want all of your personal messages to come to your work e-mail address (not recommended), or perhaps you want all of your messages funneled through one account, even though you like having multiple e-mail addresses.

Whatever the reason, using the forwarding capabilities of Gmail is easy. Like many of the other functions covered in this chapter, it starts from the Settings page. On that page, click the Forwarding and POP tab. You've seen this tab before, only this time you're looking at the top part of the page, labeled Forwarding, as shown in Figure 27-7.

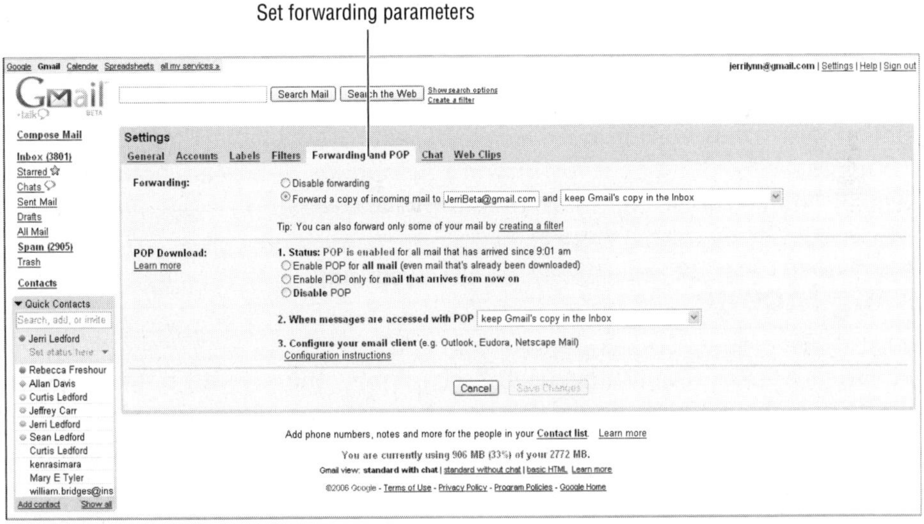

Figure 27-7: Set how (or if) you want messages in your Inbox forwarded.

In the Forwarding section, click the radio button next to Forward a copy of incoming message to. This sets your forwarding to "on." In the text box provided, enter the e-mail address to which you want messages forwarded. And then in the drop-down menu, shown in Figure 27-8, select whether you want to keep a copy of the message in your Inbox at Gmail, archive a copy, or delete the message once it's been forwarded.

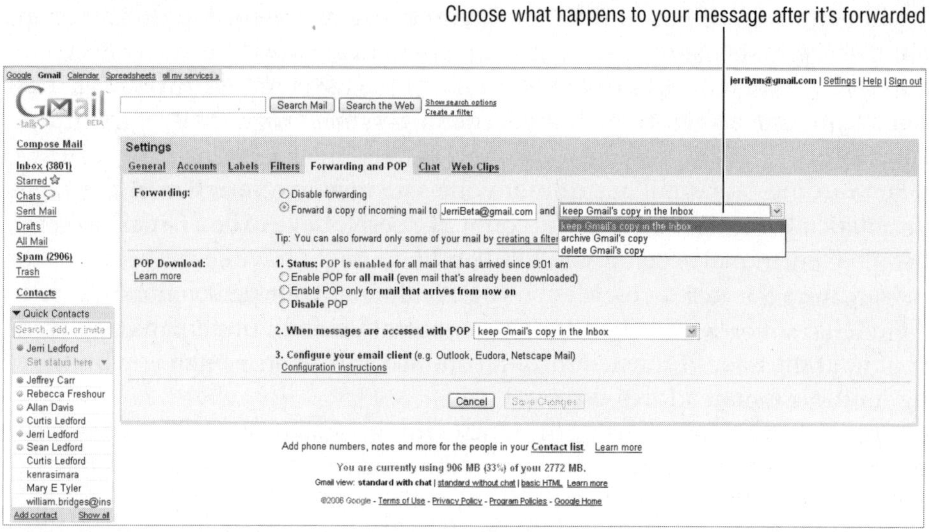

Figure 27-8: Use the drop-down menu to choose an action after forwarding.

When you're finished with these settings, click Save Changes. Your forwarding begins immediately, but you can go back at any time and click the radio button next to Disable forwarding to turn the forwarding action off.

Forwarding is a very handy capability to have. You may not need it at the moment, but when you do need it, you'll want it available right now. Most Web-mail services don't give you forwarding options, so this is a bonus feature of Gmail — one Google continues to improve and expand.

Going Mobile

One last feature you may find useful is Gmail's ability to grab e-mail from your Web-enabled mobile phone. It's true. We've become so addicted to e-mail that now we're checking it by phone when we're away from the computer. It's just a fact of the age we live in.

Unfortunately, not all Web-based mail services offer the capability to view your e-mail from your mobile phone. This requires a slightly different interface than simply using the Web because the viewing area on a cell phone is much smaller than a typical monitor or display. Google figured it out, however, so you do have the ability to access your e-mail from some cell phones if you're using Gmail. For a complete list of compatible phones, go to:

```
http://mail.google.com/support/bin/answer.py?answer=30596&topic=1580
```

If your phone is compatible with Gmail, then all you need to do is launch your Web browser from your phone (how you do this will be determined by your phone) and then go to `http://m.gmail.com`. Be sure you put the "m." in front of gmail.com or you won't be able to access the program.

If your phone is compatible and you've entered the preceding URL, you are taken to a Gmail sign-on page. Enter your user name and password and then select OK (this can vary by phone; you may need to select Send or Go To). You should be taken to the mobile Gmail Web site.

Navigating the mobile site will be slightly different, because you're working in a much smaller format, with different controls, but it's pretty intuitive, so it shouldn't take you long to become accustomed to the setup.

Google-on-the-go. Could life get any better? Probably, but we'll be satisfied with small joys, right?

Moving On

A whole book could probably be written on ways to use Gmail. It's as powerful as any e-mail program on the market. Take some time to navigate through it and get to know it. You've learned the basics here, but there's plenty more available if you have time to play with the program and read through the help files.

Our time with Gmail is up, however. Now it's time to move on to the last Google program that I'll cover in this book. Picasa is Google's answer to Photoshop and some of the other graphic manipulation and organization programs that you'll find on the Web. In the next few chapters, I walk you through the basics of how to use Picasa and what to use it for. Then we'll be finished.

PART IX

Picasa

Among the fastest growing services online are Web-based picture services. These services let you upload, manipulate, share, and in some cases print your digital (or digitized) pictures with all of your friends and family. In many cases, people even use these services to manipulate pictures that they plan to use on Web sites and blogs.

Google's answer to these online photo services is Picasa. This is a full-service photo organizer. You'll find all kinds of neat uses for your photos with Google's Picasa. And this section of the book is where you'll find out about all of them.

You can make movies with your pictures, share them with other people, create digital scrapbooks, and create posters or other files that are ready to print from your desktop photo printer or by an outside printing service. And like the other Google programs, Picasa is easy to use. So keep reading to learn more about what you can do with Picasa and how to do it.

CHAPTER

28

Welcome to Picasa

Digital pictures have become so commonplace that even non–computer users are buying (and using) digital cameras. The cameras are easier to use than ever, they take much better pictures than in the past, and even graphics manipulation and organization software is getting easier to use.

There was a time when you had to buy Photoshop if you wanted to change, correct, or organize your digital photos. Photoshop is an excellent program, but it's also expensive and complicated. Google understood all this, so when the Picasa program became available (Picasa is a graphics manipulation and organization program), the company snatched it up quickly. Since then, Google has been adding functionality and usability to Picasa.

Today, Picasa is an easy-to-use (and FREE) program that anyone can access, download, and use. And it doesn't have a steep learning curve, so you can go from download to regular use in a short time.

Why Use Picasa?

Most digital cameras today come with some kind of software that allows you to perform basic changes and corrections on your photos, but those software packages are usually lacking in the area of organization. How many digital pictures do you have on your hard drive? And do you know where to find the picture of your daughter's face when she opened her birthday present without having to open every single picture you have downloaded?

Organization is Picasa's strong point. The program gives you many options for storing, rating, and even renaming your digital photos. And all those options are easy to use.

In addition, Picasa does something no other photo software does — it searches your hard drive and locates all of the pictures that you have saved (even the ones you forgot existed). Then it will show you where these pictures are so that you can organize them in a way that will keep you from losing them.

Finally, Picasa also gives you editing options for your photos. Have you ever taken a picture and wished the light had been a little different or that the car hadn't been in the background? Using Picasa, you can create the picture that you intended to take from the picture you actually captured. And it's easy.

Download and Install Picasa

Before you can begin using Picasa, you'll need to download and install the program. You can get the Picasa software by going to `www.picasa.com`. Once the page has loaded, click the Free Download link.

The download should start automatically. Select a location on your hard drive to save the file, and then click OK. When the download finishes, navigate to the place you saved the file and double-click it to begin the installation process.

When you're finished installing Picasa, it should launch automatically. The first time you access the program, you'll be prompted to scan your computer for pictures. As shown in Figure 28-1, you can either choose to scan your entire hard drive or just portions of your hard drive. After you've made your selection, click Continue and the scanning process will begin.

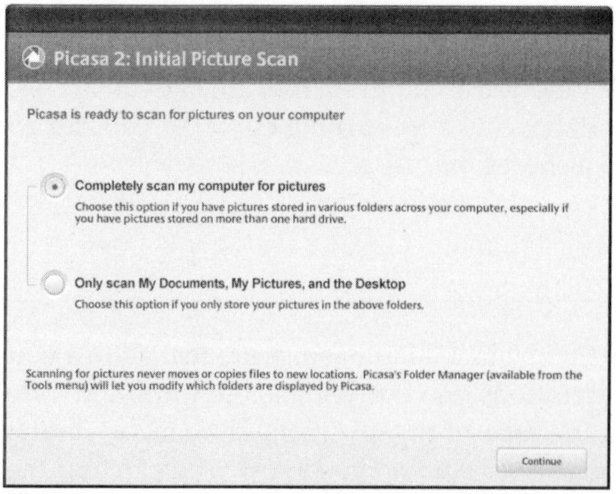

Figure 28-1: Initial setup includes scanning your computer for existing pictures.

NOTE It could take some time for Picasa to scan for pictures on your computer, especially if you're scanning your whole hard drive. During the scanning process, you can use other programs without fear of interfering with Picasa.

When the scan is finished, Picasa will be populated with all of the pictures that you have stored on your computer (in the locations you chose to scan).

Navigating Picasa

Once Picasa has scanned for your pictures and the program is populated, you'll find there are several different navigation options. The Picasa window is laid out in a way that makes it easy for you to choose what you want to do next. As Figure 28-2 shows, navigation is tiered and intuitive.

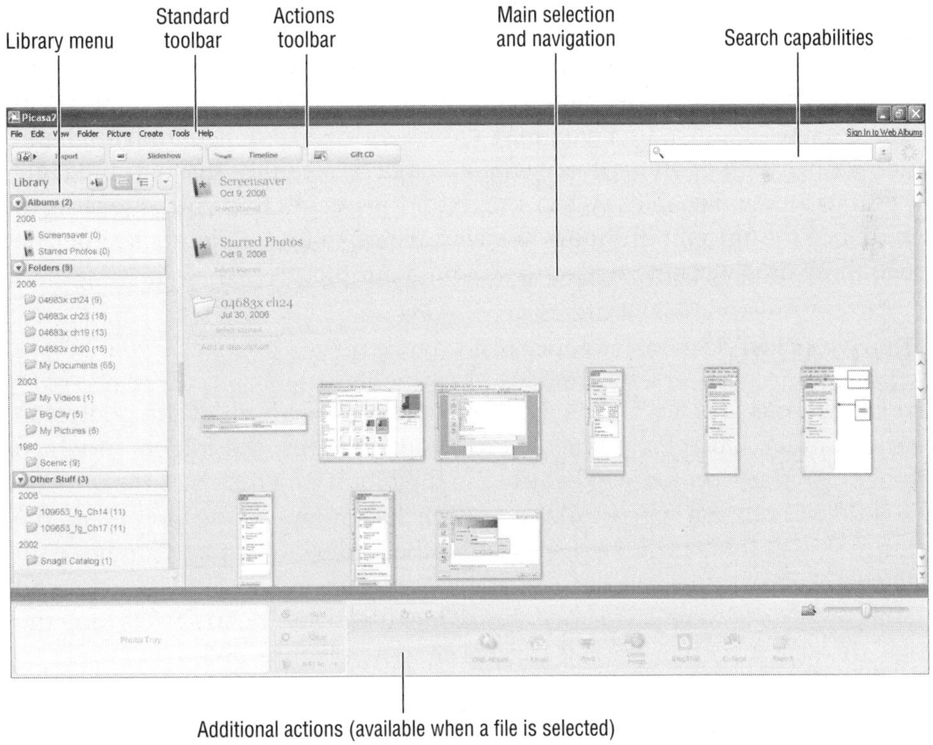

Figure 28-2: The different areas of navigation make using the program intuitive.

Standard Toolbar

The Standard toolbar is similar to the toolbar you might find on any software program. This toolbar enables you to use commands you're familiar with (such as File, Edit, and View) to perform actions you're also familiar with, such as opening a file or saving a file.

Click on any command in the Standard toolbar to see submenu options that are included in that command group.

Actions Toolbar

The Actions toolbar is a little more specific to the Picasa program. In this toolbar, you have buttons for Import, Slideshow, Timeline, and Gift CD. The Import button takes you to a page where you can import new pictures into the Picasa program. The remaining buttons — Slideshow, Timeline, and Gift CD — become available only when you are actively working with a picture.

Search Options

It wouldn't be a Google program if it didn't have a search option. And in this day of digital camera mania, you may have hundreds of images on your computer. Rather than opening every single image or scrolling through them all, the Search function enables you to search for the images that you're seeking. It will reduce the amount of time you spend trying to find a picture so you can spend more time working with and sharing your picture.

Library Menu

The Library menu is a way to navigate quickly through all of the photos on your computer. Once Picasa has logged your pictures, the folders in which those pictures are located will be listed in the Library menu.

To find a photo in a specific file, simply click the name of the file, and all the pictures in that folder will be displayed in the center of the page (in the Main navigation area).

You can expand or collapse the Library menu and submenus by clicking the small arrow to the left of the category, as shown in Figure 28-3.

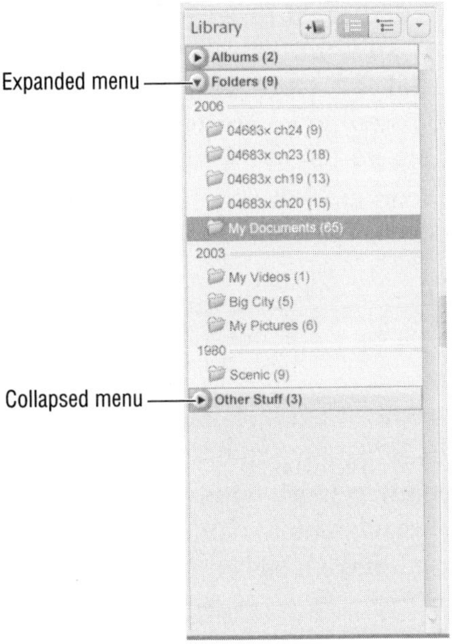

Figure 28-3: Expand and collapse menus and submenus using the arrow buttons.

Additional Actions

The Additional Actions toolbar, shown in Figure 28-4, is a feature you'll use often. This toolbar, however, is available only when you have selected a photo from your hard drive to work with.

Figure 28-4: Once you select a picture, this toolbar becomes available.

On this toolbar, you have such options as Hold, Clear, and Add to. These three options are for working with the picture in the picture tray (where the photo is displayed at the bottom of the page in the Additional Actions toolbar), and for working with photo albums.

There are also star controls, which let you mark a photo with a star. This is useful if you have several photos that are nearly exact copies. You can flip through them and select the one you like best and then star that photo so you don't lose track of it.

The biggest part of the toolbar, however, is dedicated to seven buttons that enable you to select the action you want to take with the photo that you've chosen. Those buttons are: Web Album, Email, Print, Order Prints, Blog This!, Collage, and Export. You'll use these actions when you've finished any editing of the photo.

There is also a zoom slider in the far-right corner of this toolbar. The zoom slider enables you to quickly zoom in or out of the photo on which you're currently working.

Main Selection and Navigation

The majority of your screen is dominated by the center panel of the Picasa program. This panel is your Main Selection and Navigation panel. From here, you can select the picture (or pictures) that you want to work with. You can scroll through your pictures instead of using the Library menu to navigate by folder, and you can add descriptions to your folders to make it easier to locate them.

Moving On

The basic navigation of Picasa is pretty straightforward. All of your upper-level commands, toolbars, and menus are right out in the open and they're labeled, so if you hover your pointer over them for a second or two, you'll see exactly what any link or button does.

Don't let this simple interface fool you, however. There is a lot of power in Picasa, and in the next chapter you start seeing some of that power. As you're uploading, organizing, and editing your pictures, you'll begin to understand just what you can do with the program. It all starts in Chapter 29.

CHAPTER

29

Using Picasa for Pictures

Digital pictures are the most amazing, and most useful, photographic technology to appear in a very long time. No longer do you have to shoot pictures, wait hours or days to get them developed, and then figure out what to do with all those little squares of laminated cardboard. Today, you can shoot a picture, download it to your computer, print or delete it, share it with friends, and order prints — all in just a few minutes.

Well, you can do it all in just a few minutes if you have a good software program that doesn't take you hours to figure out. The first time I used Picasa, I came up to speed on it in less than 15 minutes. It really is that easy to use.

Uploading Pictures to Picasa

Initially, Picasa will automatically search your computer for any pictures that you may have stored on the hard drive. But what if you have pictures stored on your camera or some other type of portable device? How do you upload those pictures to Picasa?

It's a simple process and, in fact, Picasa does a lot of the work for you. If you have pictures stored on a digital device, such as a USB key (Flash drive) or a CD, insert the device or disc into your computer. You'll need to plug a USB key into an available USB port. For a CD, just insert it in the CD drive.

If you're using Windows XP your computer should automatically recognize the device and prompt you with an action window, like the one shown in Figure 29-1.

Figure 29-1: When you insert a device into your computer, a prompt should appear.

Other operating systems may treat the device a little differently. Let's assume for the sake of simplicity that you're using XP.

In the action window that appears, click the Copy pictures to your computer and view them using Picasa2 option. This opens the Picasa program and begins loading your pictures into the program for you to view. If the pictures that are on the device already exist on your computer, they will appear with a red X over them, so you know you already have copies of them on your hard drive.

When the computer finishes processing, thumbnails of the pictures that are on your storage device are displayed in the Picasa program. If you want to import those pictures into Picasa, click the Import All button to import the pictures, as shown in Figure 29-2.

If you want to import only a few pictures, then you can select those pictures by clicking them. If you want to select multiple items in sequence, click the first picture in the sequence and then press and hold the Shift key. While holding the Shift key, click the last item in the sequence. All the pictures in that sequence should be selected.

Alternatively, you can select multiple images that aren't in sequence by clicking the first picture and then pressing and holding the Ctrl key. Click the additional pictures you would like to select.

When you've finished selecting the items you want to upload, click the Upload Selected button and the photos are uploaded to Picasa.

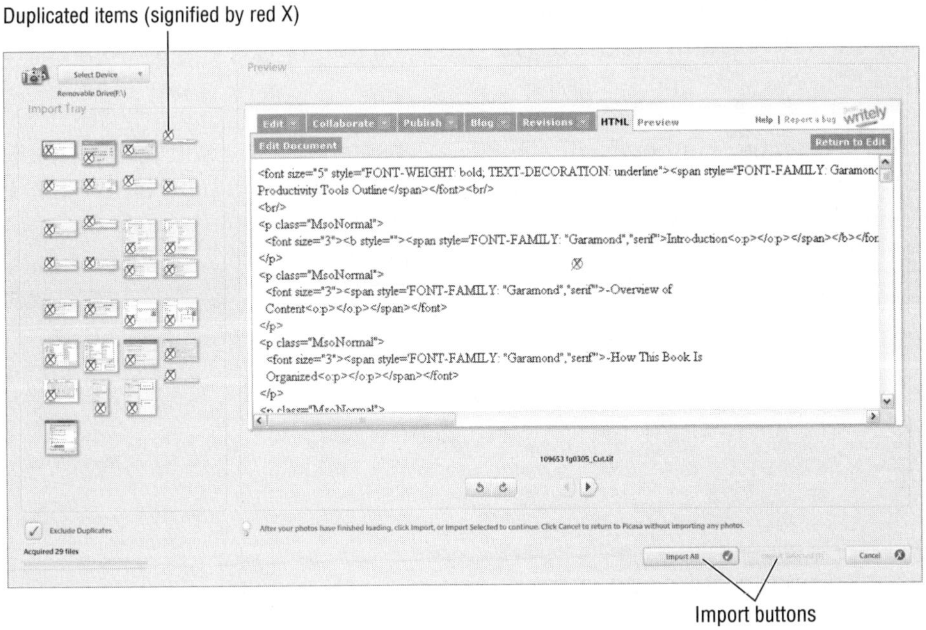

Figure 29-2: Select an Import button to import your pictures into Picasa.

Another alternative for uploading your pictures to the Picasa program is to do it from within the Picasa interface. If you're using Picasa and you want to upload files, click the Import button, shown in Figure 29-3.

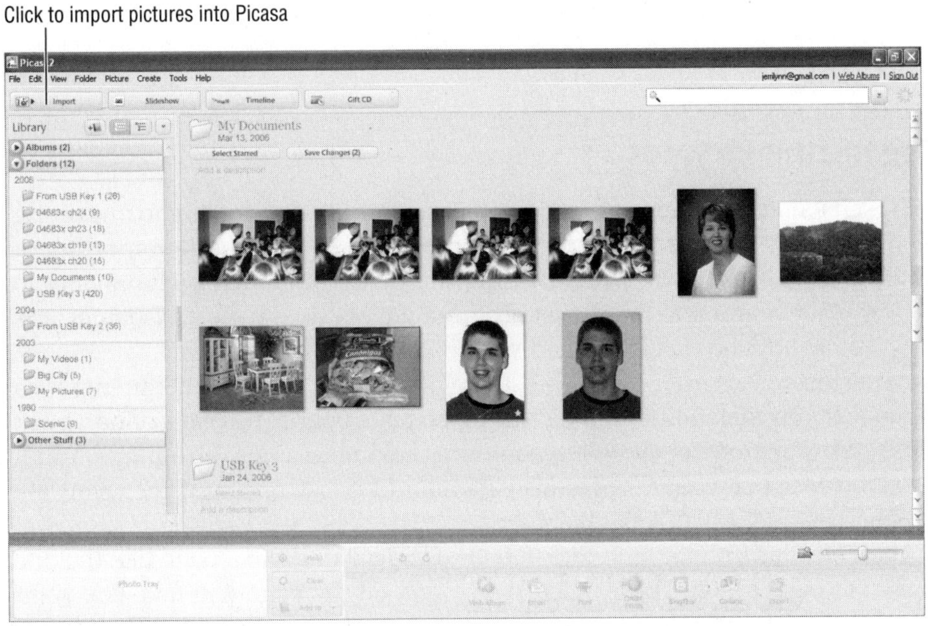

Figure 29-3: Import pictures from inside Picasa by clicking the Import button.

This will take you to a page like the one shown in Figure 29-4. The page automatically opens to the last device used, if it's still plugged into your computer. Otherwise it appears blank.

Click the Select Device button at the top of the page to select the device from which you want to import pictures. Picasa scans the device and lists pictures that are available. When it's finished, click one of the Import buttons to import the pictures you've selected.

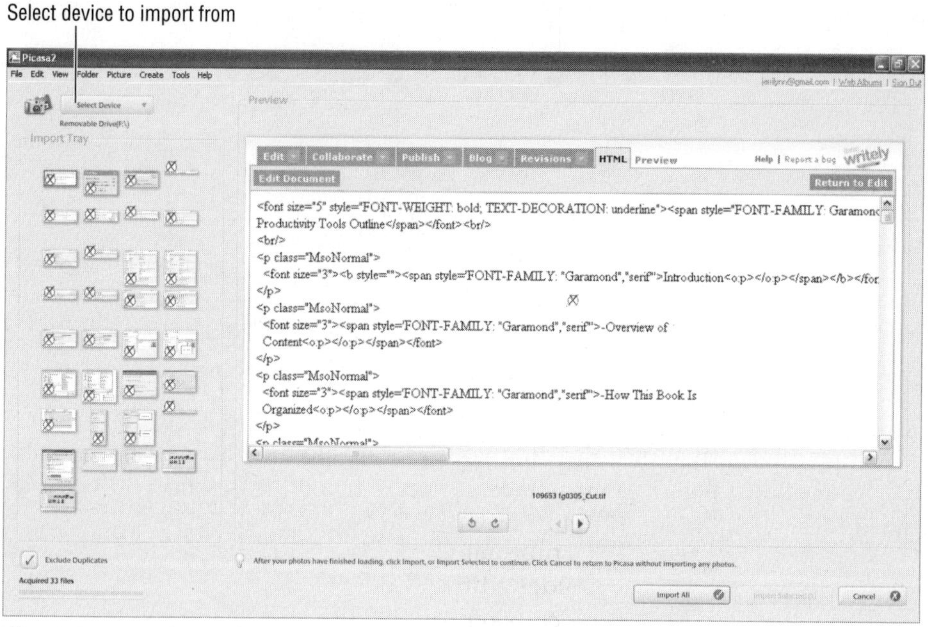

Figure 29-4: Select a device from which you wish to import pictures.

Organizing Pictures

I've been using the terms "upload" and "import" when referring to importing pictures into the Picasa program. This doesn't mean that you're importing or uploading pictures to the Web. Until now, you've uploaded pictures only to your computer and into the Picasa program. Picasa does have a Web interface, however, to which you can upload your pictures to share online.

In the top-right corner of the Picasa program, there's a link for Sign into Web albums. If you click this link, the Picasa Web page opens. You can connect your Picasa program to your Google account by clicking Enable Web albums. You'll be asked to enter your Google user name and password, and then you are given access to Picasa on the Web.

The first time you log into Picasa on the Web, you'll see a page like the one shown in Figure 29-5. The Launch Picasa link on the page will take you right back to the Picasa program installed on your computer. If you're not careful here, you could be stuck in a never-ending loop — going from your computer to the Internet and back. Instead of clicking this link, click the +New Album link in the upper-right corner of the page.

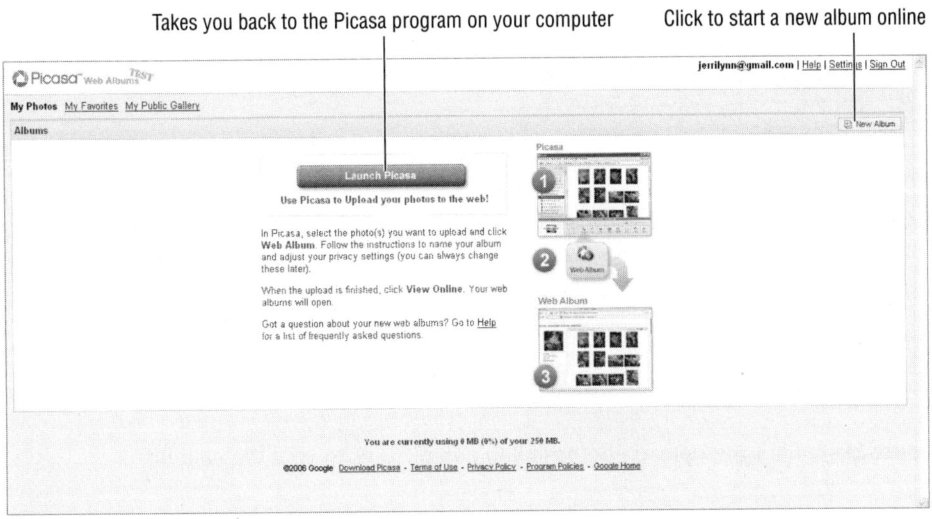

Figure 29-5: Don't get hung up in the Launch loop. Click a different link instead.

When you click the +New Album link on the Web interface, you'll be prompted to enter some basic information about the album, as shown in Figure 29-6. This information includes a title for the album, the date and description of the album, and the place taken (optional). There's also an option to make your album public or keep it private. Remember that if you make it public, anyone can see it.

Figure 29-6: Enter the basic information for your new album.

When you've finished entering the requested information, click Create. The album will then be created on your Picasa Web interface. However, it's an empty album, so if you want to add pictures to it, click the Upload Photos link, shown in Figure 29-7.

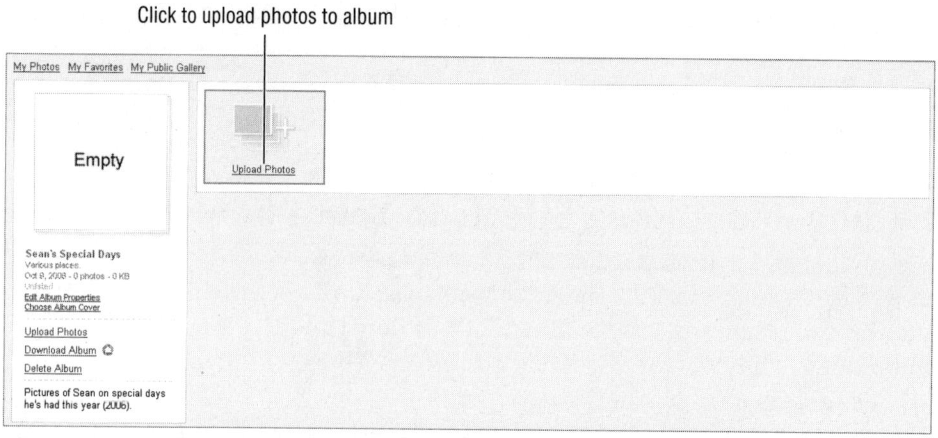

Figure 29-7: Click the Upload Photos link to add pictures to your Web album.

You are taken to a page, like the one shown in Figure 29-8. Click the first Browse button to navigate to and open a picture to upload. You can then add more pictures using additional browse buttons. When you're finished selecting your pictures, click the Start Upload button, and your photos will begin to upload to your Web album.

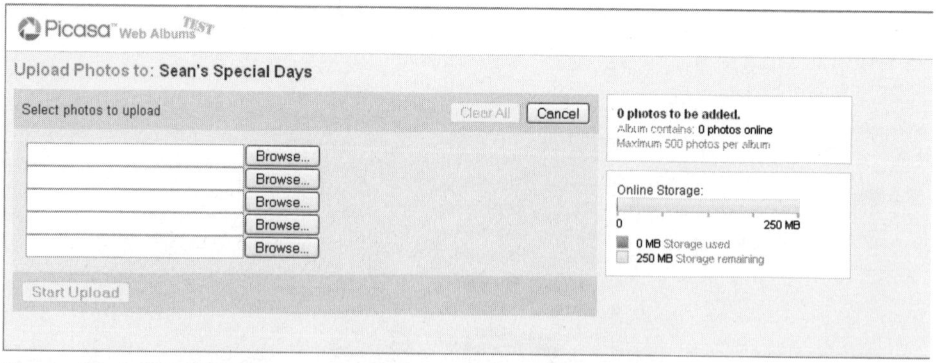

Figure 29-8: Use this page to upload photos to your Web album.

When the upload is finished, you are returned to the album view, and you should see the pictures that you've chosen to upload.

There is another way to upload photos to your Web album. From the Picasa program on your hard drive, select a picture to add to the Web album and then select the Web Album button near the bottom of the page. A dialog box appears in which you can select to start a new album or add to an album. Select one of these options, provide any additional information that might be needed, and then click OK.

The picture that you selected at the beginning of the process will be uploaded to the album that you've selected or created. Using this method, you can upload only one picture at a time. However, if you're not uploading dozens of pictures at once, this may prove to be the easiest way to upload pictures to your Web albums.

Editing and Adding Effects to Your Photos

You may also want to edit and add effects to your pictures using Picasa. I'll tell you upfront not to expect too much in this department. Picasa is serviceable, but it doesn't have as many editing and effects features as you might like. Still, what's there is useful.

Picasa also can have a user running in circles because there's no visible link to editing or adding effects to your photos. In order to access these capabilities, you must double-click the photo that you want to work on.

As shown in Figure 29-9, when you double-click a photo, you're taken to the editing screen.

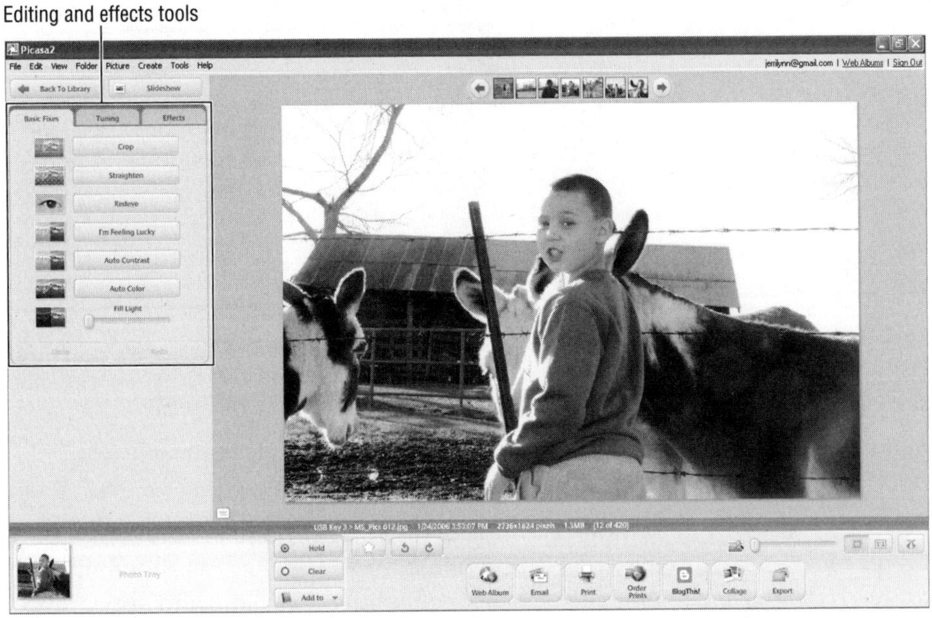

Figure 29-9: The editing screen can be accessed by double-clicking a photo.

Your editing capabilities are limited to basic fixes, such as:

- Crop
- Straighten
- Red-Eye
- I'm Feeling Lucky
- Auto Contrast
- Auto Color
- Fill Light

These are all basic functions, but the fun (and very Google-esque) one is the I'm Feeling Lucky option. If you click this option, all of your adjustments are made for you.

If you click the Tuning tab, as shown in Figure 29-10, you'll have access to some of the more precise tuning tools, such as Fill Light, Highlights, Shadows, Color Temperature, and the Neutral Color Picker.

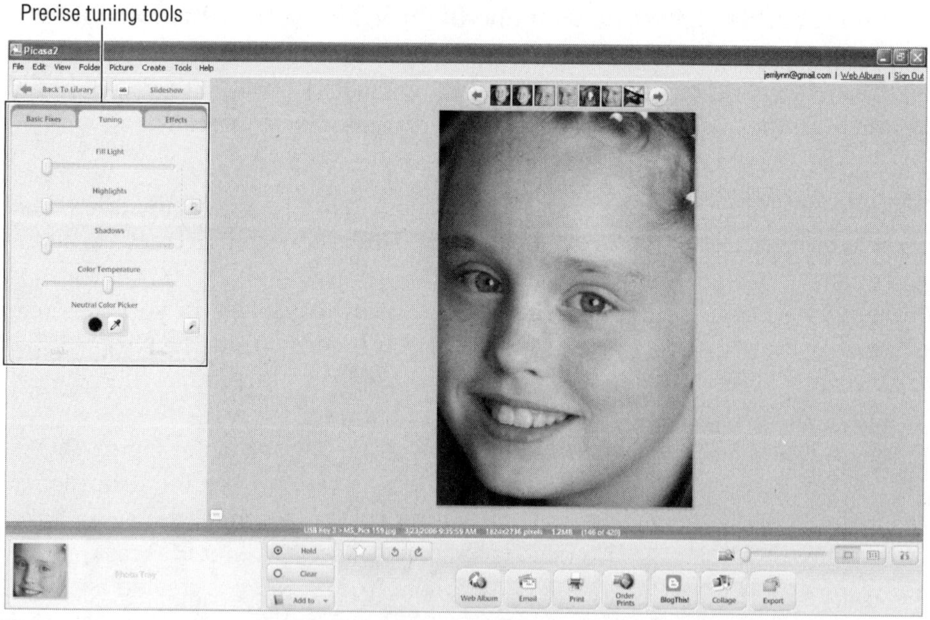

Figure 29-10: Use the precise tuning tools for detailed adjustments to your photos.

One last tab on the editing and effects menu is the Effects tab. Here you can play around with the effects of the photo you're editing, as shown in Figure 29-11. On this tab you have options for changing the colors and appearance of your pictures, although you'll find that these options aren't as far-reaching as you might like. We can hope they'll improve with time, right?

Figure 29-11: The Effects controls enable you to change how your photo looks.

In addition to these editing and effects tabs, there's another capability that you might find useful: the Collage function. This allows you to create a digital collage from your photos.

Begin by selecting the pictures that you want to include in your collage. Remember that to select multiple pictures you'll need to use the Ctrl or Shift keys. After you've selected the pictures you want to include in the collage, click the Collage button near the bottom of the Picasa screen.

This will take you to a dialog window, like the one shown in Figure 29-12. First, select a type of collage you would like to create from the drop-down menu provided. Then select the background colors you want to use and the folder where you want the collage stored. Then select a folder in Picasa where you want to add the collage, and click Create. Your collage is created and you are taken to the collage view.

When you're done, you can return to the Picasa main page. When you're ready to close out of the program, you'll be prompted to save the changes that you've made during your session on Picasa.

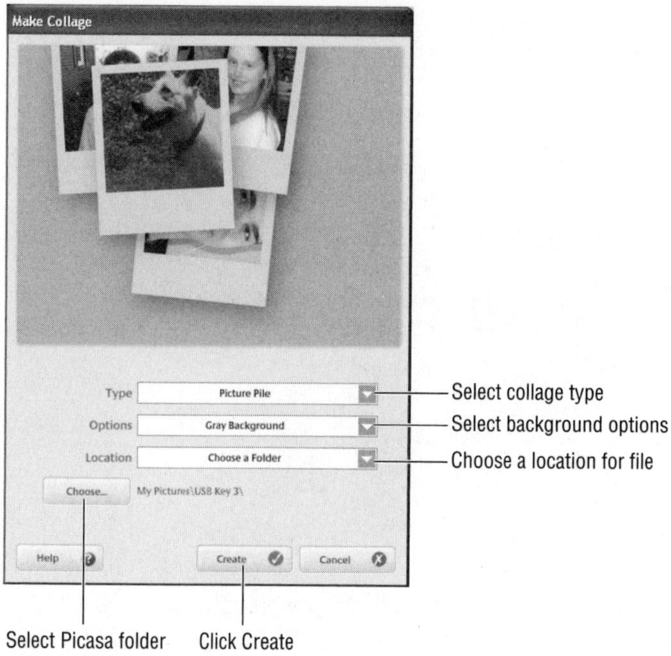

Figure 29-12: Use the collage dialog box to set the parameters for your collage.

Moving On

Like Gmail, Picasa could have a book devoted to it. However, what I've covered so far are some of the basics of uploading, organizing, editing, and creating with Picasa.

In the next chapter, you learn a few more basics: how to print, store, and create CDs from Picasa. By the time you're done with that chapter, you should know Picasa well enough to create some excellent photo projects.

CHAPTER

30

Finishing Your Photos

The coolest part of digital pictures is the ability to share them in so many ways. You can send electronic files to your friends, print them, and even create movies and slideshows and burn them to CD.

With a program like Picasa, these activities are even easier to accomplish. Picasa has some great printing and sharing capabilities, and burning a CD or a DVD with Picasa is a breeze, too.

Printing Your Photos

By now you've figured out almost everything that you need to know about Picasa in order to begin using it to edit your photos. You've even learned a little about uploading your pictures to the Web. But what if you want to print your pictures?

No problem. Picasa actually has some pretty useful printing capabilities.

To start, click on the picture that you want to print and then click the Print button near the bottom of the page. This takes you to the Print options page, shown in Figure 30-1.

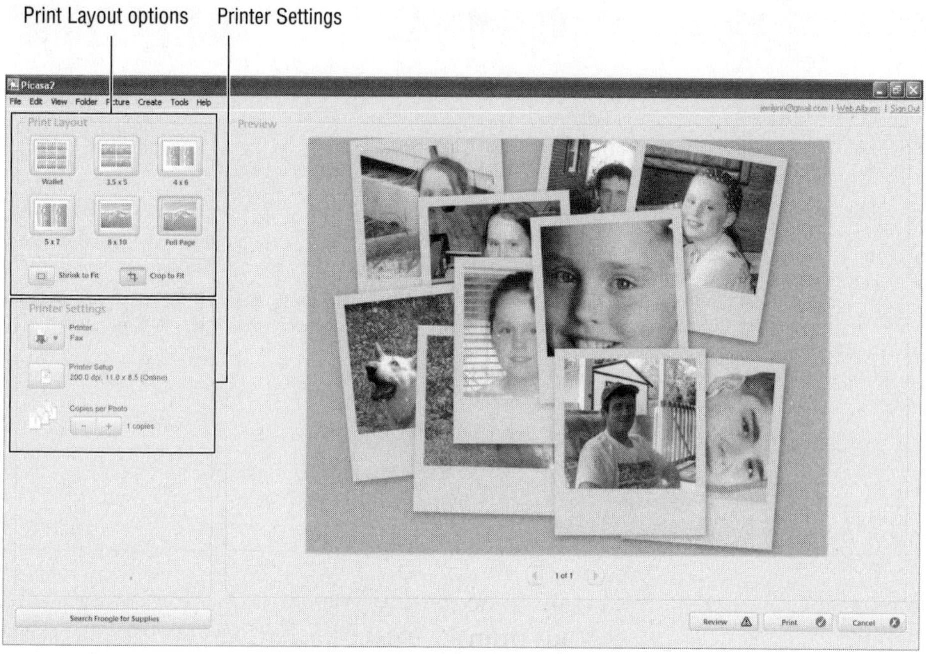

Figure 30-1: Use the print options page to set up your photo print.

The main controls on the print options page (labeled in Figure 30-1) are the Print Layout controls and the Printer Settings controls. Use these controls to change the layout of the print. For example, if you want to print wallet-sized pictures, select the Wallet button. When you do, you'll see that you have a single wallet-sized photo in the center of the page. You can change this to add up to nine wallet photos per page by changing the number of pictures to be printed in the Printer Settings area.

When you've finished setting up how you want your pictures to print, click the Review button on the bottom-right side of the page to review your pictures for printing. This opens a dialog box like the one shown in Figure 30-2 that will indicate if any of your pictures are not suitable for printing. When you're satisfied that the quality of your pictures will be good, click OK to close the Review dialog box.

When you're finished reviewing your print, you can click the Print button. Your Printing dialog box appears. Make your printer selections, just as you would when printing any other document, and click OK. The picture (or pictures) should print according to the settings that you've selected.

You can print not only the pictures that you've uploaded or imported into Picasa, but also collages that you create with those pictures.

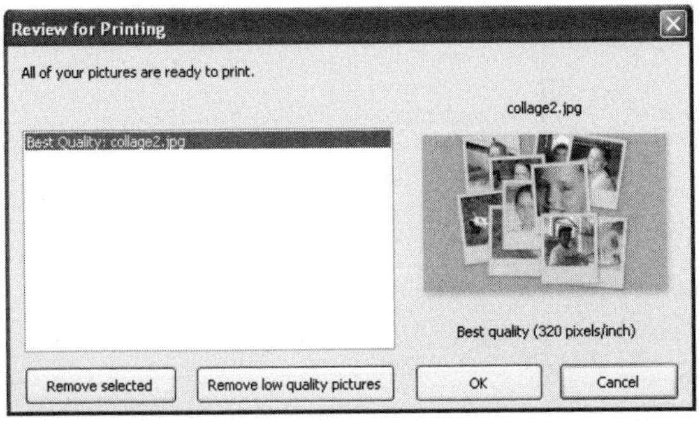

Figure 30-2: The Review dialog box tells you if picture quality is too low for printing.

Sharing Your Pictures

In Chapter 29, you learned how to access the Web interface for Picasa. This Web interface is going to be your primary means of sharing your photos with others. Remember when you created the photo album, but elected to keep your album private? If you had selected the public option, your pictures would have been made public so that anyone searching could find them.

But that's not all there is to sharing your photos. The Picasa program stored on your hard drive has several options for sharing your pictures with other people.

E-mail

Your first option is to share your pictures by e-mail. To use this option, click the picture (or pictures) that you want to send by e-mail and then click the Email button at the bottom of the Picasa page.

The first time you use this option, you are prompted to select a default e-mail program or method to send your pictures, as shown in Figure 30-3. Make your selection, and then click the small box next to Remember this setting, don't display this dialog box again. You'll be taken to your preferred e-mail editor, and you won't be prompted to choose an e-mail editor again.

Every time you choose to send pictures after this, an e-mail will automatically open, as shown in Figure 30-4. The picture is attached to the e-mail; all you have to do is enter an e-mail address (or multiple e-mail addresses), create a short message, and then click the Send button. The message, with the attached photo, will be sent.

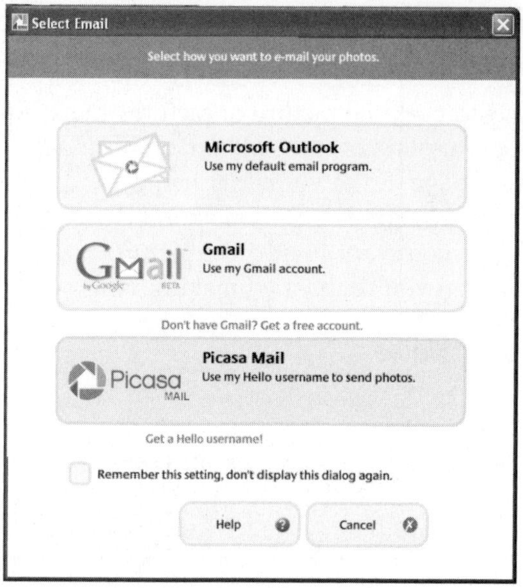

Figure 30-3: The first time you send e-mail you must choose your e-mail program.

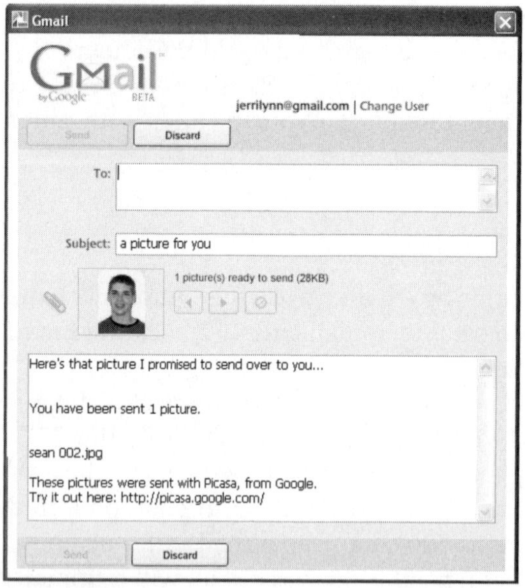

Figure 30-4: After the first e-mail, you'll see this screen.

Blog This!

Another way to share your photos if you have a Blogger account is to include the picture in your blog. Again, you need to click the picture or pictures that you want to include and then click the Blog This! link near the bottom of the page.

You are taken to the Blogger sign-in page. Enter your user name and password, click the Sign In button, and the page appears, as shown in Figure 30-5, where you can select the blog to which you want to add the picture and the way you want the picture laid out. When you're finished making your selections, click the Save Settings button.

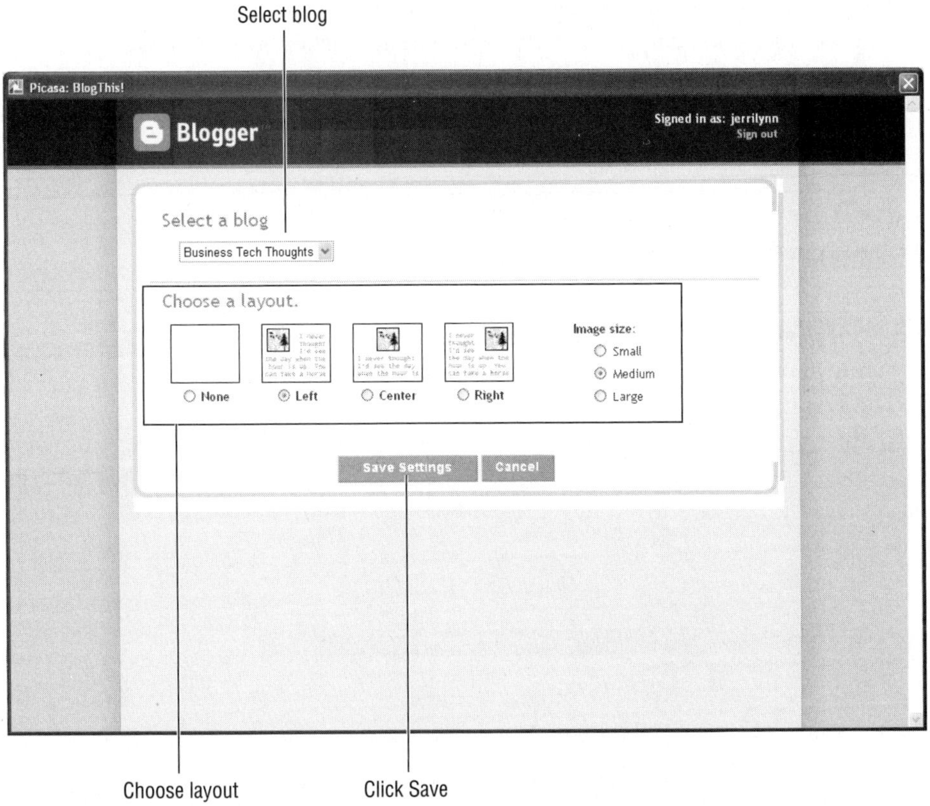

Figure 30-5: Select a blog and a layout to upload a picture to your blog.

Next you are taken to a blog entry, with your picture included. Finish creating your blog post and then click Publish to publish the blog entry, with your pictured included.

Many people have blogs. But if you're not one of them, don't despair. You can create a blog on the Blogger site in a few easy steps (see the sidebar for information on Blogger).

BLOGGER: BLOGGING MADE EASY

These days it seems that everyone has a blog. But if you're like me, you may be a little confused about exactly what a blog is and why everyone is so interested in them.

Very briefly, a blog is a place where you can create and publish your thoughts and opinions. A good blogging program will allow you to post not only your thoughts and opinions, but also photos to illustrate them, and it will allow others to post comments. The comments are a way to communicate with the people who read your blog.

Blogging as a concept seems like a difficult task, right? It's not, really. Especially if you have a program like Blogger to help you. Blogger is Google's blogging tool, and like almost all of Google's tools, it's really easy to use. Pre-designed templates, point-and-click tools, and no hosting worries make it possible for you to create your blog within minutes.

Check it out at `www.blogger.com/start`**. Blogging is fun and not nearly as complicated as you may have led yourself to believe.**

Burning CDs or DVDs

People also share or store their photos on CD or DVD. Of course, this capability requires that you have a PC or notebook computer with a CD or DVD burner. For the sake of this information, let's assume that you do.

To burn your pictures to CD or DVD, first select the pictures that you want to include on the CD, and then click the Gift CD button near the top of the main Picasa page, as shown in Figure 30-6.

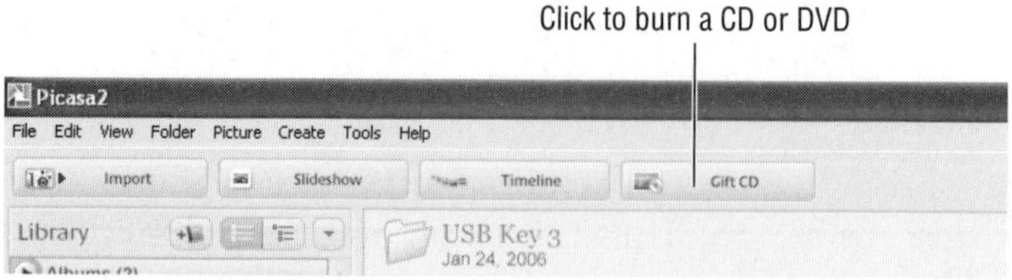

Figure 30-6: The Gift CD button leads to CD- and DVD-burning controls.

You are taken to a page, like the one shown in Figure 30-7, where you can select additional pictures from other folders to include on the CD, create a name for the CD, and decide if you want extras such as a slideshow or a copy of the Picasa software included on the CD.

When you're finished making your selections, click the Burn Disc button, and the disc will begin to burn if you've inserted a blank disc in your CD burner. If there is no disc in your CD burner, you'll receive a message prompting you to put a CD in the drive.

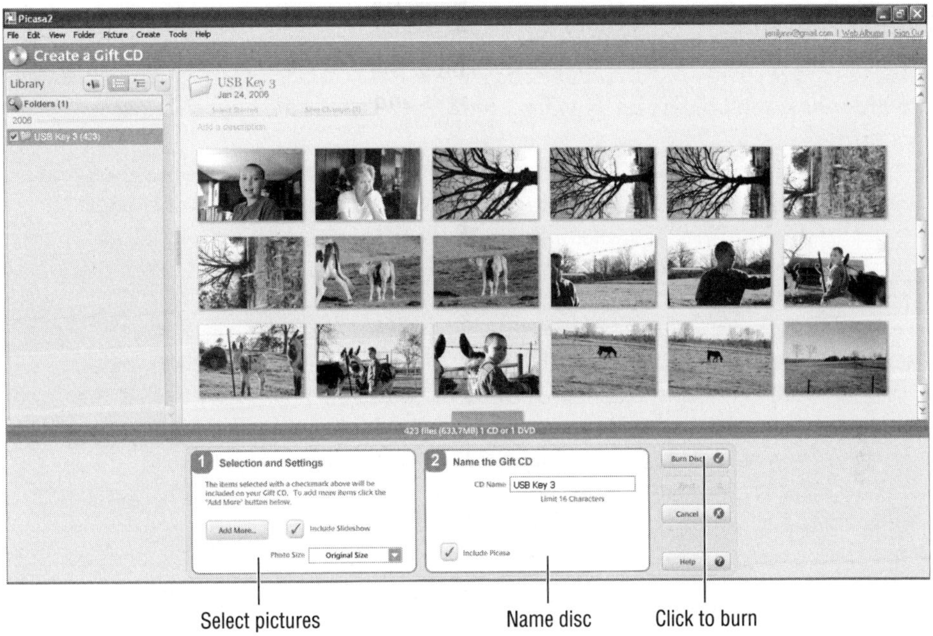

Figure 30-7: Use the controls provided to make selections concerning your photo CD.

That's all there is to it. You'll be burning pictures and slideshows to disc in minutes.

That's a Wrap!

Picasa isn't the most powerful graphics organization and manipulation program on the market. It is, however, one of the most user-friendly. And because Picasa is still in beta, there's the possibility that additional new features will be added to the program as it matures.

For now, you can organize, share, edit, and add effects to your photos and even share them by e-mail, print, and disc. There's enough functionality for most users. And the program certainly hits the right price point.

Google is constantly adding new programs, applications, and features. There's much more coming down the pipeline from Google. The productivity tools that I've covered here are just the beginning. And even as a beginning they offer loads of functionality at an irresistible price — free.

I hope you enjoy the programs you've learned about, and keep your eyes on the bookshelf because there are sure to be more Google books about new and exciting technologies heading your way.

Thanks for reading!

Index

G

Q

R

S